Politics
And The
Media
In Canada

McGraw-Hill Ryerson Series in Canadian Politics
General Editor—Paul W. Fox

Politics: Canada, 5th Ed., Paul W. Fox
Canadian Foreign Policy, D.C. Thomson and R.F. Swanson
The Constitutional Process in Canada, 2nd Ed., R.I. Cheffins and R.N. Tucker

Nationalism in Canada, P. Russell
Political Parties and Ideologies in Canada, W. Christian and C. Campbell
Pressure Group Behaviour in Canadian Politics, A. Paul Pross

Political Parties in Canada, C. Winn and J.C. McMenemy
Government in Canada, T.A. Hockin
Canadian Politics: An Introduction to Systematic Analysis, J. Jenson and B.W. Tomlin
Local Government in Canada, C.R. Tindal and S. Nobes Tindal
Public Policy and Provincial Politics, M. Chandler and W. Chandler
Political Choice in Canada (Abridged Edition), Harold D. Clarke, Jane Jenson, Lawrence LeDuc,
    Jon H. Pammett
Canadian Foreign Policy: Contemporary Issues and Themes, Michael Tucker
Canada in Question: Federalism in the Eighties, 3rd Ed., D.V. Smiley
The L-Shaped Party: The Liberal Party of Canada 1958-1980, Joseph Wearing
Politics and the Media in Canada, Arthur Siegel

FORTHCOMING

Political Parties and Ideologies in Canada, 2nd Ed., William Christian and Colin Campbell

Politics
And The
Media
In Canada

Arthur Siegel
Associate Professor of Social Science
York University

McGraw-Hill Ryerson Limited

Toronto   Montréal   New York   St. Louis
San Francisco   Auckland   Bogotá   Guatemala
Hamburg   Lisbon   London   Madrid
Mexico   New Delhi   Panama   Paris   San Juan
São Paulo   Singapore   Sydney   Tokyo

POLITICS AND THE MEDIA IN CANADA

0 D 2

ISBN 0-07-077866-3

Printed and bound in Canada

Care has been taken to trace ownership of copyright material contained in this text. The publishers will gladly take any information that will enable them to rectify any reference or credit in subsequent editions.

Canadian Cataloguing in Publication Data

Siegel, Arthur.
    Politics and the media in Canada

(McGraw-Hill Ryerson series in Canadian politics)

Bibliography: p.
Includes index.

ISBN 0-07-077866-3

1. Mass media—Political aspects—Canada.
2. Communication in politics—Canada.
I. Title.   II. Series.

P95.82.C3S53   324.7'3'0971   C82-095087-4

CONTENTS

PREFACE

In 1982, the political environment in which the Canadian mass media operate is changing. The new Charter of Rights for the first time provides constitutional guarantees for freedom of expression and freedom of the mass media. Another change is the government's far-reaching decision to make newspapers a policy area: Parliament will be asked to pass a Newspaper Act. In the broadcast sector, new policy directions are being examined.

These and other changes in the political environment come at a time when electronic technology—laser beams, computers, fibre optics and space satellites—are changing some of the characteristics of the print and broadcast press. A national newspaper, Pay-television and an enormous increase in the number of television channels available to the public are becoming new realities.

This book examines the newspaper, radio and television industries in Canada. The mass media that disseminate information, opinion and entertainment on a daily or continuing basis are studied in relation to the political, social and economic environment in which they operate. Particular attention is given to the role of the mass media in Canadian nation-building. One of the major questions examined is whether the media are vehicles for bonding the nation or instruments of fragmentation.

It is my pleasure to express my warmest gratitude to Professor Paul Fox, Principal of Erindale College, University of Toronto, who provided me with guidance, generous advice and encouragement. I want to single out for special thanks Joerg Klauck of McGraw-Hill Ryerson Ltd., whose moral support and advice helped me enormously.

I am indebted to Professor Emeritus Wilfred Kesterton, whose *A History of Journalism in Canada* has profoundly influenced my thinking about the Canadian media. Professor Kesterton read parts of the manuscript and made extremely useful suggestions.

Grateful appreciation is due to Dr. Gertrude J. Robinson of McGill University who instilled in me an interest in, and enthusiasm for, communication studies many years ago.

I have benefited from the ideas and research of a number of colleagues and friends including Professors Walter Romanow and W.C. Soderlund of the University of Windsor, Rod Chiasson and Stephen Callary. Colleagues in York University's Mass Communication Studies Programme made valuable suggestions.

The research staffs at the Canadian Daily Newspaper Publishers Association, the Audit Bureau of Circulation, the Canadian Broadcasting Corporation, the Canadian Radio-television and Telecommunications Commission and the Federal Department of Communications generously provided statistical information on Canada's communication industries.

My thanks to Mrs. Margaret Blevins, Mrs. Shirley Ormsby and Mrs. Doris Rippington for typing the manuscript.

A.S., Toronto, June 1982.

FOREWORD

Professor Siegel's book on the media is a welcome addition to the McGraw-Hill Ryerson Series in Canadian Politics. It not only examines an important subject that has not been dealt with previously in the Series but it takes a broad and assertive approach which will appeal to diverse readers. While students in journalism and communications courses may find that the descriptions and functioning of the media are most interesting to them, political scientists, economists, and sociologists will be no less interested in the discussion of the relationship among politics and the media, political institutions, the economics of the industry, and its impact on society. There is something here for everyone who is concerned with Canadian public affairs.

The author sets the scene for his broad approach by noting Canada's particular communications problems: a huge country with seven time zones, a physically divided landscape, and a sparse population living in the drainage basin of the American communications industry, which is undoubtedly the most vigorous that has ever inundated man.

Although Canada has been a leader in the field (the first voice broadcast in the world was by a Canadian and CFCF in Montreal was the first radio station), the struggle to maintain our own identity in publishing and broadcasting has been formidable and persistent. It also has been complicated by the fact that historically we have had two major languages and cultures, as well as a peculiar blend of private enterprise and government participation in the communications business.

Professor Siegel properly draws attention to the immense impact that the media have in politics by transmitting basic information, linking the populace to the government, setting the agenda for public discussion, and influencing the politicians themselves. These functions are so significant in our democratic society that the media really are a fourth branch of government. If so, they should be examined critically like any other organ of government in order to answer the basic question, how well do they carry out their responsibilities?

Professor Siegel's book is an extended reply to this question. Beginning with the media's clientele, the author notes that Canadians are among the world's greatest consumers of information. Fourteen million Canadians read a daily newspaper regularly and Canada has more radios than people. Despite the popularity of newspapers and radios, Canadians apparently get most of their information from television. The average Canadian spends five hours watching TV to every hour he devotes to reading a paper. In fact, he spends more time watching TV and listening to radio than he does working. TV is now so prevalent that there are more homes in Canada with television sets than with indoor plumbing. The public also seems to be more inclined to believe what it sees on TV than what it reads in the newspaper.

To satisfy this thirst for news, the media must have access to information, the more the better. But unfortunately in Canada, there are some obstacles which stem the flow. One of Professor Siegel's most valuable contributions is to explain in detail the legal, legislative, and parliamentary restraints on the dissemination of information in Canada. He discusses the restrictions inherent in the law of libel, the heavy hand of the Official Secrets Act, the convention of keeping the Queen's business private, budgetary secrecy, parliamentary privilege, and the reluctance of Canadian governments to adopt legislation ensuring the sort of freedom of information which the United States now enjoys.

Though Professor Siegel enlivens his account with many examples and interesting case histories, the story and its conclusion are depressing. It is clear that in the provision of public information, Canada is far from being the open democracy that many of us have assumed.

However, the author again does us a service by reminding us of our history. Neither of our mother countries, France or Britain, was dedicated originally to freedom of the press at home or abroad. New France had no media and when Britain took over the Canadian colonies, publishers survived by printing government documents rather than newspapers. Printers emigrating from the United States to Canada brought with them the doctrine of the freedom of the press found in the American constitution, but the principle was not established in this country until independent-minded journalists like Joseph Howe and William Lyon Mackenzie had engaged in protracted struggles.

When they did succeed, their victory led to an unexpected rapprochement between the press and politics. Howe became a member of Parliament and a federal cabinet minister, while Mackenzie was elected mayor of Toronto. Other journalists followed in their footsteps and journalism became a common entry-point into politics. Twenty-three of the delegates to the Charlottetown Conference that led to Confederation were journalists.

As publishing became respectable, it also became profitable. Turning from history to economics, Professor Siegel analyses the contemporary newspaper and broadcasting industries and finds that the bottom line in each is a generous profit margin. Both are big billion-dollar advertising businesses returning handsome profits to their corporate owners. To quote the author's colourful phrase, the "media have become the wrappings of advertising," which in 1980 poured $1.1 billion into daily newspapers, $625 million into television, and $418 million into radio. From 1973 to 1980, the newspaper industry earned an average annual return of 30 per cent on its net assets, a splendid rate of profit which the broadcasting industry matched in 1980.

Some of the profits came from economies of scale. The bigger the operation, the better, with monopoly being perfection. But economies of scale lead inevitably to consolidation in ownership, especially in newspaper publishing, which is not subject to the public controls imposed on broadcasting. Newspaper chains become bigger while the number of daily newspapers grows smaller. Although the population of Canada has more than quadrupled since the beginning of this century, the country now has fewer daily papers than it had in 1900. Moreover, 77 per cent of Canada's present 118 dailies are owned by 12 publishing groups, of which the Thomson empire alone has 40 papers, Southam 14, and Sterling 11.

Concentration of ownership is even more pronounced when viewed from the perspective of circulation. The six largest chains account for more than 80 per cent of the total daily circulation of 5.5 million. Two of the chains, Thomson and Southam, sell six out of every 10 English papers produced each day. "Canada," says Professor Siegel, "has a higher concentration of ownership in the daily newspaper field than in any other developed country."

Concentration is apparent regionally and locally as well as nationally. In New Brunswick, the Irving family owns all of the province's five English-language daily newspapers. Thomson controls more than 80 per cent of circulation in Newfoundland and Manitoba and 68 per cent in Prince Edward Island. Armadale accounts for 86 per cent in Saskatchewan, while Southam dominates 65 per cent in Alberta and British Columbia. In Quebec, Pierre Péladeau's Quebecor chain has nearly half of the French-language daily circulations while two other chains account for almost all of the rest.

Competition and consolidation have squeezed out rival newspapers in most Canadian cities. Only six of the country's 97 newspaper cities have competing dailies now, in contrast to the 35 cities which had genuine competition—sometimes six or eight papers each—80 years ago.

In some cases concentration of ownership has turned into interlocking ownership when publishing chains have invested in broadcasting. With 30 per cent ownership of Selkirk Communications, Southam has interests in 11 radio and five television stations in British Columbia and Alberta, as well as in cable and TV operations elsewhere. The Irving family owns TV and radio stations in New Brunswick as well as all the English papers. The Blackburn family owns the *London Free Press* and also a private radio and television station in that city.

No doubt if the market were entirely free, there would be even more instances of interlocking ownership and greater consolidation in the broadcasting industry. These trends have been forestalled by the existence of the Canadian Broadcasting Corporation, which in effect is a huge publicly owned radio and TV chain, and the Canadian Radio-television and Telecommunications Commission, which has the power to issue licences and regulate all broadcasting.

In the publishing industry, where such constraints have never existed, recent instances of large papers being phased out while chains grew bigger and fatter led to a public outcry and the appointment of a federal royal commission to investigate the problem. The Kent Report, which appeared in 1981, made some very strong recommendations to curb the power and growth of chains and to make the operation of newspapers more democratic and responsible. Professor Siegel, who has had great experience as a practising journalist as well as an academic observer, reviews these proposals and offers his comments upon them.

Whatever the outcome of the Kent Commission's recommendations, it is unfortunately likely that the Canadian press will remain "fragmented," to use Professor Siegel's well-chosen word. Like the country itself, most newspapers will continue to focus on the local scene, or at best on the region. Although *The Globe and Mail* is now striving to become truly national by publishing daily in several cities across Canada, thanks to the marvellous new technologies which Professor Siegel describes, it is doubtful that other papers will follow its example. Linking Canadians together by disseminating national news and opinion to all of them simultaneously will have to be left to the broadcasting media, at least until better technologies are developed.

As Professor Siegel points out, fragmentation in the media poses a serious problem. While Canadian nationhood depends on good internal mass communications, the country has been hobbled by regional preoccupations. Both in the past and at present, the press has tended to foster parochialism by concentrating on the local scene. Perhaps unwittingly, the media have encouraged the different perspectives on the country which have flourished in regions and local communities and divided Canada. News coverage and editorial interpretation have varied from place to place, catering to local prejudice and reinforcing self-centred attitudes. In the main, the press has thought of itself as the spokesman for its bailiwick rather than for the country at large. The result is an absence of a national voice articulating Canadian aspirations and drawing the country together. Professor Siegel documents this criticism by citing a number of illustrative instances.

It is one more example of the quality of Professor Siegel's book. *Politics and the Media in Canada* is not only an informative and useful description of the state of the media in this country. It is also an incisive commentary on the state of the nation. In both respects it will interest laymen as well as students in various disciplines.

Erindale College,   Paul W. Fox
University of Toronto,   General Editor
April 2, 1982.

To Mireille

CHAPTER I

THE CANADIAN COMMUNICATIONS ENVIRONMENT

Canada is the most communication-conscious country in the world. This pre-occupation with communication is intimately tied to the very existence of the country. Mass media play a central role in Canada's struggle to build a nation and develop an identity of its own. To this end, they can be vehicles for bonding the nation or instruments of fragmentation.

In the nineteenth century, newspapers—then the only form of mass communications—became an integral part of the political process. They politicized the population in British North America, helped foster democratic institutions, contributed to the "confederation process" and provided a support structure for the development of political parties.

In the twentieth century, first radio and later television created new opportunities for information and communication to play an even greater role in nation building and the political process. Attuned to entertainment, the broadcast media have, at the same time, become the dominant carriers of information, thought, ideas, opinions and cultural values. Radio and television can reach millions of Canadians simultaneously and were seen as the ideal agents for shaping a national identity without obliterating the linguistic, cultural and regional dimensions of Canadian society. The airwaves were envisaged as the highways of national cultural interaction. This goal, however, has not been realized. In fact, the "modern media" have become agents of denationalization by serving as roadways for foreign, largely American, cultural values. In the 1980s, Canada is searching for a mass media system that carries the cultural messages of the nation.

Modern mass communications had its beginnings with the printing press. The first newspapers came to the British North American provinces more than a century before the formation of the Canadian federal union in 1867. In the 230 years since those first newspapers, our mass communications system developed

1

distinctive features to help it deal, not always successfully, with staggering problems related to the complex nature of Canadian politics, economics, social structure and geography. These problems have not overwhelmed the communications system; rather, they have provided the dynamics for what is perhaps the most sophisticated communications system anywhere. The technical breakthroughs scored by Canada in satellite communications in the mid-1970s are but an extension of Canada's enormous involvement in the communications sphere that included Canada's financial support for Marconi's wireless experiments at Glace Bay, Nova Scotia, at the turn of the century, the first radio broadcasts in the world, the establishment of the first continental microwave communications system anywhere, and the development of such noted theorists in the communications field as Marshall McLuhan and Harold Innis.[1]

The most important aspect of communications in Canada is the problems that the mass media face. Other countries share some of these problems but Canada has a cluster of them that have to be dealt with simultaneously.

THE PROBLEMS

PHYSICAL

The physical characteristics of Canada create one set of communications problems. Canada's area is nearly 10 million square kilometres. The large size of the country, second only to the Soviet Union, and the difficult terrain impede the easy flow of communications. The country spans seven time zones and contains such natural barriers to communications as the Appalachians, the Canadian Shield, the Rocky Mountains, the Great Lakes before canalization, and the Arctic desert. Geographically, Canada is a mélange of six regions: the Atlantic provinces, Quebec, Ontario, the Prairies, British Columbia and the North. Each has distinct physical characteristics which give rise to regional interests and separate communications requirements.

Political organization reflects the geography of Canada. There are 10 provinces and two Northern Territories. Canada is the world's most decentralized federal system with each of the provinces having important political powers in the economic, social and cultural spheres. These powers often have national implications and have also, at times, resulted in provinces seeking international involvements. Sensitivity to provincial interests is an integral and dynamic aspect of Canadian nationhood but it also generates centrifugal tendencies, with provinces seeking increasing independence from Ottawa, that may be at variance with the interests of Canadian unity.

---

1. See, for example: Harold Innis, *The Bias of Communication*, Toronto: University of Toronto Press, 1951 and Marshall McLuhan, *Understanding Media: The Extensions of Man*, New York: McGraw-Hill, 1965.

POPULATION DISPERSION

Canada's 24 million inhabitants account for only one-half of one per cent of the global population but the country comprises 10 per cent of the world's living room. There are fewer than three Canadians per square kilometre compared to 1,000 persons per square kilometre in such densely populated countries as Belgium. Although most Canadians live in a narrow ribbon of land, a "people belt," parallel to the U.S. border, they are spread across a country which is 5,000 kilometres wide from the Atlantic to the Pacific. Three out of four Canadians live within 150 kilometres of the United States; most live much closer. Moreover, the huge bulk of the country to the north of the "people belt," including the Northwest Territories, the Yukon and the northern regions of six provinces, is almost empty. Although this vast region is seen as a giant storehouse of mineral and oil riches that will provide the base for future development, its present population is less than 50,000.

Maintaining the Canadian political presence in the North and developing a sense of nationhood for all Canadians, whether they live in the densely settled border area or in sparsely settled regions, is a major Canadian commitment; it involves not only showing the flag and providing administrative and social services, but also maintaining a communications link for the entire population. The very uneven population distribution tends to undermine an east-west or all-Canadian route for communications. Instead, as in economic transactions, there is a strong north-south, or Canada-U.S., pull in the communications exchange. This, in turn, gives rise to a whole series of subordinate problems related to Canadian culture and Canadian identity.

THE U.S. PROBLEM

If Canadians had any choice in the matter, they would probably pick the United States as their neighbour. We have traditionally benefitted from our neighbourly relations. Our high standards of living, rapid rate of industrial development, federal system of government and many of the most admired aspects of our lifestyle are North American in character, having been influenced by our interaction with the United States.

The two countries are each other's best customers. The formal and informal ties range across a broad spectrum of interactions that includes fishing, oil and gas swapping, labour organizations, wheat, auto trade, tourism, air and water pollution, etc. Defence links find expression in a continental air-defence system (NORAD) and the North Atlantic alliance (NATO). This closeness with the United States, however, has also created some serious problems in many sectors, especially economics and communications.

Although Canada is 10 per cent bigger in area, it has only one-tenth the population of its southern neighbour. The United States is the world's most industrially advanced nation. In both countries, the mass media in the private sector are largely financed through gross advertising spendings which in 1981 amounted to $60 billion in the U.S. and $4.3 billion in Canada,[2] a proportion of 15:1 (Table I.1). Per capita advertising expenditures are $275 in the U.S., $180 in Canada. Because of the overhwelming size of the American communications industry compared with Canada's, the mass media flow tends to be from the United States to Canada with relatively little reciprocity. Hence Canadians have easy access to American television and radio programs, films and magazines, and in fact have to fight against inundation.

TABLE I.1   Mass Communications Environment: Canada-United States Comparisons, 1981

	CANADA	UNITED STATES (including Alaska & Hawaii)
Size of Country	9,922,300 km²	9,371,829 km²
Gross National Product	CAN $328,501,000,000	US $2,925,000,000,000
Gross Advertising Spendings	$ 4,335,000,000 (1.32% of GNP)	$ 60,255,000,000 (2.06% of GNP)
POPULATION AND HOUSEHOLDS		
Population	24,343,181	225,280,000
Total Households	7,807,000	81,480,000
Television Households	7,628,000	79,900,000
Radio Households	7,702,000	80,665,000
STATIONS AND SYSTEMS		
Originating TV Stations	113	1,019
AM Radio Stations	748	4,575
FM Radio Stations	615	4,358
Cable Systems	562	4,400
Pay Cable Systems	—	3,072
Subscription Television (STV) Stations	—	19
TELEVISION AND RADIO RECEIVERS		
Television Households (% of Total)	98%	98%

2. In Canada, the publicly owned Canadian Broadcasting Corporation-Société Radio Canada is financed mostly by money made available by Parliament, although about 20 per cent of the CBC's television revenues come from advertising. The Gross Advertising Revenues in 1981 are estimates based on studies by Statistics Canada, J. Walter Thompson Company Ltd., Maclean Hunter Research Bureau, the American Daily Newspaper Publishers Association and the CRTC.

Multi-Set Television Households (% of Total)	39%	51%
Colour Television Households (% of Total)	82%	85%
Radio Households (% of Total)	99%	99%
CABLE TELEVISION		
% Households with Access to Cable TV	77%	42%
% Households Subscribing to Cable TV	57%	25%
% Households Subscribing to Pay-Cable TV	—	9%
% Households Owning Converters	24%	—
ADVERTISING ($MILLION)		
All Media Advertising Revenue	CAN $4,062	US $54,750
Television	$ 695 (17%)	$11,330 (21%)
Radio	$ 440 (11%)	$ 3,650 (7%)
Daily Newspapers	$ 967 (24%)	$15,878 (29%)
Other (Community Papers, Periodicals Outdoor, Direct Mail)	$1,950 (48%)	$23,543 (43%)
PER CAPITA ADVERTISING EXPENDITURES IN 1981	CAN $180	US $275

Sources: Canadian Radio-television and Telecommunications Commission
Maclean Hunter Research Bureau
Statistics Canada

Canadian newspapers, on a regular basis, print numerous stories about American politics, economics and culture made available through a news exchange between the Associated Press (U.S.) and Canadian Press wire services. There is often more information that either originates or is processed in the United States than there is information about Canada (especially if syndicated material such as comics, crossword puzzles, stock market quotations, advice-to-readers columns, etc. is included). In fact, our perspective of the world in the print media—and by extension, in the electronic press—is largely through U.S. eyes.[3] In the periodical sector, the American influence is impressive: of the top 20 most popular mag-

3. T. Joseph Scanlon, "Canada Sees the World through U.S. Eyes: One Case Study in Cultural Domination." *Canadian Forum* (September, 1974), pp. 34-39.

azines, 10 are published in the United States and two are Canadian editions of American parentage.[4] The top 20 magazines have a combined circulation of 12 million, with 6.5 million (or 55 per cent) either imported directly from or having umbilical ties to the United States. Since 1976, when Ottawa passed legislation (Bill C-58) to bolster its periodical identity, the circulation of magazines imported from the United States increased 18 per cent in contrast to the four per cent increase in circulation of the top 10 magazines published in Canada.

The American influence is especially noticeable in television; the most popular American programs are also at the top of the TV rating list in Canada. Some of the famed American television personalities of the last decade—Farrah Fawcett, Ed Asner as Lou Grant, Alan Alda, Beatrice Arthur as Maude—are equally well-known on both sides of the border. In fact, U.S. programming dominates the Canadian scene at the prime time hours, even on the channels of the publicly owned Canadian Broadcasting Corporation. In the book and film sector, the American influence is, on a proportional basis, equally pervasive.

It is not only the economics of Canadian communications that are affected by the enormous inflow of U.S. material. Some quarters consider this mammoth inflow to be a cultural intrusion that reinforces U.S. economic influence and presumably weakens Canadian identity. The Minister of Communications, Francis Fox, has warned that by 1985 Canada would be "an occupied land, culturally," unless action was taken against the spread of U.S. television channels through satellite delivery systems. The problem is not new. More than a half-century ago, the Royal Commission on Broadcasting, headed by Sir John Aird, reported: "[T]he majority of programs heard are from outside of Canada. It has been emphasized to us that the continued reception of these has a tendency to mold the minds of the young in the home to ideals and opinions that are not Canadian."[5] This statement, made in 1929 about radio, certainly holds true for television in Canada today. (Interestingly, radio has since developed a Canadian character partly because of "Canadian content requirements" and, more importantly, because of the local orientation of radio since the introduction of television. The American influence on radio news, however, remains significant.) In both the print and broadcast media in this country, there has been some expectation that communications will serve particular Canadian needs, requiring a Canadian thrust to communications content.[6] The Aird Report emphasized these expectations: "In a country of the vast geographical dimensions of Canada, broadcasting will undoubtedly become a great force in fostering national spirit and interpreting national citizenship."[7]

How to Canadianize the content has usually been discussed in vague terms and

---

4. "Media Trends and Developments 1975-1983." Study prepared by J. Walter Thompson Company Ltd., August 1979.
5. Royal Commission on Radio Broadcasting, 1929. *Report*.
6. Frank W. Peers, "Canadian Media Regulation," in Gertrude J. Robinson and Donald F. Theal (eds.), *Studies in Canadian Communications*, McGill University Programme in Communications, 1975.
7. Royal Commission on Radio Broadcasting, *op. cit.*, 1929.

is highly controversial. There are also major economic implications. When the choice is free, Canadians are likely to choose the U.S. media. Even in the predominantly French-speaking province of Quebec, there is great interest in U.S. television fare. The sense of awareness about the U.S. scene sometimes makes it easier for Canadians to communicate with Americans across the border than with their fellow Canadians, who may live some 5,000 kilometres away.

BILINGUALISM

The fourth major Canadian communication problem stems from bilingualism. The influence of language on the communications flow is highly visible since it has produced two distinct media systems: English and French. The independence of the two communications networks may be a healthy reflection of bilingualism and biculturalism. At the same time, however, the separateness of the French and English communications networks is costly. It means a duplication of technical facilities which have the potential to serve a population far in excess of Canada's 24 million people.

Even more important are the problems as they relate to politics. Do French-speaking and English-speaking Canadians receive similar descriptions of political developments in this country? Indications are that they do not, that the English and French media portray very different images of the realities of politics and society and thereby reinforce ethnic and linguistic divisions by providing a support structure for different value systems.

THE RESPONSE

TECHNOLOGY

Canada has sought to deal with these mass media problems in a number of ways, including through technology and legislation. Technologically, our communications system is about the best in the world.

Canada was the first country to establish a domestic communications satellite system with the launching of the first in the series of Anik satellites in 1972. There are now four Aniks in permanent orbital positions 37,000 kilometres above the equator.[8] They have linked the Northern people and other Canadians living in remote areas with the national communications network. In effect, Canada has reached the point where almost everyone has access to television, radio and telephone—a rather remarkable achievement, considering the immense size of the country. Ground stations across Canada receive signals from the Anik satellites and interconnect with the international satellite network system to provide this country with a communications system that is almost futuristic in concept.

Between 1982 and 1985, Canada plans to launch five more Aniks which will expand enormously the country's telecommunications capacity. Some of these

---

8. *Anik A-1* was launched in November 1972, *Anik A-2* in April 1973, *Anik A-3* in May 1975 and *Anik B* in December 1978.

satellites may be placed in orbit by the American space shuttle, *Columbia*, using the space arm built in Canada.

Canada's pioneering work in space communications was advanced significantly by the experimental Hermes satellite launched in 1976. Hermes provided the breakthrough for the communications technology that is expected to come into widespread use in the 1980s, particularly in developing countries that lack extensive earthbound communications networks.

In the first instance, Canadian communication satellites revolutionized the broadcasting system. Distance from population centres no longer stood in the way of television and radio reception. The Canadian emphasis on electronic communications staggers the imagination. There are more than 3,000 broadcast operations. On a per capita basis, Canada has more radio and television stations, more broadcast receivers and more cable TV subscribers than any other country in the world. Canada has more television networks than the United States and by means of the highly developed cable TV system has access to the programming of the major American networks.

The Canadian Broadcasting Corporation, which is publicly owned and financed by Parliament, operates six national television and radio networks. The private sector of broadcasting in radio and television is highly profitable and competes for audiences with the CBC. There is a shortwave broadcasting service, Radio Canada International, that reaches out to five target areas—Eastern Europe, Western Europe, Africa, North America and Latin America—in 11 languages.[9] There is a Northern Service providing special programming to meet the particular needs of the Dene, Inuit, Métis and non-native people living in the North. There is an Armed Services network broadcasting to Canadian servicemen and women stationed abroad.

Moving from electronic broadcasting to the printed press, we find that historically, Canada has had no national newspapers. The country is so large that it has been impossible to transport daily newspapers from the city of publication to all other cities while the contents are still newsworthy. However, this situation is changing rapidly. In the 1960s, the Toronto *Globe and Mail* successfully conducted experiments with a facsimile process which transmitted pictures of newspages via the microwave system of the telephone company to other cities for newspaper reproduction. The process has since become cheaper, and thereby more feasible, by transmitting the signals from Toronto via Anik satellite.

In the fall of 1980, the *Globe and Mail* began publishing a national edition at printing plants in Montreal (later moved to Ottawa because of a fire) and Calgary. The network of satellite printing plants has since expanded to Vancouver

9. The languages are: English, French, German, Spanish, Portuguese, Russian, Ukrainian, Czech, Slovak, Hungarian and Polish. While RCI (Radio Canada International) programmes are beamed to specific target areas, they can be received in many other regions of the world, including Australia-New Zealand, Asia and the Canadian North. The RCI audience is estimated at about 10,000,000 shortwave listeners per week. Only eight per cent of Canadians and Americans have shortwave sets. In other countries, the percentage of shortwave radio sets in use ranges as high as 45 to 75 per cent. *RCI Brief for the CRTC*, 1978.

and Moncton in New Brunswick. In publishing simultaneously in six cities across Canada, the *Globe and Mail* has established the infrastructure for national distribution, an essential step toward becoming a truly national newspaper. The newspaper's own circulation projections indicate that it will take at least five years, and perhaps ten, to achieve a meaningful household penetration rate across the country that would clearly establish its status as a national daily.

In the absence of national newspapers, about 100 Canadian cities have their own daily papers which serve the multiple purpose of providing local, national and international news. This produces a fragmentation which is unequalled in any other country. (In the United States, the *Wall Street Journal* has national circulation through publishing simultaneously in several cities, and *The New York Times* was using satellite transmissions before the *Globe and Mail* to print out-of-city editions. In the fall of 1982, the Gannett Newspaper chain is slated to begin publishing a national daily, *USA Today*, in 15 metropolitan areas.)[10] In Britain and Japan, the national dailies in the capital cities account for 70 per cent of all newspaper circulation. The Soviet Union and France provide further examples of countries with national dailies.

It is essentially economics which explains the large number of cities in Canada with daily newspapers. But the economic factors relating to media structure, as we shall see, do not act independently. They flow instead from social and political characteristics. Canadian newspapers are private enterprises in which the profit motive is nearly always the principal *raison d'être*. This pursuit of profit has led to a high degree of concentration in the newspaper industry and has all but terminated competitive journalism in Canada. Most cities have only one daily, in sharp contrast to the way things were at the turn of the century when the newspaper field was highly competitive. This development has important implications for Canadian politics: the number of diverse media voices is reduced, and fewer people control the information flow. The political partisanship that was so noticeable when Canadian newspapers were genuinely competitive has virtually disappeared, leading to a product that attempts to be fair, or politically neutral. The decline in competition has effects beyond the newspaper field.

Newspapers in Canada play the key role in preparing the message which is disseminated by other mass media channels such as television, radio and magazines. The birth of the message in the Canadian communications process is very often linked to the newsgathering facilities of the daily newspapers and the Canadian Press wire service.

In addition to the daily newspapers, there are more than 1,000 community newspapers, usually published once or twice a week, mostly in smaller towns and rural areas. The community papers appear in English, French and 14 other languages.

More than 1,000 periodicals are published in Canada: about 800 in English, 150 in French, about 40 in both French and English, and 50 in other languages.

---

10. *Globe and Mail*, 16 December 1981.

These include about 350 "consumer magazines," some of which are national in distribution, while others have provincial or local circulations, with numerous business, agricultural and academic publications intended for more specialized readerships.

The high state of development of Canada's communications system reflects the enormous involvement that Canadians have with the mass media.[11] Surveys show that the average newspaper in Canada is read by nearly three persons, and that almost every Canadian old enough, or literate enough to read, examines a Canadian daily on a regular basis. There are more television sets than there are households and there are more radios in use in Canada than there are people.

LEGISLATION

To promote Canadian culture and Canadian identity, some legislation has been enacted in the past several decades. Parliament set up the Canadian Broadcasting Corporation (Société Radio Canada), a nationally owned radio and TV network, and the Canadian Radio-television and Telecommunications Commission (CRTC), which is a regulative agency controlling the licensing of broadcasting and the prescription of standards for Canadian content. In the mid-1970s, Parliament also enacted legislation aimed at promoting a more viable periodical industry by curtailing the tax privileges of Canadian editions of periodicals that are essentially foreign imports.[12] Consequently, *Time Canada* disappeared and the staid old magazine, *Maclean's*, changed its format to become the country's first newsmagazine. (The U.S. edition of *Time*, printed in Montreal, is now widely read in Canada and is profitable because it attracts Canadian advertisers.)

There are great difficulties in using legislation to control the mass media in a society which takes freedom of the press seriously. Canadian governments have moved most cautiously in this sphere to ensure that the promotion of legitimate national interests in the country's mass media industries does not lead to censorship or any other forms of news control which would be unacceptable to Canadians. While the Canadian Broadcasting Corporation is a publicly owned Crown corporation answering to Parliament, it appears to be effectively insulated from political interference, so much so that the CBC is regarded as the most outspoken mass media critic of governmental policies.[13]

Although there is in Canada a strong belief in freedom of the press, there are

11. In one week, the average Canadian watches 24 hours of television and listens to 19 hours of radio. Ninety-one per cent of the population has car radios.
12. Bill C-58 amended the Income Tax Act, sections 19(1) and 19(2). The legislation's impact was largely on periodicals but also affected advertising in "non-Canadian newspapers" and "foreign broadcast undertakings" (e.g., U.S. border situations). See Isaiah A. Litvak and Christopher J. Maule, "Bill C-58 and the Regulation of Periodicals," *International Journal*, Vol. XXXVI, No. 1, Winter 1980-81.
13. Arthur Siegel, *A Content Analysis. The Canadian Broadcasting Corporation: Similarities and Differences of French and English News*, Ottawa: Canadian Radio-television and Telecommunications Commission, 1977.

contradictory pressures on the independence of the media. Economic factors, which have curtailed newspaper competition, certainly affect this freedom. The economics of the newspaper industry have also led to concentration of ownership in both the French and English press: a handful of companies owns most of the country's newspapers. Ninety Canadian dailies are chain-owned; only 28 are owned by independent publishers. In eight of Canada's ten provinces, a single publisher controls at least two-thirds of the total provincial circulation. There is also concern about interlocking ownership of the printed press and broadcast media; some newspaper publishers have important interests in radio, television and cable companies.

In 1981, the Royal Commission on Newspapers (Kent Commission) warned that concentration of ownership was a threat to freedom of the press: "In a country that has allowed so many newspapers to be owned by a few conglomerates, freedom of the press means, in itself, only that enormous influence without responsibility is conferred to a handful of people."[14] The Commission declared in its opening statement that freedom of the press is a right of the people, not a property right of owners.

The Kent Commission's far-reaching recommendations will, if adopted, introduce an element of governmental supervision and intervention in the editorial and managerial practices of newspapers that may be incompatible with the independence of the press as it has evolved in Canada. The record of government in Canada at both the federal and provincial levels on press freedom issues has not always been reassuring, especially in times of stress.

One of the unresolved dilemmas of Canada which is shared by many other countries is how to reconcile freedom of the press with the pressures of the commercial system that finances it. This is a matter that we will explore when the ideological underpinnings of the Canadian media system are examined later.

Perhaps more pertinent than economics in shaping the political role of the press is the nature of the political system. The role of the press in an authoritarian society is quite different from its role in a democratic society. Yet even where freedom of the press is not only espoused as a principle of prime importance but is also practised, there are restraints on the flow of communications resulting from the political system. Later chapters will explain how Canada's parliamentary system, federalism and bilingualism help establish the parameters in which the mass media operate.

In 1982, as the government was examining the merits of a Canadian Newspaper Act (recommended by the Kent Commission), there were other significant developments in the interaction of media and politics. Most important was the "freedom of the press and other media of communication" provision in the new Canadian Constitution; it will, in the long term, bring about an expanded role for the courts on matters relating to the independence of the media. Furthermore, Parliament enacted Freedom of Information legislation aimed at providing the

14. Royal Commission on Newspapers, 1981. *Report*. Ottawa: Minister of Supply and Services, 1981, p. 217 (Kent Report).

public (and the media) greater access to government documents and thus encourage more open, and less secretive, government.

THE FUNCTIONS OF MASS COMMUNICATIONS AND NATION BUILDING

This book focuses on daily newspapers, radio and television—the mass media that disseminate information on a daily or continuing basis.

The essential activities of mass communications can be summarized for convenience in four words: information, interpretation, entertainment, and education.[15] The daily media are collectors and disseminators of information for the purpose of what the political scientist Harold Lasswell has called the surveillance of society.[16] Since raw news would be a confusing collection of massive amounts of information, the media also interpret the messages they carry and put them in a meaningful context. This interpretative activity is also referred to as correlation, editorializing and persuasion. Mass media have an entertainment function: watching television, listening to radio and reading newspapers are the principal leisure-time activities in society. The educational function of mass communications involves the transmission of culture, values, and social norms.[17]

The British sociologist, Denis McQuail, has observed that there is agreement that a major function of the media is "to increase integration and consensus in a society, to bridge social gaps and maintain continuity over time."[18] This integrative function is not one of the essential activities of the media; rather, it is expected to be the sum total result of all the media activities.

SUMMARY

The complexities of Canada's political system, the country's mixed economy in which publicly-owned sectors compete with private enterprise, the heterogeneous nature of the society, and the four major problems—geography, population dispersion, U.S. influence and bilingualism—facing communications make Canada an unusually fertile field for mass media research. How Canada copes with its staggering communications problem is of great importance to the country's search for unity and a sense of identity.

15. For a discussion of mass communications in society, see Charles R. Wright, *Mass Communication: A Sociological Perspective*, New York: Random House, 2nd edition, 1973, pp. 9-22. See also Morris Janowitz, "The Study of Mass Communications," *International Encyclopedia of the Social Sciences*, New York: The Macmillan Company and Free Press, 1968.

16. Harold D. Lasswell, "The Structure and Function of Communication in Society," in L. Bryson (ed.), *The Communication of Ideas*, New York: Harper and Brothers, 1948, pp. 37-51.

17. For a discussion of the media as part of the ideological system, see John Porter, *The Vertical Mosaic*, Toronto: University of Toronto Press, 1965, pp. 457-490. See also F. Elkin, "Communications Media and Identity Formation in Canada," by B. Singer (ed.), *Communications in Canadian Society*, Toronto: The Copp Clark Publishing Company, 1972, especially p. 229.

18. Denis McQuail, *Review of Sociological Writing on the Press*, British Royal Commission on the Press, Working Paper No. 2, London: Her Majesty's Stationery Office, 1976, p. 66.

CHAPTER II

THE MEDIA: POLITICAL POWER, IDEOLOGY AND ECONOMICS

Canadians, like people in most other countries, see the world beyond their immediate personal sphere through the mass media.[1] Few of us personally know the Prime Minister, the provincial premiers or other political personalities. Our relationship with politicians has become even more distant since World War II, although government today penetrates many more facets of our lives. Bigger government and more complex problems mean a correspondingly greater need to explain government and politics to the public. But parliamentary sessions are longer and MPs have responsibilities in Ottawa almost year round. The media fill the gap created by the politician's absence and distance from the home riding; they occupy new territory that was previously associated with the drama and literature of the hustings.

Much of what we know about political affairs comes from the media; they are carriers of information, ideas, thought and opinion. Robert Stanfield, the elder statesman of the Conservative Party, observed: "Canadians are getting the kind of political discussion their media are encouraging."[2] The political power of the media has been bolstered by broadcasting, as national audiences of millions can be reached simultaneously. This chapter deals with the sources and nature of the political power of the media and focuses on related ideological and economic factors. We also examine the interaction of newspapers and the broadcast press in relation to news flow.

---

1. For development of the argument that the expanse of our knowledge of public affairs comes from the media, see: William L. Rivers and Wilbur Schramm, *Responsibility in Mass Communication* (revised edition) (New York: Harper and Row, 1969), p. 14.
2. Robert Stanfield, "The Media and Politics: The Trend in Distributing," the *Globe and Mail*, October 2, 1980, p. 7.

SOURCES OF POLITICAL POWER OF THE MEDIA

Mass media political power flows from five major sources: the media as providers of information, the political linkage role, the agenda-setting role, the editorial offerings and the direct influence the media have on political actors.

Provision of Basic Political Information. The media are powerful because they provide basic information; they survey the society, including the political sphere, and transmit a continuous account of politics that includes warning signals about threats and dangers on the national and international scene, thus preparing the public for future developments.

Another example of media power stemming directly from their function as providers of information is that they make people famous, with persons singled out for newspaper or TV coverage receiving public recognition; this is called the "status conferral" role. Furthermore, persons who are "well-informed," largely through the media, are often regarded as influential, becoming important message carriers and image shapers for their friends on political matters.[3]

Political Linkage. A second source of political power is that the media are the major link between the public and the government. The nature of this linkage shapes in part the public's involvement in the political process and helps to define the "democratic nature" of the governmental system. The free flow of political communications is one of the major building blocks—perhaps the most important—in democratic societies. If voters are to make rational choices in elections they must have meaningful information and discussion of public issues; they depend on the media for this information and discussion.

Agenda Setting. The media do not transmit all the news that they have collected and that is made available by the press services; they are selective. In choosing and displaying news, editors and others who help shape media content must take into consideration the resources at their disposal, time factors and space considerations. Not only do the media describe the events of the political world as the editors perceive them, but they also pick and choose the events they regard as important. In effect they prepare the news menu, thus deciding the issues of the day that are to receive public attention. This is referred to as the agenda-setting function of the media.[4]

The press, says Bernard Cohen in his study of the press and foreign policy, "is significantly more than a purveyor of information and opinion. It may not be suc-

---

3. Elihu Katz and Paul Lazarsfeld, *Personal Influence* (New York: The Macmillan Company, 1964).
4. For an interesting account of the historical development of the agenda-setting concept, see Jack M. McLeod, Lee B. Becker, and James E. Byrnes, "Another Look at the Agenda-Setting Function of the Press," paper presented to the Theory and Methodology Division, Association for Education in Journalism, Ft. Collins, Colorado, August 1973. For application of the agenda-setting concept in international studies, see George Gerbner, "Press Perspective in World Communication: a Pilot Study," *Journalism Quarterly*, Vol. 38, Summer 1961, pp. 313-322. For application of agenda-setting in Canadian studies, see Walter C. Soderlund, Ronald H. Wagenberg, E. Donald Briggs, Ralph C. Nelson, "Regional and Linguistic Agenda-Setting in Canada: A Study of Newspaper Coverage of Issues Affecting Political Integration in 1976," *Canadian Journal of Political Science*, XII:2, June 1980.

cessful much of the time in telling people what to think, but it is stunningly successful in telling readers what to think about."[5] The consequences of this are of vital importance. For, as Cohen puts it:

". . . the world looks different to different people, depending not only on their personal interests, but also on the map that is drawn for them by the writers, editors, and publishers of the papers they read. . . ."[6]

These observations apply also to the electronic press.

If, as is argued here, the mass media are by far the most important—if not the only—information source about politics for the general population, then agenda setting is of critical importance in the analysis of the political process. The media exert influence through the choice of certain issues for emphasis in news presentation and editorial comment, as well as through the omission of others. Furthermore, the priorities of the media, "indexed by [the] day-by-day pattern of selection and display of the news, become over time the priorities of the public."[7]

Editorial Offerings. Another source of political power is derived from the editorial offerings. In newspapers this is especially visible in the form of editorials, background stories that discuss political issues and their merits, columns by political columnists, interpretive stories and political cartoons. What emerges is persuasion. The "ideological" perspective is not limited to editorial pages in newspapers and the commentaries of the broadcast press, as journalists often argue, but also shapes the general content of the media: selection of stories and pictures and the prominence of display. The persuasive power is directly related to the correlation function of mass communications; the media help to put the vast amount of information they collect into a "meaningful picture," and provide a support structure for a point of view.

Influence on Political Actors. Politicians recognize only too well the impact mass communication can have in generating public opinion, and as a result pay close attention to the coverage of politics and the editorial views expressed in the media. Consequently, the media influence politicians themselves.[8]

A number of examples illustrate this media power. Politicians will make statements in time for TV newscasts or newspaper deadlines; in other words, the media partly control the time frame for major political pronouncements and planned political events. It is a two-way relationship, with politicians and journalists trying to use each other for their own best interests. The role of the media in election campaigns is so important that how to "use" the media effectively, especially television, is a key element of political party strategy.

Mr. Stanfield has referred to another facet of media influence in elections

---

5. Bernard C. Cohen, *The Press and Foreign Policy* (Princeton: Princeton University Press, 1963), p. 13.
6. *Ibid.*
7. See also Maxwell McCombs and Lee Becker, *Using Mass Communication Theory* (Englewood, N.J.: Prentice-Hall, 1979), p. 121.
8. Colin Seymour-Ure, *The Press Politics and the Public* (London: Methuen, 1968), p. 301. See also Colin Seymour-Ure, *The Political Impact of the Media* (London: Constable, 1974).

stemming from his experiences in the unsuccessful effort to lead the Progressive Conservative Party to power in 1974. A photograph showing Mr. Stanfield fumbling a football was used widely by the media and became a symbol of his election campaign. Another area of difficulty for Mr. Stanfield was the 40-second TV clip inserted in the national newscasts; as he himself noted at a Conference on the Media and Politics, he is more famous for the 40-second *pause*.

"For a politician," says Mr. Stanfield, "the image is the maker or the breaker. It is more important for a politician to have a good media image than a good idea."[9] This is one of the reasons why politicians use the "planted leak" or "trial balloon" to see how a policy proposal or political appointment will be perceived by the media, and possibly the public, before making a formal decision. The image issue also arises when politicians are subjected to ridicule in the press over such matters as the way they walk, the size of their chins or the fact that their luggage was lost on an international tour.

One of the consequences of the greater importance of image over idea is that it tends to transform the statesman to an actor. Acting ability may be more important than truth in establishing credibility. Furthermore, television has "domesticated" the head of government and other leading political figures who are now seen in the living room and not on the hustings; this "false" familiarity has implications for the image of authority.

The sources of political power discussed here mean that the media strongly influence the political, social and economic environment. In fact, the media are an essential part of political life in industrial societies. It is not a one-way flow of influence, for the media do not operate in a vacuum: the institutions of mass communications and the information flow are shaped by the political system and economic features of the society. There is, then, a reciprocal relationship between the media and the political-social systems, each reflecting and influencing the other.

In studying the Canadian mass media system, it is useful to examine the ideological and economic conditions that help set the parameter of mass media operations. In a later chapter, we will analyse the constitutional and legal features that help shape mass media content. Only then can we proceed to evaluate the specific political role and influence of the media in Canada.

IDEOLOGY

The kind of linkage the media provide between the government and the public depends in large part on ideology, or the basic beliefs and assumptions which the society holds. There are at least five different ideological models affecting press operations: Authoritarian, Libertarian, Social Responsibility, Soviet-Communist and Developmental Journalism. The first four of these press styles or theories are described in *Four Theories of the Press* by Fred Siebert, Theodore Peterson and Wilbur Schramm. The authors argue convincingly that the media take on complementary characteristics of the social and political structures within which they

---

9. Stanfield, *Globe and Mail, op. cit.*

operate; "they reflect the system of social control whereby the relations of individuals and institutions are adjusted."[10]

The Authoritarian press style is the oldest of the media theories and is still characteristic of the press systems in many countries today. Within this style, the media operate "from the top down." The rulers use the media to inform the public while strictly controlling the content. Uncontrolled printing was seen as a potential threat to the authorities almost from the time that printing was first introduced by Gutenberg in the middle of the fifteenth century. In its modern form, the Authoritarian theory recognizes the political power of the media (print and broadcast) and governments seek to control the media to further their own interests. The media, whether privately or publicly owned, are subservient to the interests of the state. To ensure governmental control, there is a sophisticated arsenal: licensing of the media, censorship, pre-publication censorship, monetary (fines) and jail penalties, confiscation of newspapers and nationalization of the privately owned press sector.

The Libertarian theory emerged in the seventeenth century Age of Enlightenment, in company with political democracy, religious freedom, expansion of free trade and travel and the acceptance of a laissez-faire economy. In fact, the Libertarian press style was a prerequisite to political democracy. Both put their faith in a free exchange of ideas among well-informed individuals who would make the correct choices. The Libertarian theory is associated with freedom of the press as it is defined by the Anglo-American countries and other western nations.

The theory of Social Responsibility, which has its roots in the United States, is a mid-twentieth century outgrowth of the Libertarian theory and seeks to deal with some practical problems relating to the free marketplace of ideas. Freedom of the press has not quite lived up to expectations and, in some ways, the free marketplace of ideas has remained elusive, since all interests in the political and economic spectra have not had meaningful access to the mass media to make their voices heard. Social Responsibility places the burden on the mass media to be fair, politically as well as economically. The media must accommodate the interests of individuals and groups that may stem from linguistic, cultural, religious and ethnic rights, among others. Conflicts of interest between the society and the media also arise from advertising, especially misleading advertising, which has tarnished media credibility. There is much idealism in Social Responsibility and certainly the name has an enviable ring to it. But the theory raises some serious problems and carries with it elements of authoritarianism when it tries to find a mechanism to *ensure* that the press is responsible and will provide all the necessary information on important public issues.

The Communist theory asserts that the press should act in the interests of the state and party. These interests are seen as coinciding with the interests of society. In fact, the press does not function outside of the state; it is part of the state. In this way, there can be no oppression of the press, which can then serve as an

---

10. Fred Siebert, Theodore Peterson and Wilbur Schramm, *Four Theories of the Press* (Urbana: University of Illinois Press, 1963), pp. 1-2.

important instrument in furthering the cultural, educational and political doc-
trines that move from the top down. Critics see the Communist press theory as an
extension of authoritarianism, and indeed a purer form of the Authoritarian
theory, because state or party control is theoretically absolute. There is no private
ownership of media.

To these four theories of the press must be added a fifth: Developmental Journalism.[11] Many of the third world countries—the so-called uncommitted nations
in the ideological struggle between capitalism and communism—argue that there
is a need to restrict the free flow of news reporting in the developing countries
and eventually replace it with government-controlled information. The reasoning
is that the news about developing countries comes mostly from the international
news agencies which, since they are dominated by western news organizations,
distort the dissemination of news. Developmental Journalism argues, as the
Communist nations do at the United Nations, that governments should control
the news about the cultural, economic and social developments in their respective countries.

These theories of the press provide some insights and reference points for
comparison in the evolution of the Canadian media system. The Libertarian and
Social Responsibility theories prevail in Canadian mass media operations today.
But the theoretical glove does not always have a good fit. The mandate for the
public sector of broadcasting, for example, speaks of the public interest, laud-
ably fostering a sense of Canadian identity and promoting regional communication interaction. Does this mandate, if actively pursued, impose media restraints
that are incompatible with Libertarian theory? Furthermore, although Canada has
loudly proclaimed its opposition to Developmental Journalism at meetings of
UNESCO (United Nations Educational, Social and Cultural Organization), we
share with the third world countries the problems stemming from communications imperialism.

CANADA AND THE MEDIA

In Canada today, we place considerable emphasis on the responsiveness of our
political leaders and institutions of government to the attitudes and aspirations of
the public. It appears that governments and opposition parties are influenced
more by public opinion polls than by proceedings in Parliament. Examples
include the use of public opinion polls in the Quebec referendum debate, the
Ottawa-Alberta oil price dispute and the Canadian debate on constitutional
change.[12] In the 18-month period between March 1979 and September 1980,

---

11. For an interesting discussion on Developmental Journalism, see Robert Stevenson, Richard Cole
    and Donald L. Shaw, "Patterns of World Coverage: A Look at the UNESCO Debate on the
    'New World Information Order,' " paper presented to Association for Education in Journalism,
    Boston, August 1980.
12. In the Alberta-Ottawa oil dispute, the *Toronto Star* (October 4, 1980) had a front-page headline
    story declaring that most Canadians support raising the domestic price of oil to world levels. The
    poll, commissioned by the Alberta government, was released by Premier Peter Lougheed in the
    wake of failed oil-price talks.

federal government departments commissioned 141 public opinion surveys, an average of eight a month. The provincial governments, for their part, are equally adroit at using such polls. Only selected results are made public through the media and there are major problems with the interpretation given to the findings.[13]

The great battleground for public opinion is, of course, the mass media. The media carry messages from the government to the people. Their function, however, is not just to transmit the message, for then they would be little more than spokesmen and propaganda outlets for the authorities. Instead, the media select what they regard as important (although there may be a lack of context and continuity), and then attempt to put the information into a meaningful perspective. By focusing attention on particular events, the media help to define the political issues of the day and to determine the relevance of politics for the individual.[14] In this way they become the watchdogs for what they themselves define as the public's interest.

The concept of free press incorporates the mission of the media to search out missing elements that are part of the truth. The journalist sees himself as "an exemplary democrat" and "as the agent of the sovereign people." But actually it is the government and the opposition that represent the people according to the choices made at election time. Consequently the press cannot be only a critic or negative communicator. Ithiel de Sola Pool has argued that society as a whole "must have media that are the government's voice as well as media voices that oppose it.[15] If there are no media that express the government's goals and that are willing to disseminate explanations and support of them, the government's policy cannot possibly work and the government cannot function."[16]

The media are also "positive communicators" within the government itself. Douglas Cater draws our attention to this in the *Fourth Branch of Government*, noting that the press serves as a major instrument of communications in the policy-making process by linking different parts of the bureaucracy, the legislative and executive branches, as well as the government and the people.[17] Seen in this way, the press provides the necessary information for achieving coordinated action. In Canada, the informal linkages between the federal and provincial levels of government provided by the media are especially important.

The adversary view of the media, then, is only one side of the triangular relationship among the political sphere, the media and the people. In practice, the political journalist develops a close working relationship with the politician. The result is that the media are both friend and foe to the politicians. Politics has a

---

13. For an example of media problems about polls, see "Poll Referred to Foreign Sales," *Toronto Star*, October 11, 1980, p. 2.
14. V.O. Key, Jr., *Public Opinion and American Democracy* (New York: Knopf, 1961), pp. 390-405.
15. Douglas Cater, *The Fourth Branch of Government* (Boston: Houghton-Mifflin, 1959).
16. *Ibid*.
17. Ithiel de Sola Pool, "Newsmen and Statesmen," in William L. Rivers and Michael J. Nyham (eds.), *Aspen Notebook on Government and the Media* (New York: Praeger, 1973), pp. 12-50.

seductive influence on the journalist, but the liaison must not become too close. Press and politics cannot live without each other but they must also keep their distance if the public's interest is to be safeguarded.

This notion of the media as both friend and foe of political leaders is borrowed from the United States and Britain. In the American case, the adversary relationship is stressed. It finds its roots in the presidential-congressional system of government, which calls for checks and balances throughout the political system. American politics operates on the principle that people in power should not be trusted, that they should be watched closely to keep them honest. The presumption is that all those in power are corruptible. A good example of corruption in high places is provided by the celebrated Watergate case which led to the resignation of President Nixon. In Canada, where we have close access to American television fare, we are fascinated by this American brand of politics. It is politics in the open and politics in the raw, particularly acute in presidential election years.

In the British parliamentary system, on which Canada's governmental practices are based, there is a loyal opposition elected by the people. In theory, the press in the parliamentary system is more friend than foe to the political leadership, both in the government and the opposition. There is a strong "old boy Establishment" tradition in this kind of politics. It thrives on secrecy, which may well be the soft underbelly of the parliamentary system. Secrecy undermines the watchdog role of the media. Brian Chapman in *British Government Observed* argues that secretiveness has contributed to a weakening of Britain's capacity to cope with economic, social and foreign problems of the contemporary world.[18] Canada, as we will see later, is even more secretive than Britain.

There is a problem with borrowed concepts in that they may not be applicable to the Canadian case. The press theories associated with Britain and the United States are essentially normative prescriptions that do not have a good "ideological fit," nor do they apply to political conditions in both French- and English-speaking Canada. It will be argued later that our media system is American in style, while our political system is British in character. This presents an avenue of conflict in the interaction of press and politics in Canada. It may well be that Canadian students of the relationship between mass communications and the political system should ask different questions than those being raised in more homogeneous societies.

NATION BUILDING AND THE MEDIA

The most critical question relates to the very existence of Canada: the role of mass communications in nation building. Mass media have usually been seen as a major positive force in national cohesion. The traditional argument is that the media help foster a sense of identity and unity and mobilize consensus for the political culture of the society.

---

18. Brian Chapman, *British Government Observed* (London: George Allen and Unwin Ltd., 1963).

Wars of independence and revolutions also help to develop a sense of political community. Canada's identity crisis is not unique; the historical experience of most well-established and stable nations show that the sense of community developed over time. Canada—a product of negotiation and reasoning—had no war of independence or similar experience to unify the nation. Because of this background, our mass media carry an especially heavy burden in fostering a sense of nationhood. "If the sense of 'we-feeling,' of community, 'fails to emerge and deepen over time . . . it may leave a system extremely vulnerable to stress.' "[19] The identity problem does not stalk us continuously; rather, it surfaces and becomes a crucial issue at times of crisis. Our experiences in World Wars I and II, the Front de Libération du Québec (FLQ) Crisis of October 1970, and the unity crisis precipitated by the election of the separatist Parti Québécois in 1976 are some examples.

A key aspect of community, observes Karl Deutsch, is that people have learned to communicate with one another well beyond the mere exchange of goods and services. Efficient internal communications among a whole people seems to be one of the requirements of nationhood.[20] If the inhabitants of a given political unit exchange ideas more with other people in the same unit than with those outside it, prospects for national viability are better than if political lines cut across principal lines of communications.[21] If the picture of Canada portrayed by the mass media varies in important ways, and the variations are identifiable with population clusters that have a geographic or political base, then the communications flow has an unsettling effect on integration. It follows from this argument that the mass media are *not always* unifying bonds in a society. On the contrary, they can be divisive if they reinforce such nation-threatening differences as language or region. In examining communications in relation to Canadian identity, Canadians have in recent years been preoccupied with the external threat of a cultural intrusion by the United States that presumably weakens Canadian identity. We have overlooked the internal communications factors threatening Canadian unity, the question of gaps in communication within the country itself. In Karl Deutsch's terms: "People are marked off from each other by 'marked gaps' in the efficiency of communications."[22]

It is precisely to foster the national interest—recognizing the enormous importance of mass communications in creating this nation—that Canada established a public sector in the modern communications sphere: the electronic press. The mass media, the carriers of words and images, were seen as the ties that would help to bind Canada together during this century much as the railways and inland waterways were perceived as the links to physical union in an earlier period.

The setting-up of the first radio network in Canada in the 1920s by the Cana-

19. David Easton, *A System Analysis of Political Life* (New York: John Wiley, 1965), p. 187.
20. Karl W. Deutsch, *Nationalism and Social Communications* (Cambridge: M.I.T. Press, 1953), pp. 1-14.
21. *Ibid.*
22. *Ibid.*, p. 100.

dian National Railways to serve the travelling public was a cultural mission with an important political dimension. This network of transmitting stations providing for radio reception on the trains meant that many Canadians with radio receivers at home could also tune into the broadcasts. It was no accident that the CNR, a publicly owned Crown corporation, moved into the radio field. There is a natural link between land communications (transportation) and mass communications:[23] the former involves the communication of bodies and substances, while the latter relates to communication of words and images. There was a cultural mission in the establishment of the Canadian Broadcasting Corporation-Radio Canada in 1936, much as there was a cultural mission in the creation of the Crown-owned National Film Board. In fact, this common thread of cultural mission can be seen in the creation of the Massey Royal Commission on Culture, the Fowler Commission on Broadcasting, the establishment of the Canadian Radio-television and Telecommunications Commission (CRTC) and a whole host of other developments in the communications industry, including our emphasis on communications satellites. In 1982, the Federal Cultural Policy Review Commission was preparing its Report on the most comprehensive review in 30 years of Canadian cultural institutions and cultural policy.

In emphasizing the cultural dimension of communications there is a tendency to overlook the political. Granting a broadcasting licence, the Fowler Commission noted, is essentially a political act. We talk of culture as something that is disembodied and can apply to a state. Actually, culture applies to the people within the state. The culture of a society is strengthened through openness, for woven into the cultural fabric are strands from other cultures.

Canada's internal lines of communications—including canals, telegraphs, railways, airlines, broadcasting and the Canadian Press news agency—were for the most part political rather than cultural in nature in the first instance. Identity is cultural in nature; unity is a political dimension. We seek a co-terminus or a congruence between the political and cultural streams. Identity and unity imposed artificially on each other produce uniformity, which tends to weaken rather than enhance cultural richness.

If cultural mission was a crucial element in Canadian communications policy, fear of cultural disintegration played an important role in the evolution of Harold Innis' thought in this area.[24] A country like the United States, with a powerful communications system, can extend its powers far beyond its borders through ideas and values. In this sense, it is argued that American cultural imperialism is

---

23. For a discussion of the links between transportation and communication, see Douglas Hartle, "The Regulation of Communications in Canada," *Government Regulation: Issues and Alternatives 1978* (Toronto: Ontario Economic Council, 1978).
24. Innis, *Bias of Communication, op. cit.* See also Harold Innis, *Empire and Communication* (Toronto: University of Toronto Press, 1972). For a sensitive discussion of the contributions of Innis and Marshall McLuhan to Canadian communication theory, see Donald F. Theal, "Communication Theory and the Marginal Culture: The Socio-Aesthetic Dimensions of Communication Study," in Donald F. Theal and Gertrude Robinson (eds.), *Studies in Canadian Communications, op. cit.*, pp. 7-26.

imposed on Canada.[25] Innis' opposition to cultural dominance—it threatens Canadian national life—should not be interpreted as an anti-United States bias, since he was close to American culture and, in terms of political organization, he was close to the republic. But he recognized the force of empire and he dealt in realities. One reality to which he gave very little attention is the cultural dimension of Quebec nationalism.

Innis, who died in 1952, is a much-celebrated Canadian economic historian whose work on the course of Canada's economic and political development, revealing as it did its dependency relationship with the growing American imperial power, imposed on him the more global questions about the general state of health of western civilization. Ultimately, this interest generated his unique approach to the study of society and social change, whereby he concentrated on the dominant communications technology in a given society and assessed its cultural, economic and political impact. A range of techniques and consequent social patterns formed the basis for his development of a theory of society and social change, which he called the bias of communications.

Innis concluded from his research and analysis that "stable and creative civilizations were those that successfully balanced time factors and space factors. Time factors involve transmission of culture and values from one generation to another, creating a sense of continuity with its historical predecessors," while space factors "refer to those administrative institutions and techniques that are required for managing and governing a given territory."[26] The media of communications, broadly defined, are the major mechanisms for promoting human cohesion over time and space.

Innis found he could now explain an important source of the weaknesses and deficiencies of western civilization. Unfortunately, he could not predict the elimination of these shortcomings, for every feature of the most modern mass media tended to emphasize the spatial dimension, the mass media reach to span the country (and even beyond) in a process of centralization that stresses the immediate interests in politics, economics and entertainment. The vitally important influences of culture and traditional values that have local and regional roots are de-emphasized. Hence the Canadian case was only a specific problem within the context of a much broader and more severe condition that found its roots in the commercialization of mass communications.

Changes in communications technology, Innis showed, change the nature of the society, and new social systems emerge. It is in this sense that Marshall

25. Writing in 1952, Innis said that in the Depression the American government learned much of the art of propaganda from business and exported new technological devices such as the radio. He noted that in World War II, the American instruments of propaganda were enormously extended. "The effects of these developments on Canadian culture have been disastrous. Indeed they threaten Canadian national life." Harold Innis, *Changing Concepts of Time* (Toronto: University of Toronto Press, 1952), p. 18. For an overview of the intellectual foundations of Canadian communications, see James W. Carey, "Canadian Communication Theory: Extensions and Interpretations of Harold Innis," in *Studies in Canadian Communications, op. cit.*, pp. 27-59.
26. Sally F. Zerker, "Harold Innis and Past and Present in the Middle East," *Middle East Focus*, September 1978.

McLuhan's oft-quoted saying "the medium is the message" takes on profound meaning: mass media are the carriers of our cultural stamp. They reflect the society of our times and in turn mold it.

ECONOMICS

Much attention has been given in Canada to the economics of mass communications. In idealistic terms, the mass media are variously referred to as the Fourth Estate, the Fourth Branch of Government and an essential pillar of democracy. There is a tendency, on the part of political scientists, sociologists and even the public at large, to think of the media as social institutions, enjoying perhaps semi-official status, with defined rights and privileges. Seen this way, the media exist for the public good; in political terms, they are support structures for the modern political states. These viewpoints do not pay sufficient attention to economic considerations.

In Canada, as in many other western societies, mass communications is essentially a profit-making industry. Canadian media have been incredibly profitable, so much so that they have served as a springboard from which integrated corporate power emerged. The most dramatic example of this is provided by the late Lord Thomson, who started with modest means in Canada. Thomson's very small newspaper investment developed into the world's largest mass communications empire, including Canadian newspapers, papers in the United States and numerous media holdings (print and broadcast) in Britain and other countries. The Thomson enterprises today include department stores and North Sea oil. (In 1981, Thomson was an unsuccessful bidder for Abitibi-Price, the world's largest newsprint manufacturer.)

A further illustration of more recent origins is provided by Sterling Newspaper Limited, which went on sale in 1978 for $14 million. For this sum, Sterling was willing to part with 18 newspapers: nine small town dailies, and nine weeklies and bi-weeklies. (The deal between Sterling and Maclean Hunter, one of Canada's biggest communications companies, fell through at the last moment. In 1981, the Sterling holdings were worth an estimated $18 million.)

Sterling Newspapers began as a minor operation with the purchase of the *Sherbrooke Record* in Quebec province in 1969 for less than $50,000. Owned by David Radler (a management consultant), Gerald Peter White (a London, Ontario, lawyer) and Conrad Black (a financier who became president of the giant Argus conglomerate in 1978), Sterling was able to turn the *Sherbrooke Record* around and show a profit within four months. In nine years, Sterling expanded to a multi-million dollar corporation. The company's principal purpose had nothing to do with social function, politics or other high ideals; it was to make money. Based on Thomson's successful formula, Sterling's approach was to buy out barely surviving small newspapers in small communities. The local newspaper managers were told to find out what kind of newspapers their customers wanted and to give it to them. After that, the local newspapers invariably prospered. The Thomson and Sterling cases are classical examples of the profit-making approach to journalism. For others, see Chapter VI.

The mass media, then, are perceived differently by politicians, academics, newspaper owners, journalists and the public. To the politician, the media are the link to the people, the battleground for political party support and the vehicle for hoped-for political success. The academics most often concern themselves with the functions and dysfunctions of mass communications, dealing with such important issues as violence in the media, pornography and the stereotyping of women. The public, in the main part, looks to the media for entertainment and information. To the media owners, the main purpose of the media is usually profit, as Lord Thomson was honest enough to acknowledge. The Canadian mass media have an outstanding profit record. They are the envy of media owners in many other countries.

In their search for profits, the mass media face all the dangers of the commercial world. The keys to success have been monopoly, achieved by absorbing local competitors in the newspaper field, chain ownership of newspapers and multi-media ownership. These very ingredients may be detrimental to democracy. The many voices of the free marketplace become stilled. Only a few loud voices are heard and these have each carved out their own area of operation so that only one voice can be heard in each community. Because of the central role of newspapers in the news and information process, this situation has major implications for the entire flow of public communications in Canada. In practice, the media owners have been careful to separate profits from politics and ideology and, by focusing on profits, have sought to produce the most palatable product that will sell well, thus providing ever larger audiences for the advertisers. Even critics of concentration of ownership readily admit that when a chain buys a newspaper, the paper tends to become more efficient and, because of technological improvements, often also more attractive.[27] In general, the key to success has been the Thomson and Sterling motto: Give the public what they want, since that sells best. In this way, the media have become all things to all men.

There have been dramatic changes in the newspaper field since the 1950s. Qualitative changes have come in large part as a result of competition that the newspapers face from the broadcasting industries for audience attention and consequently for advertising revenues. Equally important changes flow from the computerized systems that have become commonplace in the industry. In the newsroom, the video display terminal is replacing the reporter's typewriter and paper. The editor is using electronic dots instead of a blue pencil. Molten lead in the newspaper plant has given way to the "cold type" system which uses photographic methods for newspaper composition. Laser beams are now working their way into Canadian dailies. In the circulation department, the computers are helping to produce information that reflects a newspaper's individuality and local

27. For example, see N.R. Kleinfield, "The Great Press Chain," *New York Times Magazine*, April 8, 1979.

characteristics and at the same time is providing what Anthony Smith has called that air of mechanized assurance that a well-run airline provides for its customers.[28]

In 1982, newspapers were moving in new and radical directions that included a "national daily" and delivery to the home of electronic "pages" and ads via television sets and home computers. The new technology brought a significant degree of automation to a labour-intensive industry; it required large capital expenditures but at the same time increased profit potential.

Canadian newspapers have been at the forefront in computerization and in adapting new labour-efficient print technology. By June 1980, 85 Canadian dailies (70 per cent) had already switched to the offset printing process in which a newspaper page is photographically reproduced on a thin metal plate, which is curved to fit the revolving cylinder of the printing press.

Newspaper owners are reluctant to discuss the degree of unionization among journalists, composing room staff, pressmen, truck drivers and office workers in their operations. It is clear, however, that unionization in the newsroom came late in Canada and did so in piecemeal fashion. (The printers and pressmen in Toronto were unionized early but here also the union factor has been less important in recent years compared with Britain and the United States. For example, three Toronto dailies continued publishing during a seven-year strike from 1964 to 1971 by the mailers and pressmen and succeeded in ousting the unions.) Unionization led to higher wages and better working conditions for journalists and other employees. Non-union newspapers matched and even surpassed union salaries, partly in order to keep out the unions. Canadian newspapers generally have been determined to prevent unionization wherever possible and, where unions are in place, to override objections to automation that make some jobs obsolete.

The conflict between newspaper owners and unions resulted in numerous publication interruptions in recent years, lasting nine or ten months for some papers. Table II.1 shows a dramatic increase in strikes beginning in 1970, when the impact of automation began working its way through unionized dailies. In the five-year period from 1965-69 inclusive, no newspapers were shut down by strikes. There were 36 strikes in the 1970s. In cities with newspaper competition, the shutdowns resulted in mass defection of readers to rival papers, which the struck papers were never able to fully recoup when they resumed publication. In fact, strikes have sometimes been fatal for newspapers in competitive markets. Examples are the permanent closings of *Montréal-Matin* and the *Montreal Star* in 1979. In contrast, newspapers without competition have suffered little long-term damage.

---

28. Anthony Smith, *Goodbye Gutenberg* (New York: Oxford University Press, 1980), p. 107.

TABLE II.1   Strikes Resulting in Publication Interruptions in Canadian Daily Newspapers, 1964-1982*

YEAR	NAME OF NEWSPAPER	STRIKE PERIOD
1964	*La Presse*, Montreal	June to December (7 mths)
1970	*Windsor Star*	December 2 to 18 (16 days)
	The Province & The Vancouver Sun	February 14 to May 15 (3 mths)
1971	*La Presse*, Montreal	October 27, 1971 to February 10, 1972 (3 mths 10 days)
	Sudbury Star	April, May & June (14 days)
1972	*La Presse*, Montreal	(See 1971)
1973	*La Voix de l'Est*, Granby	October 18 to December 31 (2½ mths)
	Le Soleil, Quebec	May 5 to 11 (6 days)
	Sudbury Star	October 4 to November 2 (1 mth)
	Windsor Star	May 22 to 31 (9 days)
	Victoria Colonist & Victoria Times	December 1, 1973 to May 31, 1974 (6 mths)
1974	*Brantford Expositor*	June 19, 20 & 21 (3 days)
	Ottawa Citizen	June 13, 14 & 26 (3 days)
	Ottawa Journal	June 13, 14 & 26 (3 days)
	Sudbury Star	April 18 to July 31 (3½ mths)
	Windsor Star	May 15, 18 & 19 (3 days)
	Victoria Colonist & Victoria Times	(See 1973)
1975	*Le Quotidien du Saguenay Lac St. Jean*, Chicoutimi	November 14 to November 28 (14 days)
	Le Devoir, Montreal	November 12 to December 11 (1 mth)
	The Montreal Star	May 30 to July 8 (1 mth)
	Kamloops Daily Sentinel	March 18 to December 8 (9 mths)
	Kelowna Courier	March 18 to December 8 (9 mths)
	Nanaimo Free Press	May 6 to December 6 (7 mths)
	Penticton Herald	March 18 to December 8 (9 mths)
1976	*Le Nouvelliste*, Trois Rivières	March 1 to April 27 (2 mths)
	The Province & The Vancouver Sun	August 6 to August 20 (14 days)
1977	*La Presse*, Montreal	October 7, 1977 to May 8, 1978 (8 mths)
	Montréal-Matin	October 7, 1977 to May 8, 1978 (8 mths)
	Le Soleil, Quebec	August 29, 1977 to July 8, 1978 (10 mths)
1978	*L'Evangeline*, Moncton	May 18 to May 24 (4 days)
	La Presse, Montreal	(See 1977)
	Montréal-Matin	Ceased publishing January 3, 1979
	Le Soleil, Quebec	(See 1977)
	La Tribune, Sherbrooke	May 3 & June 13 to July 4 (22 days)
	The Montreal Star	June 13, 1978 to February 12, 1979 (8 mths)
	The Province & The Vancouver Sun	November 1, 1978 to June 29, 1979 (8 mths)
1979	*The Montreal Star*	Ceased publishing September 25, 1979
	The Sudbury Star	June 27, 1979 to November 3, 1979 (5 mths)

	The Province & The Vancouver Sun	(See 1978)
	The Evening Telegram, St. John's	August 2, 1979 to November 15, 1979 (3 mths)
1980	Oshawa Times	March 26, 1980 to May 2, 1980 (1½ mths)
1981	Le Devoir, Montreal	April 7, 1981 to June 10, 1981 (2 mths)
	Le Quotidien du Saguenay Lac St. Jean, Chicoutimi	October 20, 1981 to November 9, 1981 (17 days)
1982	Le Droit, Ottawa	March 5, 1982 to March 26, 1982 (18 days)
	La Tribune, Sherbrooke	April 9, 1982 to April 21, 1982 (10 days)
	Le Nouvelliste, Trois Rivières	April 10, 1982 to April 14, 1982 (4 days)

Source: Canadian Daily Newspaper Publishers Association

*Table valid to April 1982

The broadcast sector has also been affected by technological developments and unionization, with major impact on news and public affairs programming. Electronic cameras and satellite hook-ups, among other innovations, have made television news programming more immediate and flexible. These costly developments come at a time when television audiences are increasingly fragmented, because of the wide choice of offerings made available through cable delivery systems. Unionization is especially high in the public-sector Canadian Broadcasting Corporation and thus helps set wage scale patterns that also affect the privately owned stations.

With higher wages in the news operations of newspapers and broadcasting, a new breed of journalist is developing. The old high school graduate who worked his way up in the newsroom, almost in apprentice fashion, has given way to those who spent two or three years at college and most recently to university graduates. In the 1950s, reporters on small Canadian dailies were earning $40 a week and editors at the press agencies, about $55. Journalism was often a passing stage for the ambitious, with reporting being viewed as a preparation for the writing jobs in public relations and government information services. In the 1980s, journalism is a respectable career in itself. Though jobs in newspapers are becoming increasingly scarce, the journalism departments at universities have record enrollments. The working journalist, in print and broadcasting, does not resemble the bohemian characters of Bill Weintraub's novel *Don't Rock the Boat* or the movie *The Front Page*.

The better-educated reporter has found some measure of security (except, of course, where newspapers folded) and a good salary, especially if he belongs to the Canadian Newspaper Guild (affiliated with The Newspaper Guild in the United States). The union had its start in the United States in 1933, but it was not until 1949 that the *Toronto Star* became the first Canadian daily to sign a guild contract. The Guild established a permanent Canadian Regional Office in 1972.

Newsroom salaries (print and broadcast) in Canada vary considerably, depending on size of city and union affiliation. For example, a reporter at the Thomson-owned Toronto *Globe and Mail* probably earns twice as much as his colleague at a small Thomson paper without a guild contract. The highest salaries in 1982 at newspapers that have guild contracts were at the *Montreal Gazette*, where reporters with five years' experience were earning a minimum weekly wage of $650. The salaries at other unionized dailies were as follows: *Vancouver Sun* and *Vancouver Province* $621, *Victoria Times-Colonist* $635, *Toronto Star* $533, *Ottawa Citizen* $540, *Sudbury Star* $421 and *Oshawa Times* $412. On average, the highest-paid journalists are the unionized editors and reporters at the Canadian Broadcasting Corporation.

News, as was observed earlier, is an expensive commodity. The public is unwilling to pay the actual costs of newspaper or broadcast media production and prefers to subsidize them indirectly through the added costs of products they buy, that is, through advertising. (Before general advertising became a major source of income, newspapers in Canada were largely supported by printing government announcements and similar type of official work.) In strict economic terms, the media exist as message bearers for people who want to sell something to newspaper readers, radio listeners or television audiences. Advertising accounts for 78 per cent of the revenues of newspapers in Canada and nearly all of the income of the private sector of radio and television. And Canadians—whether French- or English-speaking—are apparently satisfied with this arrangement. In a sense then, media have become the wrappings of advertising.

The importance of advertising in mass media is clearly illustrated by the advertising spending figures in Canada (see Chart II.1). In 1981, Canadian advertisers funnelled nearly $1 billion into daily newspapers, $695 million into television and $440 million into radio. The total advertising spendings for the year were over $4 billion; 38 per cent went to the print media (dailies, weeklies and magazines), 28 per cent was directed to television and radio and outdoor advertising and other kinds of advertising accounted for the rest. Advertising spendings in 1981 were more than double the spendings in 1975.

There is, understandably, suspicion that the editorial line is influenced by the revenue sources. Certainly, there are some examples of this in Canadian dailies. The high profit special sections of newspapers (e.g., real estate, travel) are built around a theme and frequently carry news stories that are little short of open advertising. But, by and large, newspapers have become so economically viable and, with the advertisers' choice limited because of the monopoly situation, the risks of advertising dictating editorial content is very much neutralized. Peter Worthington, the *Toronto Sun's* outspoken editor-in-chief, has cited four major examples of companies that tried to show their displeasure about *Sun* coverage of their affairs by withholding advertising, "but they soon returned" with their business.[29] The advertiser will not go away because there is virtually no competition in the newspaper field. In proof of this, major advertisers—the auto

---

29. Peter Worthington made his comments on the CITY-TV program *The Shulman File*, October 5, 1980.

CHART II.1.   **Advertising Revenues in Canada, by Medium, 1981**

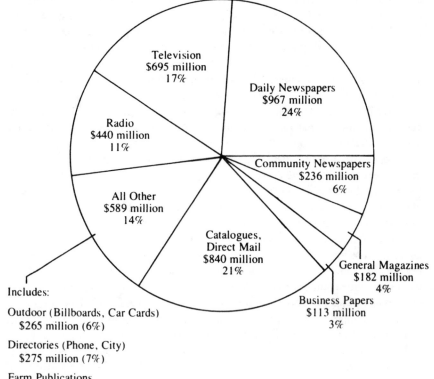

Television
$695 million
17%

Daily Newspapers
$967 million
24%

Radio
$440 million
11%

Community Newspapers
$236 million
6%

All Other
$589 million
14%

Catalogues,
Direct Mail
$840 million
21%

General Magazines
$182 million
4%

Business Papers
$113 million
3%

Includes:

Outdoor (Billboards, Car Cards)
$265 million (6%)

Directories (Phone, City)
$275 million (7%)

Farm Publications
Religious, School
$28 million (1%)

Weekend Supplements $21 million (.5%)

Total Advertising Revenues, 1981 = $4.1 billion

Source: Maclean Hunter Research Bureau

industry, liquor distilleries, the cigarette industry, chemical manufacturers, and the oil industry, among many others—have come in for considerable criticism in the media in recent years. Consumer interests have received better press than did the image of the giants of industry that was sometimes tarnished by problems related to pollution of the environment, windfall profits, etc.

While there may be little, if any, direct interference by the advertisers in editorial content, advertising has an indirect impact. Of critical importance to the advertiser is the size and spending power of the audience. While newspapers are thriving, the success stories of Sterling and Thomson have whetted the profit appetites of other newspaper chains. In the 1970s, the newspaper publishing industry increasingly made use of opinion polls in order to find out what the readers want. The judgements of the editors as to what is newsworthy are being challenged.

The advice of the media consultants and the pollsters has brought change to the content of Canadian dailies with "soft news" do-it-yourself features, gossip columns and petty crime stories replacing the "hard facts" reporting that is generally regarded as important in producing well-informed citizens. Doug Fetherling observes that major Canadian newspapers have reversed their order of priorities—soft news instead of hard news—almost to the exclusion of staff-written national and international news.[30] Such policies are aimed at increasing newspaper circulation generally and among young persons specifically. The *Ottawa Citizen*, for example, in 1978 became a conspicuous convert to the soft news approach with three sections "feeding the readers' appetite for trivia": the daily TEMPO section, the weekly TGIF and Neighbourhood News.[31] The purpose of newspaper supplements and special sections is to reach specific audiences and the *Citizen*'s TGIF section was described in a management memorandum as "some attractive bait to dangle in front of the large group of non-readers, from high schoolers to young adults, who do not have the newspaper reading habit." The 18-34 age group, extremely important in the consumer market, is a notoriously difficult audience for newspapers to reach. Supplement sections such as business, travel, real estate, books, homes, etc. are aimed at specific demographically defined readers. Also, newspapers have developed "zoning" patterns with one section of a paper directed to one area or suburb, thus making it economically easier for advertisers to reach a specific market, a phenomenon that is related to market segmentation. One apparent consequence of "soft" news emphasis and other changes related to marketing and public opinion surveys is that Canadian newspapers are in the process of becoming magazines, while television and radio provide the "hard" news.

There is also some evidence that hard news, as presented in Canadian newspapers, is not all that meaningful. Our political system, with its division of powers between the federal and provincial levels, and parliamentary traditions that may be rich in history and tradition but not always understood by the public, provide us with such a complex form of government that Canadian political news, as traditionally presented, often loses its meaning. The federal government's Task Force on Government Information in 1969 found that many Canadians were poorly informed about public affairs, especially in relation to federal-provincial jurisdiction. It is a sad commentary on the involvement of Canadians in the political process that only one-third of the adult population knows the name of one cabinet minister other than the Prime Minister. There is also a question of mood. The Canadian environment, and the world generally, has become so complex that people may be turning off from the details about the "real world," and a quick summary on radio or TV may be all the public wants. Newspapers, then, are transforming their editorial content because of such interacting factors as market conditions, computerization and the advice of pollsters. All affect the relationship between the print and broadcast media.

30. Douglas Fetherling, "All the News that's Soft Enough to Print," *Maclean's*, October 30, 1978.
31. *Ibid*.

THE PRINTED AND ELECTRONIC PRESS: INTERACTION

Broadcasting, and especially TV, is generally perceived as the most important sector of the Canadian mass media in shaping public opinion today. Canadians appear to put greater trust in broadcast news than in what they read in the newspapers. A national Gallup Poll in 1978 found that if there are conflicting reports of an event, Canadians will believe television rather than the printed press.

This tendency for more Canadians to rely on the broadcast media for news rather than on the newspapers is confirmed in a number of studies, including one carried out by the CRTC in 1975 (see Table II.2). This enhanced broadcast role for news dissemination is especially strong for Quebec. The Davey Special Senate Committee Study on the Mass Media (1970) observed that French-Canadian culture, and the media that help to define it, seems to reflect an oral bias. [32]

TABLE II.2   **Preferred Media Reliance of Canadians for News, by Language**

MEDIA	ENGLISH-SPEAKING	FRENCH-SPEAKING	TOTAL CANADA
TV	36%	53%	40%
Radio	25%	15%	22%
Newspaper/ Magazine	39%	31%	37%

Source: Research Branch, CRTC Fall '75 National Survey

In recognizing the importance of the broadcast media for news dissemination in Canada, we should not underestimate the role of the printed press in the mass communications process. The printed press, especially the daily newspapers, provide the depth to news collection. In Canada, as in Britain, the United States and most other countries, broadcast journalism has not yet produced a comprehensive news service that is independent of the newspaper system (and its support structure, the wire services). [33] There is some indication that, in the present state of media development, societies without a highly developed daily newspaper system are communications-deprived.

When newspaper strikes occur at critically located geographic sources of news collection, the impact on the electronic media is easily observed. This was the case in Quebec province in 1977-78 when Montreal's *La Presse* and *Montréal-Matin* were closed for eight months and there was a ten-month shutdown of *Le Soleil* in Quebec City. Another example was the strike that closed Vancouver's

---

32. *Report of the Special Committee on Mass Media, op. cit.*, Vol. 1, p. 95.
33. Ben H. Bagdikian, *The Information Machines* (New York: Harper and Row, 1971), p. 138. For another view of the factors that help shape broadcast news, see Edward Jay Epstein, *News From Nowhere* (New York: Random House, 1973). This book is based on Epstein's doctoral dissertation in political science at Harvard University in 1968.

two dailies for six months in 1978-79. Local news was especially hard hit. It virtually disappeared in Vancouver and declined sharply in Quebec, although competing papers continued publication. Furthermore, when there are no newspapers, the television stations are deprived of their major reference points as to what is newsworthy.

It is no accident that the Canadian content of broadcast news declines appreciably during the weekends. This happens because there are few Sunday newspapers. Consequently, the Canadian Press news agency, which to a large extent depends on the news collected by daily newspapers, carries little Canadian news. It is international news that tends to dominate weekend and holiday broadcasts. Canadian TV newscasts, for example, will give detailed coverage to accidental deaths during long holiday weekends (e.g., July 4th, Labour Day, Christmas, etc.) in the United States with comparatively little about the accident rate in Canada. The limited amount of news available on Sundays was especially noticeable in the FLQ crisis of October 1970, when some of the most traumatic events took place on weekends. The Quebec Labour Minister Pierre Laporte was kidnapped on the long Thanksgiving holiday weekend, so that most Canadians did not receive newspaper accounts until the following Tuesday. Mr. Laporte was murdered on Saturday evening one week after his kidnapping. The overall meaning of what had taken place that black weekend in Canadian history, the editorial perception of the events and some guidelines to the public as how Canada should move to cope with these problems did not emerge until the newspapers reappeared on the streets. In Quebec province, one newspaper, the French-language *La Tribune* of Sherbrooke brought out a special Sunday edition. *La Tribune* is a small paper and would normally rely on Canadian Press for its major out-of-town stories. Most of *La Tribune*'s stories about the Laporte death were based on what the reporters and editors gleaned from television and radio.[34] The Sunday CP news file has improved since 1970, when there was only one Sunday newspaper in Canada; in 1982, there were nine.

Canadian newspapers, especially because of their local character, provide the best source of continuous coverage of the local environment. Canadian dailies carry a triple load: they cover the international, national and local scene. They can present details in their news coverage which the broadcast media, with their strong emphasis on entertainment, cannot match. Furthermore, newspaper journalists have a strong sense of civic responsibility that has not yet evolved in as sharp a form among broadcasters.

There are many things the broadcast media can do better than newspapers: they can reach the public faster, even simultaneously, in emergencies and for the first accounts of very important developments such as the murder of Pierre Laporte and the assassination of President Kennedy. No newspaper account could match the direct television transmissions from the lunar module as the first man stepped on the moon. The broadcasting of important political events provides average Canadians with the opportunity to see the Prime Minister at a press

---

34. Information based on interviews with editors and reporters in 1973.

conference or, more recently, to view the proceedings of budget presentations and other activities of Parliament. Political leaders have used these occasions with great skill to bypass some of the filtering process involved in news handling. The planned broadcast exposure of such figures as the Prime Minister and the leader of the opposition are normally stage-managed and not nearly as open and frank as the public assumes, but they do give viewers an enhanced sense of involvement in political affairs. Prime Minister Trudeau, Quebec Premier Lévesque and the late John Diefenbaker are examples of Canadian politicians with broadcast skills. Examples of effective use of radio in the United States were President Franklin Delano Roosevelt's so-called fireside chats.

Politicians hardly get excited when they see the reporter with his notebook. It is the TV cameras that make the politicians take notice: the quick smile appears. Yet broadcasters, the best paid in the journalistic profession, were not considered real "newsmen" in Canada until rather recently. It was only in 1959 that radio and TV reporters were allowed into the Parliamentary Press Gallery in Ottawa, by far the most important institution in the political communications flow in Canada. The TV journalists have since become media stars.

The broadcast media and the print media do not appeal to different audiences among the adult population; they reach the same group. The news reports in the electronic media are aimed mainly for the ears, while the newspaper messages are eye-oriented.

Radio and television reports would hardly ever get into a newspaper the way the texts are written. They may be fair and accurate but they often lack depth. Some of what we hear on TV or radio may make sense to the ear but when seen in print appears almost illiterate.

In newspapers, there is a wall separating the reporter who bears the message from the message itself. The public receiving the newspaper account is not likely to have any idea as to what the reporter looks like or his personal attitudes to issues. Much of TV news may be straight hard facts, but it also consists of reporters raising questions, drawing conclusions and forecasting events. David Brinkley, whose newscast audiences in the United States ran into the millions, in speaking about the differences between the newspaper and TV media, says: "Words lying down are more remote than a person talking in living colour."

In broadcasting, the audience cannot go back and have another look at the previous sentence. Either the message is received as it comes or it is lost. The listener is hardly in a position to separate the facts from interpretation since it all moves rapidly, with punditry interwoven with the hard facts. Newspapers may make the same points as television but the approach is different. In a well-written newspaper story, all of the available facts are incorporated and readers draw their own conclusions, although they receive considerable guidance in arriving at them.

The timeliness of broadcast news and even its lack of depth may have its own appeal to the audience, since most people are not interested in details unless they have a personal involvement in the event. The public is so engulfed in communications messages that members can appreciate a digested briefing more than the detailed accounts. Because of film presentation in TV, the audience has the impression that it is getting the news first hand and this sense of being almost a witness to important events makes television "believable." It appears that people attach more credibility to someone they can hear and see than to cold print on paper.

The public's impression, however, does not correspond to the realities of the news handling process in the 1980's when broadcasting remains largely dependent on the print media for the agenda. In most instances, broadcast journalists receive their first reports about news breaks from the wire services—Associated Press, United Press International, Reuter, Agence France-Presse and Canadian Press—which are all an integral part of the print news system. Compared to broadcast news reports, where balance may be sacrificed as a story is processed, newspaper accounts are more detailed and by inference more meaningful. In broad terms, there is a hierarchy of information penetration. Television has been compared to strip mining, radio digs somewhat deeper and newspapers provide details, context and continuity. This hierarchy may be in the process of realignment as a result of the soft news emphasis in newspapers and the increasing popularity of tabloid dailies.

In 1982, the CBC introduced a national TV newshour which includes the magazine-type program *The Journal* (five times weekly, except in summer). In opting for a 10 p.m. rather than an 11 p.m. newshour, CBC TV was asserting itself in what is a prime-time entertainment period. (The CBC's innovative step is being watched with great interest by major networks in North America.) CTV's *W5*, a weekly public affairs programme, is a further example of the "magazine format" aimed at dealing with some of the "depth problems" of broadcast news.

There is an umbilical tie between the printed and electronic media. They do not operate independently of each other, but instead complement each other. Radio, for example, hastened the end of the famed special editions of newspapers with vendors attracting consumers with their shout: "Extra, extra, read all about it." When television came along, radio developed a new character and became increasingly local and personal in orientation. There were corresponding changes in the consumer use of media and these in turn brought new patterns of advertising spending. It is significant, however, that the amount of money that the consumer devotes to media and the amount of leisure time taken up by media consumption have remained fairly constant as a percentage of disposable expenditure and total leisure time. Furthermore, advertising spendings have also held steady at about 1.3 per cent of the Gross National Product. The media pie may be sliced differently, but its size, relative to corresponding economic and leisure-time factors, has remained fairly constant in North America.

In examining media in relation to politics and society in Canada, it is important to appreciate the interaction between the printed and electronic press. Mass communications is the most efficient channel for the continuing flow of information, persuasion, cultural transmission and entertainment to the public. The printed press no longer reigns supreme in any of these functions. Canadians spend about five hours in front of the television set for every hour they spend with a newspaper.[35] A Statistics Canada survey in 1978, based on a sample of 20,000 persons aged 15 and over, tends to substantiate Jean-Louis Servan-Schreiber's conclusions that the importance of the press in modern society is decreasing: "It has lost its monopoly on mass communications to the air waves."[36]

For many centuries, print was the only form of mass communications: first in books, later in newspapers and periodicals. In Canada, the newspaper and periodicals were the only mass media from 1752 until about 1930. In the past 50 years, radio and television successively became competitors with print and each other. In the 1970s, cable distribution, video tape and satellite transmission were used largely in the electronic media to extend their reach. In the 1980s, these new technologies are reshaping the printed press. Consequently, new economic realities are being created and with them must come new perspectives to such important considerations as freedom of the press, the competition of ideas in the marketplace of democratic societies and the role of media as support structures for our national interests and indeed our very existence as a nation.

---

35. Yvon Ferland, "How Can We Develop Reading: What Some Studies Tell Us," in Dick Mac-Donald (ed.), *Reading, the Future and Us* (Toronto: Webcom, 1979), pp. 77-92.
36. *Ibid*.

CHAPTER III

FREEDOM OF INFORMATION: CONSTITUTIONAL RESTRAINTS

Freedom of the press loses some of its meaning in Canada because of the secretive nature of the Canadian government. In 1982, however, Parliament in Ottawa finally enacted Freedom of Information legislation aimed at providing the general public and the media with the right of access to government documents. A walk through the offices of senior civil servants at the Privy Council Office leaves an unforgettable impression: large combination locks on the filing cabinets. There are similarly locked filing cabinets in all of the departments and agencies of government at both the federal and provincial levels across Canada. Unlocking these filing cabinets and making most of the documents they contain available to the media and the public is what Freedom of Information legislation is all about. ''Access to documents,'' ''open government,'' and ''right to know'' are phrases closely related to freedom of information and are sometimes used interchangeably. The democratic ring to them is not accidental, for the adoption of Freedom of Information legislation is generally seen as a step fostering democratic practices. This chapter examines the tradition of secrecy in Canadian government and the increasing pressures for open government.

The case for general access to government documents, with relatively few and well-defined exceptions, is strong. The conventional argument is that access to documents helps provide meaningful information about the political process because it enhances the notion of responsible government, makes government more accountable to the governed, and helps to protect the public against government arbitrariness.

The late Harold Laski observed in *A Grammar of Politics*: ''A people without reliable news is, sooner or later, a people without a basis for freedom.''[1] In Canada, Pierre Trudeau said, some years before he became a member of parliament

---

1. Harold Laski, *A Grammar of Politics* (New Haven: Yale University Press, 1925), pp. 146-47.

and prime minister: "Democratic progress requires the ready availability of true and complete information. In this way people can objectively evaluate the government's policies. To act otherwise is to give way to despotic secrecy."[2] The Conservative Party leader, Joseph Clark, before he became prime minister, warned in the House of Commons: "There is excessive power concentrated in the hands of those who hide public information from the people and Parliament of Canada."[3] Before he became president of the United States, Richard Nixon said: "The plea for secrecy could become a cloak for errors, misjudgements and other failings of government."[4] The appreciation of the importance of information in the political sphere is not new. One of the classic quotes on the subject comes from James Madison, a founding father of the United States and fourth president:

> A Popular Government, without popular information, or the means of acquiring it, is but a Prologue to a Farce or a Tragedy, or perhaps both. Knowledge will forever govern ignorance: and a people who mean to be their own Governors, must arm themselves with the power which knowledge gives.[5]

OPEN GOVERNMENT AND FREEDOM OF INFORMATION

Information has been described as the currency of democracy, and it is argued that the sword of democracy is blunted by the indifferent voter who is ignorant about what is going on in his country. The conventional argument is that, without an informed public, political accountability is illusory. In order to play any meaningful role in the political process, the voter needs information about political affairs and for this usually turns to the mass media, the professional collectors and disseminators of information in society. This wisdom lies behind the pressures in democratic societies to follow the long-standing example of Sweden and, more recently, of the United States, for legal provisions (constitutionally enshrined in Sweden) whereby the public and consequently interested individuals, the political opposition, the mass media, scholars, business groups and interest groups have access to government documents. The legal guarantee for access to documents is called freedom of information legislation.

The very definition of "open" and "closed" government is based on the presence or absence of freedom of information legislation in a country.[6] In the "open" system of government, there are legal requirements that give the public access to government documents, and all documents are available on demand except those in limited and special categories, where disclosure would be con-

---

2. Pierre Elliot Trudeau, 1964. Quoted in *Bulletin*, CAUT, Vol. 26, No. 3, May 1979, p. 13.
3. *Debates*, House of Commons, June 22, 1978.
4. *New York Times*, May 10, 1969.
5. Quoted in Michael Singer, "United States," in Donald C. Rowat (ed.), *Administrative Secrecy in Developed Countries* (London: Macmillan Press, 1979), p. 309.
6. For a discussion on the meaning of "open" and "closed" government, see Donald Wraith, *Open Government: The British Interpretation*, London: Royal Institute of Public Administration, 1977.

trary to national interests (for example, defence, security or equally compelling reasons). In the closed system, all documents are secret except those that the government releases at its own discretion, when it believes that making the information available would be in the public interest.

SECRECY

There are contradictory pressures for secrecy and openness in Canada. Political traditions, federal-provincial politics, bilingualism and biculturalism, international considerations, economic interests, and a strong belief in democratic practices have interacted to bring about what Professor Donald Rowat has called a "schizophrenic conflict" between secrecy and openness: "Among the developed countries of the world, Canada seems to rank about midway between those having the most administrative secrecy and those enjoying the least."[7]

The support structure for secrecy comes from constitutional factors (cabinet and civil service secrecy), the nature of Canadian federalism, the practice of elite accommodation in the political process, economic considerations and the tradition of individual privacy.

A. Constitutional Factors

Canada's parliamentary system inherited the traditions of secrecy from Britain and in some ways we have made it even more secret. The main decision-making centres in Canadian government are the Cabinet and Civil Service; both are surrounded by a cloak of secrecy.[8]

(i) Cabinet Secrecy

At the cabinet level in Canada, the proceedings and deliberations are secret. Cabinet Ministers take the Privy Councillor's Oath, which imposes a strict obligation not to disclose information. It would appear that the Official Secrets Act could be applied—although it has never occurred—for a breach of cabinet secrecy. There are two reasons for cabinet secrecy. One is constitutional, theoretically based on the concept that the cabinet is the body of advisors to the Queen and the Crown's business is confidential.[9] Information cannot be made public until the time has come to announce a decision. The second reason for cabinet secrecy is pragmatic: confidentiality encourages full and frank discussions aimed at achieving compromise and consensus.[10]

---

7. Donald C. Rowat, "Canada," in *Administrative Secrecy, op. cit.* p. 279.
8. James R. Mallory, *The Structure of Canadian Government* (Toronto: Macmillan of Canada, 1971), p. 111.
9. *Ibid*, p. 91.
10. Wraith argues that the obligation for cabinet secrecy rests on convention and not on law. See Wraith, *Open Government, op. cit.*, p. 33. Sir Ivor Jennings reflects a similar point of view when he says that neither the Privy Councillor's Oath nor the Official Secrets Act is the effective sanction to maintain cabinet confidentiality. "The rule is, primarily, one of practice." Ivor Jennings, *Cabinet Government*, Cambridge: Cambridge University Press, 3rd edition, 1961, p. 267.

When Cabinet deliberates the decisions of government, there are bound to be opposing views, for the very task of cabinet-making involves bringing in disparate voices. The representative principle, reflecting provincial representation, religion, regional economic interest and special interest groups, is deeply embedded in the Canadian Cabinet.[11] The members of the Cabinet must be able to speak freely and raise considerations that may stem from provincial or regional interests or other factors. Not even successor governments have access to the records of discussions of the Cabinet or cabinet committees.[12]

The different views of ministers emerge as one voice when Cabinet arrives at a policy decision, whether it be by consensus or decreed by the Prime Minister. The Cabinet as a whole takes responsibility for policy, and ministers must give their public support or resign. This is the concept of collective responsibility, a convention of parliamentary government. Collective responsibility would be impossible without secrecy.

Collective responsibility arose out of necessity. The practice received some acceptance in eighteenth-century England, where it was assumed by the government that the Monarch would be more hesitant to disregard the advice of a minister who had the backing of a full cabinet.[13] But it was not until the rise of the two-party system in the second half of the nineteenth century "that collective responsibility became part of the unwritten convention of the constitution"[14] in Britain and in Canada. As Professor Franks points out, the extension of the franchise, the development of mass parties and rigid party lines were factors that led to collective responsibility.[15]

Collective responsibility plays an instrumental role in keeping governments in office. It means that the Cabinet stands together or falls together in Parliament. If Members of Parliament withdraw their support from a minister on an important matter that is considered one of confidence, they are bringing down the government and probably precipitating a general election. This usually occurs only when there is a minority government, because government supporters hardly ever vote against their own party. Collective responsibility thus contributes to party discipline, since members vote along the lines dictated by the leadership. In practice, the secrecy that exists at the cabinet level filters down to the party level and into caucus and should therefore be properly identified as political secrecy.[16]

Political secrecy serves the interests of the various political parties vying for power. It enables the Government to shape policies away from the glare of publicity and keeps the Opposition in the dark. The Opposition, for its part, is

11. Paul Fox, "The Representative Nature of the Canadian Government" in Paul Fox (ed.), *Politics: Canada* (Toronto: McGraw-Hill Ryerson, 1977), 4th edition, pp. 414-419.
12. *Debates,* House of Commons, May 3, 1966, p. 4627.
13. Colin Seymour-Ure, *The Press Politics and the Public* (London: Methuen, 1968), p. 189.
14. Patrick Gordon Walker, "Secrecy and Openness in Foreign Policy Decision-Making: A British Cabinet Perspective," in T.M. Franck and E. Weisband (eds.), *Secrecy and Foreign Policy* (Toronto: Oxford University Press, 1974), p. 46.
15. C.E.S. Franks, *Parliament and Security Matters* (Ottawa: Supply and Services, 1980), p. 17.
16. Seymour-Ure, *The Press Politics and the Public, op. cit.*, p. 186.

equally secretive: it also wants to present a unified image so that it will be seriously considered as an alternative government. Furthermore, secrecy also helps the Opposition to develop parliamentary strategies that might catch the Government off-guard. Political interests rather than any legal restraint are the basis for political secrecy. Disclosure of confidential discussions in caucus may lead to hard feelings and intra-party feuds but it is a secrecy that has no constitutional or legal support.

(ii) Secrecy at the Public Service Level

Secrecy in the decision-making and advisory process at the officials' level, that is, by senior civil servants in the various departments of government, stems from the constitutional principle of individual ministerial responsibility.[17] This principle, which is far older than collective responsibility, requires that individual ministers be responsible to Parliament for their own actions and for the public servants over whom they have management and control.[18] Parliamentary praise or criticism pertaining to a department is directed at the minister. Departmental employees act in the minister's name and on his authority. It is from this inherited principle of the British governmental system that the practice of civil service anonymity has grown up. Students of Canadian politics have shown that the involvement of senior civil servants in the policy process in this country has been as close and continuous as anywhere in the world.[19] The enormous growth of governmental activity since 1940 has brought about a greatly expanded need for decision making at the civil service level, with a corresponding increase in the power of the administrative machinery of government. A minister's effective management and direction of his department is open to question.[20] But the departments continue to speak through the minister only; they are to a large extent out-of-bounds to the public and journalists seeking information.

(iii) Some Modifying Factors: The Leak and the Ministerial Resignation

There is, of course, another side to the story, and that is the lifting of the veils of secrecy. As Gordon Walker, the former British Foreign Secretary observed, collective responsibility is to some extent a mask worn by the Cabinet to cover up

---

17. For a detailed discussion of ministerial responsibility, see Kenneth Kernaghan, *Freedom of Information and Ministerial Responsibility*, Research Publication 2, Toronto: Ontario Commission on Freedom of Information and Individual Privacy, 1978. Franks observes that Canada has not refined the theory and practice of ministerial responsibility. Ministers have frequently not resigned when faults have been discovered in their departments and ministers have also at times acknowledged errors by civil servants without taking the blame themselves. See Franks, *Parliament and Security Matters, op. cit.*, p. 18.
18. Royal Commission on Financial Management and Accountability. *Report.* Ottawa: Supply and Services, 1979, p. 372.
19. James Eayrs, *The Art of the Possible* (Toronto, 1961), p. 32. See also J.E. Hodgetts, "The Civil Service and Policy Formation," *Canadian Journal of Economics and Political Science,* XXIII, No. 4, November 1957, p. 467.
20. Royal Commission on Financial Management and Accountability. *Report, op. cit.*, p. 373.

divisions that have not been wholly reconciled.[21] It is the demands of politics—the need for leaders to let their followers know about their political views—that is one reason for the unattributable leak. Walker sees the leak as a natural outgrowth of the self-same conditions of mass democracy that gave rise to collective responsibility. Cabinet ministers, and even sometimes officials, use leaks and trial balloons, as they are called, to influence the course of argument before a question is settled in Cabinet, the bureaucracy, and even caucus.

Leaks, as we will see below, are accepted as a way of life in Canadian politics and, in fact, were institutionalized in our parliamentary form of government at the time of Confederation. Leading politicians in the Government and the Opposition ranks had special relationships with particular newspapers supporting them. Members of the Parliamentary Press Gallery were often informal advisors to ministers and were aware of some cabinet deliberations.

The point being made here is that all government secrets are not of the same order; some matters can be leaked, others not. In practice, a distinction can be made between ordinary leaks and disclosures of true state secrets. The best examples of state secrets are security matters, decisions on altering the value of the Canadian dollar vis-à-vis other currencies and the budget.

The reason for choosing national security is obvious, although it has often proven difficult to precisely define national security. In the case of devaluation or revaluation of currency, any premature disclosure would undermine the very purpose of the moves and in fact could have ruinous implications for the economy and the fiscal structure. This brings us to the question of the budget leak. Advance information on fiscal measures can transform financial speculation to a "sure thing" and result in loss of revenues for the government treasury. For the past 40 years, the budget has been presented in the evening, after the closing of all security and commodity markets in Canada.[22]

In Canada, there is no direct evidence of a federal budget secret ever having been compromised. The closest we came to a "budget scandal" was in 1963, when Finance Minister Walter Gordon used three consultants from private industry to help prepare the budget. The consultants were working temporarily for the Department of Finance and had been sworn to secrecy, but they were being paid by their regular employers. The Opposition felt that the principle of budget secrecy had been breached. Mr. Gordon offered his resignation but Prime Minister Lester Pearson refused to accept it.[23]

In the British Parliament, breaches of budget secrecy have always been

---

21. Patrick Gordon Walker, "Secrecy and Openness in Foreign Policy Decision-Making: A British Cabinet Perspective," in *Secrecy and Foreign Policy*, Franck and Weisband (eds.), *op. cit.*, pp. 42-52.
22. In 1941, the last time a budget was presented in the afternoon, the Finance Minister announced new taxes on sugar that were to go into effect at midnight. The Vancouver markets were still open, leading to massive sugar sales before the tax became effective. See Sharp, "How the Budget Estimates are Prepared," *op. cit.*, p. 223.
23. Hugh Finsten, "Background Information on Government Secrecy, Financial Measures and Parliamentary Secretaries." Appendix "F." *Proceedings*. House of Commons Standing Committee on Privileges and Elections, August 11, 1975, p. 73.

severely punished. In 1947, Hugh Dalton, Chancellor of the Exchequer, disclosed some details of his budget to a newspaperman, a lobby correspondent, shortly before the budget was to be brought down. No one could have benefitted from the disclosure and no improper motive was attributed to the incident. However, Dalton admitted that it was a grave indiscretion and he promptly resigned. The resignation was accepted. In 1936 J.H. Thomas in his capacity as a minister betrayed budget secrets to friends. He resigned and left public life.[24]

There is no doubt that the budget contents are among the most inviolable of government secrets in Canada. Mitchell Sharp, who has had considerable experience with budget preparations as Finance Minister, says that even the cabinet colleagues are not made aware of the budget proposals too far in advance of the event.[25]

There are special legislative procedures for financial measures in Parliament. They must be introduced in the House of Commons by a minister. The Cabinet's responsibility in all financial matters is complete; it is a responsibility from which it cannot escape.[26] Cabinet secrecy and collective responsibility are indivisible when it comes to the budget. But no similar tradition seems to exist for breaches of secrecy on other government legislation, even measures that may be introduced in the wake of the budget.[27] There is, then, a difference in degree, in what is regarded as secret in a sacred sense.

As noted before, national security, currency realignments and the budget are the most important matters that cannot be leaked. Little else is sacred. The doctrine of collective responsibility is not sufficient to hold back the ordinary cabinet leaks which often involve differences between ministers, subject matters under discussion and cabinet decisions. It is the political interests of the individuals involved, and to some extent the ingenuity of the press, that determine the leakage from the highest levels of government.[28]

A few examples suffice. The leak on government strategy in the federal-provincial negotiations on the new Constitution created headlines across the country. In 1982, some ministers even took to writing letters to disassociate themselves from parts of the November 1981 budget. In May 1982, a cabinet document labelled "Minister's Eyes Only," dealing with the Government's response to the recommendations of the Royal Commission on Newspapers, was leaked to a parliamentarian who turned it over to the press.

---

24. *Ibid*.
25. Mitchell Sharp, "How the Budget Estimates are Prepared," in *Politics: Canada*, Paul Fox (ed.), (Toronto: McGraw-Hill of Canada, 1966, 2nd edition), p. 222.
26. R. McGregor Dawson, *The Government of Canada* (Toronto: University of Toronto Press, 1970, 5th edition), p. 212.
27. Finsten, "Background Information on Government Secrecy, Financial Measures and Parliamentary Secretaries," *op. cit*.
28. For an interesting discussion on leaks of cabinet documents in 1970 and 1971, see Gordon Robertson, "Official Responsibility, Private Conscience, and Public Information," *Transactions of the Royal Society of Canada, 1972*, Vol. X, University of Toronto Press, 1973, pp. 149-162. For examples of cabinet leaks in Britain see Walker, "Secrecy and Openness in Foreign Policy Decision-Making," *op. cit.*, p. 48.

The trial balloon, a particular kind of leak where the Prime Minister or other Cabinet Ministers test public reaction to proposed policies, appointments, and so on, has become a political tool that is used with considerable skill.[29] The morality of employing leaks that mislead the press (and public) and using them for political expediency is questionable.

In addition to the leak, there are other institutionalized methods to lift the veil of secrecy. The most significant of these is the resignation speech of a minister. Resignations by cabinet ministers stemming from differences over policy occur with much greater frequency in Canada than in the U.S.[30] In Canada, as in Britain, "the system accommodates and to some extent encourages a public statement of those differences, and in the course of such a statement considerable hitherto secret information may be aired."[31] In Canada, there is an instance of a cabinet resignation leading to the airing of matters that could be regarded as being within the defence classification. This is clearly illustrated in Mallory's account of the resignation of J.L. Ralston from the Cabinet of Mackenzie King in November 1944.[32] It should be pointed out that a resigning minister cannot assert for himself the right to reveal cabinet secrets and, in fact, the Governor-General must give his consent, who will in turn be acting on the advice of the Prime Minister. No Prime Minister could, however, take the political risk of refusing a resigning minister the opportunity to give his version of the controversy. Aneurin Bevan observed in the House of Commons at Westminster in 1953 that the practice of disclosure upon resignation is "one of the immemorial courtesies" of Parliament.[33]

The leak and the ministerial resignation can provide openings to the decision-making centres but they are usually politically motivated. On balance, the constitutional traditions are firmly entrenched on the side of secrecy.

B. Federalism

Another important factor that contributes to secrecy in Canada is the nature of our federal system. Canada has perhaps the most decentralized federal system in the world. The former Prime Minister, Mr. Clark, described Canada as "a community of communities." The provinces have formal constitutional powers of an extensive nature over vitally important matters, including natural resources,

---

29. Michael Barkway, Ottawa correspondent for the *Economist* in the early 1960s, a period of numerous leaks, observed that the media had been victimized by "calculated leaks . . . whose source can be traced directly to Mr. Diefenbaker himself." Barkway, commenting on trial balloons, said: "If the reactions are favourable, the highly placed proceed with their plans. If unfavourable, the press correspondents are accused of irresponsible speculation." Barkway is quoted in W.H. Kesterton, *A History of Journalism in Canada* (Toronto: McClelland and Stewart, 1967), p. 251.

30. Thomas Franck and Edward Weisband, "Dissemblement, Secrecy, and Executive Privilege in the Foreign Relations of Three Democracies: A Comparative Analysis," in *Secrecy and Foreign Policy, op. cit.*, p. 424.

31. *Ibid.*

32. Mallory, *Structure of Canadian Government, op. cit.*, p. 86.

33. Bevan is quoted in Franck and Weisband, *Secrecy and Foreign Policy, op. cit.*, p. 424.

social welfare and education. The 10 provincial capitals are political powers in their own right, with such factors as population size, industrialization and natural resources being aspects of the power configuration. The coordination and cooperation requirements of federalism necessitate significant exchanges of information between the two levels of government. There is at the same time a strategic withholding of information in the ongoing federal-provincial bargaining. The practices of secrecy that flow from parliamentary government are as applicable to the provincial governments as they are to Ottawa.

The 10 Canadian provinces account for a relatively limited dilution of provincial power as compared to the United States, where there are 50 states. This, combined with decentralization, the secretive nature of governmental systems and other factors, brings about a situation where federal-provincial relations have some of the characteristics of international politics. Diplomacy involved in this kind of interaction usually thrives in secrecy, since compromises are far more feasible before public positions have been defined. Political information exchanges and bargaining occur at meetings of federal and provincial ministers, usually behind closed doors. Further reflecting the international flavour aspect of Canadian federalism are the so-called heads-of-government conferences that bring together the federal prime minister and the 10 provincial premiers. The importance of confidentiality in these negotiations has long been appreciated by the participants and going public is perceived as an obstacle to agreement. Premier René Levesque, in his first major statement after the defeat of the Sovereignty-Association referendum, indicated that Quebec would take part in constitutional negotiations in "good faith" but made it clear that if things did not go the way he wished, he would bring in the press.

C. Elite Accommodation

A characteristic of the Canadian political process that finds its base in the demands of federalism, regionalism, corporate interests, religious and cultural pulls is "elite accommodation." Professor Donald Smiley argues that "elite accommodation in Canada is facilitated by the dominance of bureaucratic traditions and relative weakness of liberal individualism."[34] The interests of the bureaucracy are enhanced by the practice of secrecy.

D. Economics

Canada's economic structure also encourages secrecy. While ours is a mixed economy with private industry often competing with nationally owned corporations such as Air Canada and Canadian National Railways, both the private and public sectors emphasize the rules of confidentiality in the competitive business world. Canada has laws that safeguard the secrecy of information collected by the government on private industries. The government's involvement in business

---

34. Donald Smiley, *The Freedom of Information Issue: A Political Analysis,* (Toronto: Ontario Commission on Freedom of Information and Individual Privacy, 1978), p. 41.

ventures and in providing social services is very much respected in Canada and is related to attitudes of trust toward the authorities. In Canada's pioneering origins, government usually came before society. As Franks has observed, ''There were tremendous needs for government services in Canada's difficult environment, and the origins of the country are so recent for these influences still to be pronounced.''[35]

E. Individual Privacy Tradition

At the personal level, there is also a support structure for secrecy in the strong Canadian tradition of individual privacy. Governments at both the federal and provincial level have accumulated on computers vast amounts of personal information dealing with such matters as age, health, education, religion, income, property ownership, taxes, legal violations and convictions, customs declarations, among many other matters. The widespread use of the Social Insurance Number, or SIN, as it is called, gives governments extraordinarily easy access to information about our personal lives. There are growing pressures in Canada to safeguard the confidentiality of this information.

The pressures for secrecy stemming from a variety of sources—constitutional factors, federalism, economics and individual privacy—are in combination a formidable obstacle to the easy flow of communications from the political sector.

OPENNESS

The pressures for openness in Canadian society are also extremely strong. They include the democratic characteristics, the requirements of Canadian unity and the American influence.

A. Democratic Characteristics

Canada is a constitutional democracy. The governmental institutions have fully developed democratic characteristics:
- —The voters judge the government at regularly required elections.
- —The government is ''responsible'' to the peoples' elected representatives in Parliament.[36] This ''accountability'' provision is somewhat tempered by party discipline and in fact Parliament rarely defeats cabinets and never impeaches them.[37] (A Royal Commission recently warned that there has been a grave weakening of the accountability of government to Parliament.)[38]
- —Parliament is open to the press and public and the proceedings of Parliament, as recorded in Hansard, can be freely published in the media. The

35. Franks, *Parliament and Security Matters, op. cit.*, p. 13.
36. For a discussion of ''accountability,'' ''responsibility'' and ''answerability,'' see Smiley, *Freedom of Information, op. cit.*
37. Franks, *Parliament and Security Matters, op. cit.*, p. 18.
38. Royal Commission on Financial Management and Accountability, *Report. op. cit.*, p. 21.

televising of parliamentary proceedings, the ''electronic Hansard,'' as it is called, has further increased public awareness of Parliament.

—The courts are independent, insulated from political interference and open.

—There is freedom of the press. The International Press Institute, Freedom House and other respected institutions that concern themselves with civil rights around the world invariably rank Canada near the top among the very limited number of countries that have press freedoms.

—The government actively seeks to encourage greater public involvement in political decision-making in what has been called ''participatory democracy.'' This participation requires an informed public and the government has a highly developed publicity system which directs its attention to the mass media and the public generally. The government controls what it publishes but the government's legitimacy in a democratic society is related in part to the public's trust in the information that surfaces.

B. Canadian Unity

The requirements of Canadian unity also set off pressures for openness. Bilingualism and biculturalism in Canada require that both the French- and English-language populations must be supplied with adequate political information that would engender trust in the political institutions. This political information is especially pressing for French-speaking Canadians who, it may be argued, have in the past felt left out from the mainstream of Canadian federal politics. There is ample evidence that French Canadians have traditionally related to the personalities in power at the federal level of government rather than to parliamentary institutions.[39] On the other hand, English-speaking Canadians have a greater affinity for parliamentary institutions, which they see as part of an inherited tradition. This situation is changing. Extensive exposure to American mass media (television, film, magazines) means that many Canadians are more familiar with American presidential/congressional politics than they are with the complexities of the parliamentary/cabinet system. Furthermore, federalism requires good internal communications on a national basis about the federal political process to help domesticate the strong fragmenting influences of regionalism.

C. The American Factor

The so-called American factor also provides direct pressure for openness in Canadian politics. ''Canada,'' says Mallory, ''has been nourished by the same stream of constitutional ideas, and in many respects, the same constitutional atmosphere, as the United States.''[40] American ways are much admired in Canada and the demonstration effect of the openness of the U.S. political process has a significant influence on Canadian attitudes towards politics. The freedom of information issue was widely debated in the United States as a result of the

---

39. This matter will be discussed in greater detail in Chapter X.
40. Mallory, *Structure of Canadian Government, op. cit.*, p. 1.

Watergate disclosures which led to the resignation of President Nixon. It was partly because of Watergate that Congress in 1974 amended the U.S. Freedom of Information Act to make it a formidable instrument for public disclosure. The spillover effect of the American example, combined with ongoing pressures for "democratization" in other western societies such as Britain, Australia, France and West Germany, is helping to shape Canadian attitudes about openness.

PARLIAMENT AND INFORMATION

Administrative secrecy puts governments in a privileged position: they have the means to "look good" and explain policy decisions through selective release of documents. Secrecy does not have to be justified. In 1968, a New Democratic Party member of Parliament told the Task Force on Government Information, "In Canada there is a tendency on the part of governments to be partisan in the papers made public. If it's good news, the government releases it when it's advantageous, but if it's bad news, the government doesn't want it known."[41] Nearly a decade later, John Turner, after resigning from Parliament following service as Justice Minister and Finance Minister in the Trudeau cabinet, admitted this practice: "Certainly, in politics there is a vested interest in presenting any policy or any decision in the most favourable light. This sometimes means selecting facts. It often means managing or manipulating information. It often involves orchestrating the timing. Full and immediate revelation of all the facts can be embarrassing. I know—I've been there."[42]

Parliament's role in the political process is the core of our democratic practices. It is important to recognize that in Canada there is parliamentary sovereignty, but no tradition of popular sovereignty. The electorate selects a new Parliament at least every five years and it is the arithmetic of party politics that determines the Government. In this sense, Parliament has an elective function and legitimizes the Government; its own party composition determines the Government. A second function of Parliament is to consider and pass legislation, to shape the laws of the land. Thirdly, there is the education function: both the Government and the Opposition party present their cases to the public, thus making the Opposition a viable alternative to the Government. The fourth function of Parliament is surveillance of the Government with the purpose of making it accountable.

The accountability of the Government to Parliament and ultimately to the Canadian people "is the essence of our democratic form of government."[43] The administrative activities of the Government are thus subject to the scrutiny of the Commons. The requirements for information disclosure in the parliamentary process are considerable.

Parliament is the great receiver of Government information. It is on the floor

---

41. Task Force on Government Information (Ottawa: Queen's Printer, 1969), *Report*, Vol. II, p. 26.
42. To Canadian Bar Association, August 30, 1976. Quoted in *Globe and Mail*, October 25, 1979.
43. Royal Commission on Financial Management and Accountability. *Report, op. cit.*, p. 21.

of the House of Commons that the government announces its policies and tables its legislation. The practice of "first disclosure" in the House also applies to White Papers, Green Papers, Royal Commission Reports and Task Force Reports, among other documents. The controlled information-release procedure, in terms of setting and time frame, contributes to secrecy and causes delays. In the last 10 years or so, a further cause of delay has been that nothing could be tabled in the House until it could be produced in both languages, and the delays in the translation bureau often delayed matters further.

Ministerial responsibility, party discipline and the rules and customs of Parliament interact to put the focus of attention on the House of Commons, away from the real centres of decision-making: the Cabinet and the Civil Service. This parliamentary bias promotes the vested interest of government and has a pronounced effect on the political communications flow.

Governments are criticized if they disregard the rules and traditions of Parliament and provide journalists with information on which the House has first claim. As Professors Jackson and Atkinson note, if the Government goes directly to the media, the prestige of Parliament suffers and the floor of the Commons loses some of its importance as the centre of political debate.[44]

The formal Canadian practice is that the media work in the shadow of Parliament. The information flow is from the ministers to Parliament and simultaneously, because Parliament is a very open forum, to the media. This flow is the critical element in the process of accountability. In the final analysis, the Cabinet and all members of the House of Commons are accountable to the Canadian people. The general election is the day of reckoning.

Question Period. The most publicized part of Parliament's business is the Question Period. The daily, 45-minute session enables members of the House of Commons to get information by asking the minister directly. These oral questions are usually posed without giving previous notice and the period is a "freewheeling affair, with tremendous spontaneity and vitality."[45] In the Question Period, ministers are regularly made accountable to the House through their "obligation" to answer questions pertaining to matters that are under the jurisdiction of their departments. The House is filled for Question Period as are the Press Gallery and the Visitors Gallery. The oral questions often provide the leads for newspaper stories. The major television and radio newscasts frequently include excerpts from the Question Period. When the Question Period ends, the media interest in Parliament declines sharply and there is almost a mass exit by the press. The Public Gallery also empties and many of the Members of Parliament leave the chamber to attend other business.

Budget. Parliament is the guardian of the national purse. It grants supply, making money available for governmental operations, and authorizes taxation. Perhaps the most important event in the parliamentary calendar is budget night,

---

44. Robert J. Jackson and Michael M. Atkinson, *The Canadian Legislative System,* (Toronto: Macmillan of Canada, 1974), p. 74.
45. Franks, *Parliament and Security Matters, op. cit.,* p. 28.

when the government presents its spending plans and its projected incomes. In the budget and the review of the budget that follows, parliamentarians have an opportunity to focus on government activities. Traditionally, Canadian governments have limited their budget projections to the spending revenues for the coming year. In the fall of 1979, the budget brought down by the Conservative Party government of Joe Clark for the first time ever presented a four-year projection that went beyond general spending and revenue figures to focus also on specific items in some detail. The budget and the accompanying research paper set a precedent in government openness that future governments will find difficult to disregard.

Ombudsmen.   On money matters, parliamentarians have the advice of the Auditor General, an officer of Parliament who has the independent standing of a judge with special powers of access to government documents and financial statements. The Auditor General's Report, which at times provides devastating examples of poor government judgement in money management, is examined largely by the Public Accounts Committee. It is significant that, since 1958, Canada has followed the British example and the chairman of the Public Accounts Committee is a member of the Opposition.

On language questions, specifically the use of French and English in government departments, there is the Official Language Commissioner. An officer of Parliament, he has tenure and investigatory powers that cut across departments. A more recent development of a somewhat similar nature is the appointment of a Human Rights Commissioner. Both the Official Language Commissioner and the Human Rights Commissioner report to Parliament and are responsible to Parliament.

Committees

Government in Canada has become too big for the House of Commons to be a meaningful watchdog over the administration's activities. There are more than 400 departments, Crown corporations, agencies, boards, commissions and councils. Robert Stanfield believes our governmental system is overloaded. He said, "The demands on our national government and the consequential scope of its deliberations, decisions and activities are far greater than the ministers can competently cope with, and far beyond the supervision of Parliament, to which the Government is supposedly responsible."[46]

While Parliament has traditionally been reluctant to dilute its collective powers, its work demands have made it necessary to turn over many of the scrutiny responsibilities to the committees of the House. In the past 10 or so years, detailed discussion and examination of government policies and programs have shifted largely to these committees.[47] The committee system has been strengthened considerably. For example, research facilities have been improved, civil

---

46. Quoted in *Report*. Royal Commission on Financial Management and Accountability, *op. cit.*, p. 28.
47. *Ibid.*, p. 398.

servants are now allowed to appear before committees, and the proceedings of committees are published. The greater role of committees in the legislative process and in the scrutiny responsibilities of Parliament is important.

But there are also major shortcomings. The committees have become the workhouses of the House—so much so that the committee members have more work than they can handle. The number of MPs under the new formula is 282, but there are about 450 seats to be filled on more than 20 committees. Not all members are actively involved in committees and some members carry extremely heavy loads.

In his examination of the committee system, Professor Franks points to a number of other problems.[48] Firstly, committees are not insulated from government control, in that committee membership reflects party strength in the House. Secondly, the chairmen of the committees (except Public Accounts) belong to the ruling party. Thirdly, ministers appearing before committees are not obliged to give more detailed answers than they provide in the House Question Period. Fourthly, civil servants speak for the minister and there is little likelihood that they will contradict views expressed by ministers. On balance, it would appear that the potential for scrutiny and control has not fully materialized.

Canada's parliamentary system has adopted a number of practices that are specifically aimed at generating information.

Commissions of Inquiry

The first Canadian Commission of Inquiry was appointed in 1868.

There are two types of commissions. One has an advisory purpose and usually gathers information on a broad issue. The other focuses on a specific problem, such as an alleged wrongdoing in the activities of government.[49]

Commissions of Inquiry set up to examine "wrongdoings" are usually the result of demands made by the Opposition when there is reason to believe that the Government is withholding information in Parliament on an important matter. The Government then determines the mandate of the Commission and appoints its members. The Commissions have special investigatory powers and "are vehicles for the disclosure of documents and information."[50]

From time to time, Royal Commissions are appointed by the Cabinet to investigate areas of special concern, draw conclusions and make recommendations. Governments are not obliged to implement these recommendations, but the very fact that the Royal Commission has been appointed is an indication of the importance of the problem. Royal Commissions frequently launch extensive research, hold public hearings and produce a report as well as studies on aspects of the

48. Franks, *Parliament and Security Matters, op. cit.*, pp. 32-35.
49. Canada. Law Reform Commission. *Commissions of Inquiry.* Working Paper No. 17. (Ottawa: Supply and Services, 1977), p. 13.
50. Rowat, "Canada," in *Administrative Secrecy, op. cit.*, p. 29.

problem being examined. Adopted from Britain, Royal Commissions have been used in Canada since the nineteenth century.[51]

The Task Force inquiry is adopted from the United States and was first employed by Finance Minister Walter Gordon in 1963. A Task Force is less formal, less expensive and usually faster than a Royal Commission. The Task Force on Government Information, which produced the report "To Know and Be Known," examined among other matters the flow of political communication in Canada. In the wake of the election of the Parti Québecois in Quebec, the Federal Cabinet set up the Task Force on Canadian Unity, which reported in 1979.

Canadian governments also make use of White Papers and Green Papers to provide Parliament and the public with information on important matters. White Papers are statements of basic policy where the government has decided on central principles but has an open mind on lesser points. These papers are part of a process of stimulating national debate and promoting broad support for proposed legislation. First introduced in Canada in 1939, White Papers have been used frequently in the past 20 years. Since 1967, the Government has experimented with the Green Paper, a broad discussion of a variety of policy approaches about which the Government has not yet made final decisions. It is assumed that the Government has an open mind on the issue discussed in the Green Paper (for example, Freedom of Information) and is interested in further consultation with the Opposition parties, interest groups, experts and the public generally. The White Paper and Green Paper experiments could result in wider consultation and participation in shaping governmental legislation, but the assessments to date have been mixed.[52]

Moving beyond the parliamentary process but related to it is the government practice over the past fifteen years of establishing advisory bodies such as the Economic Council of Canada and the Science Council of Canada. The government has created its own critics, says G. Bruce Doern, and these advisory bodies are set up "to bring debate in their respective domains out of the closed executive-bureaucratic deliberations and into a somewhat broader public arena."[53]

In summary, the House of Commons has undergone many reforms, especially since 1965. These changes include the introduction of the electronic Hansard (televising of Parliament), the strengthening of the committee system, and the availability of research funds to the parties. An important reform made the Speaker of the House more independent from government control. The White and Green Papers and more detailed research papers for the budget are examples of an increased flow of information about government policies. But these developments and others have come at a time of enormous increase in governmental activity in Canada. There are doubts that the balance between Parliament and Government has been significantly affected.[54]

---

51. "Commissions of Inquiry and Task Forces," Library of Parliament Information and Reference Branch. Unpublished document. April, 1979.
52. G. Bruce Doern, "Canada," in I. Galnoor (ed.), *Government Secrecy in Democracies*, (New York: Harper and Row, 1977), p. 153.
53. *Ibid.*
54. Franks, *Parliament and Security Matters, op. cit.*, p. 14.

A major factor is the inadequacy of the flow of information in the form of administrative documents to Parliament, the media and the public. Parliament, including the committees, receives massive volumes of information from many different arms of government. But is it information of the right kind? The Royal Commission on Financial Management and Accountability does not think so:

"The mass of information it [Parliament] receives is so overwhelming, complex, and often irrelevant that it fails to provide any basis for measuring the performance of departments and agencies against objectives."[55]

Administration secrecy contributes to this flow of irrelevant information. Information that may be politically controversial or that might expose blunders in the government can often be kept conveniently locked up in the filing cabinets.

CONCLUSIONS AND GENERAL OBSERVATIONS

The search for a balance between the people's "right to know" and the needs and preferences of government for confidentiality is not unique to Canada. Administrative secrecy tends to be the general rule in most democratic societies, although the closed governmental systems are under increasing pressure to unlock their filing cabinets. The constitutionally enshrined Swedish provisions for Freedom of Information and the quasi-constitutional American Freedom of Information legislation are in a class by themselves; there are final appeals to impartial adjudicators (the courts in the United States, the Supreme Administrative Tribunal or the Parliamentary Ombudsman in Sweden) in cases where administrative secrecy is challenged. Other countries, such as Norway and Denmark, have quasi-information laws called publicity acts that are not as far-reaching, in that appeals are to administrative bodies of the Civil Service and not to legal bodies.[56] Austria, France and the Netherlands adopted access legislation with limiting provisions in the 1970s.

The progress toward Freedom of Information legislation in Canada has been extremely slow, considering the strong declarations of support from political leaders, the media, interest groups (including the Canadian Bar Association), and the public. But Canada has clearly moved in the direction of more open government. An important break with the tradition of discretionary secrecy was advocated in the 1969 Report of the Task Force on Government Information, which declared in its first recommendation that Canadians have a right to "full, objective and timely information" to government activities. The Trudeau government accepted this recommendation. Another important development in 1969 was the announcement by government of its new 30-year rule whereby most official records would be transferred to Public Archives and released to the public after 30 years. (There were some exceptions in the 30-year provision relating to

---

55. Royal Commission on Financial Management and Accountability, *Report, op. cit.*, p. 29.
56. Tom Riley, "Freedom of Information—An International Perspective," unpublished paper, p. 11.

the release of documents which could adversely affect Canada's national security and external relations or which might violate the rights of privacy of individuals.) The archives provisions are of particular importance to researchers who now have even earlier access if there is ministerial approval.

The Federal Courts Act of 1970 brought some limitations to Crown privilege and enhanced the power of the courts to force the production of government documents needed by litigants or defendants. The exceptions are where the minister certifies that disclosure could be harmful for matters of national defence, international relations, federal-provincial relations or the revealing of a cabinet confidence. In 1971, Parliament passed the Statutory Instruments Act, which elaborated on governmental requirements in publication of regulations and provided for increased parliamentary scrutiny for such regulations. The Federal Court Act and the Statutory Instruments Act are complementary in terms of greater "openness": one enhances legal review procedure, the other strengthens Parliament's hands. A further important development was the 1973 announcement by the government of a new set of guidelines for the release of documents to Parliament. The general principle in these guidelines was that departments of government should make available to Parliament as much information as possible, providing such information release did not compromise effective administration, the security of the nation and the right to privacy.

In 1973, the government took the unusual step of referring a Private Member's Bill on freedom of information introduced by Mr. Gerald Baldwin to Parliament's Joint Committee (Senate-House of Commons) on Regulations and Other Statutory Instruments. Mr. Baldwin had been pressing for such legislation over almost his entire 22-year career in Parliament (1958-80), but until 1973 his Private Member's Bill had always been allowed to die on the floor of the House. The Joint Committee set out on a wide-ranging study on freedom of information, in which it heard evidence from ministers, senior officials and experts in governmental secrecy, leaks, etc. At the end of 1974 it recommended that Canada should have Freedom of Information legislation. The House of Commons approved the Committee Report in February 1976. It took another 15 months before the government declared itself for Freedom of Information legislation by issuing a Green Paper: *Legislation on Public Access to Government Documents.*[57]

The Green Paper presented alternative approaches to Freedom of Information legislation and thus invited a public debate. There was general praise for the "principle of openness" in the Green Paper, but much criticism of the detailed provisions. There were indications that the government would opt for a weak law with broad exemptions for documents that would not have to be made public.[58]

---

57. John Roberts, *Secretary of State* (Ottawa: Supply and Services, Canada, 1977).
58. Donald C. Rowat, *Public Access to Government Documents: A Comparative Perspective,* (Toronto: Ontario Commission on Freedom of Information and Individual Privacy, 1978), p. 92.

The Green Paper was studied by the Joint Committee which reported its recommendations, favouring a strong Freedom of Information Act, in June 1978. At the opening of the next session of Parliament, the Throne Speech announced that Freedom of Information legislation would be forthcoming. This did not materialize. In the election in May 1979, the Liberal government of Prime Minister Pierre Trudeau, which had taken Canada some distance along the road to Freedom of Information legislation, was defeated.

During the brief Conservative administration in 1979, the Clark government introduced a far-reaching Freedom of Information Act as its first major piece of new legislation. While there were some broad exemption provisions, there was no direct reference to the often troublesome "national interest." The legislation provided for final appeals to the court following an examination by an Information Commissioner. All parties supported the legislation in principle and Parliament was expected to give quick approval, but the thirty-first Parliament ended abruptly with the defeat of the government in a non-confidence motion on the budget.

Mr. Trudeau's Liberal government, elected in February 1980, introduced its own version of Freedom of Information legislation in the thirty-second Parliament in July 1980. Bill C-43, the Access to Information Act and the Privacy Act, contains many of the provisions of the Conservative bill of the previous year. The proposed Liberal legislation has been criticized for being too long and containing too many exemptions that enable documents to be kept from the public, and praised for allowing appeal to an Information Commissioner and finally to the Federal Court.

All parties in Parliament supported the 98-page bill in principle. The bill received final approval in June 1982.

It has taken a dozen years to progress from the acceptance of the principle that Canadians have a right to full, objective and timely information on government activities (as recommended in the Report of the Task Force on Government Information) to the point where Freedom of Information legislation has become a reality. The beneficial expectations may be somewhat inflated, considering the exemptions and the technical difficulties of declassifying hundreds of thousands of separate documents. Governments will certainly continue to look after their vested interests and present their policies and decisions in the most favourable light. Freedom of Information legislation, however, will make decision-makers aware that the public can obtain information to better assess government activities.

It will, thus, generate new attitudes among officials and government leaders, since the general rule will be disclosure and openness rather than administrative secrecy. Equally important, Freedom of Information legislation will put the onus on the mass media to be more searching and investigative in reporting on the affairs of government. It is hoped that old practices in government as well as in the media will gradually give way to a more meaningful interaction, and one that will be of benefit to the public.

CHAPTER IV

THE LEGAL RESTRAINTS: THE MEDIA, POLITICS AND THE LAW

On July 24, 1975, the Montreal *Gazette* carried a headline spread across all eight columns of page one, which read: BUDGET LEAKED TO BUSINESSMEN. Reporter Jacques Hamilton declared that John Reid, parliamentary secretary to the president of the Privy Council, was fed advance details of the federal budget which he shared with manufacturers who could gain from the information. The *Gazette* claimed that it had found out the details of these events through an interview with Mr. Reid himself. "His admissions," said the *Gazette*, "leave him open to prosecution under the Official Secrets Act. His disclosure of the leak, if parliamentary precedents hold, could force the resignation of Finance Minister Turner and lead to the prosecution of the informant under the Official Secrets Act—even if the informant is the minister himself." Reporter Jacques Hamilton's story went on to say that maximum penalty for violation of the Act is 14 years' imprisonment. He also made the argument, which he claimed was based on information he had received from senior authorities on parliamentary procedure, that Privy Council President Mitchell Sharp "is technically responsible for the actions of his parliamentary secretary and could also face a demand for his resignation."[1]

The spectacular *Gazette* story touched off consternation in Parliament. John Reid, speaking on a question of privilege on the day that the *Gazette* story appeared, categorically denied that he had obtained and passed advance details of the federal budget.[2] He demanded a retraction and apology from the Montreal *Gazette* and asked that the matter be referred to the House of Commons Standing Committee on Privileges and Elections if the newspaper did not comply. The *Gazette*, for its part, offered a partial retraction in an editorial on July 25th in

---

1. Montreal *Gazette*, 24 July, 1975
2. House of Commons, *Debates*, 24 July, 1975

which it said that Reid "disclosed advance information not about last November's budget itself but about a later amendment to the budget. We apologize for putting this disclosure in the wrong time frame. . . ." But the *Gazette* editorial went on to argue that the divulgence of inside information on a tax change prior to public announcement "is just as serious whether the tax change is included in the budget or in an amendment."[3]

The question of privilege raised by Mr. Reid was referred to the Commons Standing Committee on Privileges and Elections. Mr. Reid also initiated legal action claiming he had been libelled by the *Gazette*. In the course of the proceedings of the committee, which held ten meetings, fundamental questions about the interaction of the media and government in Canada were raised. The tradition of secrecy, parliamentary privilege, budget leaks vis à-vis other kinds of leaks, the Official Secrets Act, libel, and the rights of newspapers to carry excerpts from Hansard were among the issues discussed. The Reid case did not have any major political or legal repercussions; there were no ministerial resignations, no one was prosecuted under the Official Secrets Act, the libel action initiated by Mr. Reid never went before the courts, and the Standing Committee on Privileges and Elections did not think there was either a leak from the budget or from an amendment to the budget.[4] All the same, the Reid incident is unusually interesting for political scientists and students of communications, for it focused attention on legal restrains (e.g., the Official Secrets Act, parliamentary privilege, laws of libel) that affect the flow of political communications.

In this chapter, there will be an examination of five restraints that help set the legal parameter for mass media coverage of politics. The five facets in the complex interaction of press, politics and the law will be discussed in the following order: revealing of sources, the administration of justice and the right to fair trial, the Official Secrets Act, parliamentary privilege and laws of libel.

REVEALING OF SOURCES

Journalists usually consider it essential to protect the identities of their confidential sources of information. The traditional argument is that the unattributable leak would dry up if reporters were required to make public the names of their sources. News-gathering organizations and journalists generally do not have to identify their sources but at the same time they do not have the protection for confidentiality provided by "shield laws" in the United States. "There is no legal privilege for source protection in Canada."[5]

There are, in fact, situations when journalists are required to reveal sources. The Canadian practice, says Professor Kesterton, "has been to evaluate each

---

3. Montreal *Gazette*, 25 July, 1975.
4. For the *Report* see House of Commons, *Votes and Proceedings*, 17 October, 1975.
5. Peter Grant, "The Press and the Courts," in Dick MacDonald (ed.) *The Canadian Legal System*, Toronto: Canadian Daily Newspaper Publishers Association and Canadian Institute for the Administration of Justice, 1978.

revealing of sources situation on its merits,'' with the judiciary having the discretion to enforce disclosure or permit confidentiality.[6] Kesterton identifies three situations when Canadian journalists may have to name names of their sources, or face imprisonment. One such situation is when a journalist has information that may be pertinent to a public inquiry such as conducted by a Royal Commission. A second situation is in a police prosecution when the stories prepared by a journalist—and the identity of sources for the story—may be pertinent to determining the guilt or innocence of the accused. A third situation that requires source disclosure arises in a libel case where the journalist's legal defence is based on the belief that what he published was true.

Professor Peter Grant has commented that the law is very clear in Canada that if the identity of confidential sources is relevant to the inquiry, ''there is no way the reporter can get out from under by asserting some kind of privilege.''[7] Prosecutors in Canada have, however, been hesitant to push the demands for disclosure of sources and the number of test cases have been few, usually touching off controversies about interference with freedom of the press.

It is important to note that freedom of the press finds its roots in time-honoured traditions and precedents.[8] The legal counsel for the Canadian Daily Newspaper Publishers Association, J. J. Robinette, says that ''freedom of the press means the right to publish without prior consent of the government involved; and that is it.''[9] Under the law, Mr. Robinette said in a freedom of the press debate at the Toronto Press Club in 1978, members of the media have no more rights than the average citizen and therefore have no justification for refusing to supply material or answer questions under court subpoena.

In recent years, journalists in North America have come in for considerable criticism for the broad use—''overuse'' might be a better term—they make of ''confidential sources.'' The haphazard use of such anonymous sources tends to undermine the credibility of the media. In the United States a number of sensational stories—including a 1981 Pulitzer Prize-winning story on the use of drugs by children and a story alleging that President Carter eavesdropped through an electronic bug on conversations between President-elect Reagan and Mrs. Reagan who were staying at the Presidential guesthouse—have been based on ''confidential sources'' but not necessarily true facts.[10] In Canada, stories of this kind tend to be quickly forgotten unless they give rise to libel suits. There is much suspicion that the all-too-frequent story on politics which is based on ''sources in Ottawa'' or ''according to reliable sources'' may come from no more reliable a source than the journalist himself or the opinion of a fellow reporter. The unethi-

---

6. Wilfred H. Kesterton, ''Secrecy and Openness in Three Canadian Media-Related Situations,'' paper presented to the Canadian Communication Association, Halifax, N.S. May, 1981, p. 12.
7. Grant, ''The Press and the Courts,'' *op. cit.*, p. 94.
8. *Newsletter*, Canadian Daily Newspapers Publishers Association, October-November, 1978.
9. *Ibid.*
10. Both of these stories appeared in the *Washington Post*, one of the most respected newspapers in the United States.

cal use of sources that are either nonexistent or not reliable is more of a "responsibility of the media" than a disclosure of sources issue.

Another complicating element that is tied to the revealing of sources issue has been the increasingly frequent attempt by the police to use journalists' notes or film clippings from TV stations as evidence for possible police prosecutions. There have been a number of searches of newsrooms for this kind of evidence. These police actions have been referred to in the media as "fishing expeditions" to establish a *prima facie* (at first sight) case that would otherwise fail.[11] When Ronald Basford was Minister of Justice, he reportedly regarded such police raids as not consistent with the free-press tradition in Canada.[12]

The distinguished Canadian broadcast journalist, William Cunningham, is one of the strongest critics of "the police in the newsroom"; he argues that the media collect information in the public interest and not as a police back-up: "It is important that the public perceive the role of the press and the role of the police as two different things."[13] A different perspective of police searches is that they fall in line with public expectations of police convicting criminals as well as clearing those suspected of crimes.[14] As the law stands, police must first obtain a search warrant from a Justice of the Peace. Proving that the police did not have just cause for seeking a warrant could be a difficult matter.[15]

THE ADMINISTRATION OF JUSTICE, FAIR TRIAL AND FREE PRESS

The open court is one of the pillars of liberty in democratic societies. The public and the media play an important role in the judicial process, for their very presence in the courtroom means that the courts—one of the three branches of government—do not operate in secret. The public (i.e. the press) in the courtroom is a support structure for the independence of the judiciary and the independence of the bar. As Gordon Henderson of the Canadian Law Information Council has pointed out, the public today relies almost entirely on the media to find out about what is happening in the courts.[16] But although a free press and a free judiciary complement each other, there are times when the interests of those two institutions are in conflict. In Canada, the interests of the administration of justice and the right to a fair trial come before the right of freedom of expression.[17]

Parliament itself respects the traditional practice that "a matter which is under jurisdiction by a court of law cannot be brought before the House by motions or

---

11. Kesterton, "Secrecy and Openness," *op. cit.,* p. 16.
12. *Ibid*, p. 17. Kesterton quotes from Stuart Keate, *Paper Boy,* Toronto: Clarke, Irwin, 1980, p. 180.
13. *Newsletter,* Canadian Daily Newspaper Publishers Association, *op. cit.*
14. *Ibid.*
15. *Ibid.* Remarks attributed to J.J. Robinette.
16. Gordon Henderson, "People in the System," in *Canadian Legal System, op. cit.,* pp. 25-36.
17. Peter Grant, "The Legal Perspective: Recent Developments in the Law of Freedom of Expression," in Richard R. Cole (ed.) *Border Impact and Canadian Identity,* International Communication Division, Association for Education in Journalism, 1976. p. 12.

otherwise.''[18] There are situations, however, where the rights of Parliament to investigate (for example, in an inquiry into a breach of parliamentary privilege) are concurrent with the rights of the court. In a case in 1913, Parliament ordered Mr. R. C. Miller to be committed to jail in Ottawa for contempt of Parliament on the charge of refusing to tell the Public Accounts Committee about whom he had bribed to secure public contracts. Mr. Miller's contention that he did not have to answer because the matter was before the courts was not acceptable. Parliament's power to punish for contempt of Parliament is independent of the court process.[19]

The restraints on journalists that flow from the "higher interests" of the Court are important in the interaction of the media and the political system since the judiciary is an integral part of the political system. In the interests of the administration of justice, journalists can be found in contempt of court—a criminal offence—for undue criticism that scandalizes the Court or members of the judiciary.[20] Abusive comment about judges, allegations of bias, or insults can lead to prison terms. Ron Atkey points out that "contempt convictions for scandalizing the Court have generally been reluctantly imposed on the Canadian mass media." The practice is that "the press has been allowed a certain degree of freedom in criticizing both individual judges and the judicial system, and the courts have tended to be tolerant of journalistic impertinence."[21]

There is little judicial tolerance where the rights of an accused to a fair trial are concerned: the right to a fair trial takes precedence over the free press tradition. "Trial by press," especially where a jury is involved, raises serious problems and journalists can be held in contempt of court for interference in the judicial process. News of political importance can be affected in differing ways. It is almost impossible, for example, for the media to make public the findings of their "own investigation" on matters that are before the courts. There are restrictions on reports of confessions, a matter that has sometimes been overlooked by the media and has led to contempt of court citations.[22] Publishing information about the criminal record of an accused before the conclusion of the trial is not allowed. The press and public may be excluded from the Court where this is in the interest of public morals, national security, the maintenance of order or the proper administration of justice.

The safeguards in the judicial process to protect an accused person can delay for long periods of time the dissemination of important information of great public interest on matters (including political scandals) where criminal charges have been laid. Some of the restraints on the media apply until after the conclusion of

---

18. *Proceedings,* House of Commons Standing Committee on Privileges and Elections, August 11, 1975, Issue No. 25. Information provided by J.P.J. Maingot, Parliamentary Counsel and Law Clerk.
19. *Ibid.*
20. Ronald G. Atkey, "The Law of the Press in Canada," in G. Stuart Adam (ed.) *Journalism, Communication and the Law,* Scarborough: Prentice-Hall of Canada, 1976 pp. 125-126.
21. *Ibid,* p. 127.
22. Grant, "The Legal Perspective," *op. cit.,* p. 12.

an appeal. The restraints on the media in the interest of fair trial are not always clearly defined. This can lead to inconsistencies in judicial interpretation.

THE OFFICIAL SECRETS ACT

The impact of the Official Secrets Act on the press in Canada has been overlooked; newspapers and broadcasters were generally complacent until the late 1970s. Official Secrets Acts have been in Canadian statute books since 1890, and for 88 years—which included such stressful times as World War I, the Great Depression, World War II, the Korean War, the Cold War and the Front de Libération du Québec (FLQ) Crisis—the Acts were never invoked against the mass media. Not until 1978, when the *Toronto Sun* and its two senior executives were charged under the Act did journalists in Canada begin to show any great concern. In Britain there had been highly controversial prosecutions against journalists under similar legislation and these should have served as a warning. But Canada's mass media after World War II were more conscious of American court cases involving the government and the mass media than freedom of the press cases in Britain.

The previous chapter focused on the constitutional characteristics that make Canada's parliamentary system secretive and closed in comparison to the more open American presidential form of government. The constitutional thrust on secrecy gives rise to a whole series of administrative and legal provisions that reinforce confidentiality. They include:

— Cabinet Ministers are sworn to secrecy.[23]

— Members of the civil service swear not to release any document or information without permission.[24]

— There are reinforcing provisions for secrecy in numerous Acts, including the Income Tax Act, the Railway Act, the Hazardous Products Act, the Defence Productions Act, etc. (In many instances the confidentiality provisions are aimed at protecting the privacy of individuals, in others they safeguard secrecy in government.)[25]

— The government's classification of documents system sets the guidelines for the degree of secrecy of particular documents: "Top Secret," "Secret," "Confidential," and "Restricted."[26]

The Official Secrets Act, with its specified sanctions, stands in the background as a legal support structure for confidentiality.[27]

---

23. Privy Councillor's Oath.
24. Public Service Employment Act, R.S.C. 1970, c. p. 32, Schedule III.
25. Several Acts including the Atomic Energy Ltd. Act, the Bank of Canada Act, the Central Housing and Mortgage Act, The Surplus Crown Assets Act, the Industrial Development Board Act require civil servants to take a special oath of secrecy. See M. L. Friedland, *National Security: The Legal Dimensions,* A study prepared for the Commission of Inquiry Concerning Certain Activities of the Royal Canadian Mounted Police, Ottawa: Minister of Supply and Services, 1980. pp. 56, 153. For a listing of prohibitions against the release of government information contained in Canadian statutes, see F. Pepin, Appendix "SRI-17," Standing Joint Committee on Regulations and Other Statutory Instruments, April 18, 1978.
26. See Report of the Royal Commission on Security (the MacKenzie Report) 1969.
27. *Proceedings,* Standing Committee on Elections and Privileges, *op. cit.*

The Official Secrets Act encourages the practice in Canadian politics of the public's right to know depending in large part on what the government is willing to tell. The awesome title, the Official Secrets Act, suggests that the legislation deals specifically with the innermost secrets of State, the revealing of which would cause serious injury to Canada's defence, internal security and international relations involving defence. Instead, the Official Secrets Act is drawn up in sweeping terms. It contains "broad and ambiguous language" that *can* cover nearly all unauthorized (that is, illegal) disclosures of government information, even on insignificant matters. The fact that it has been invoked only once against the press belies its long-term constraining effect on political communications; the impact is mostly indirect and unseen. The Official Secrets Act restrains openness in Canadian government and contributes to an atmosphere of secrecy.

The history of Official Secrets Acts—Canada has had three—provides an explanation for the unacceptable features of the legislation. It is a troubling story of parliamentary failure to closely examine far-reaching legislation introduced in times of international tensions.

THE BRITISH CONNECTION: THE FIRST ACT

All Canadian Official Secrets Acts are based on British legislation. The first Canadian Act of 1890 was passed by Parliament in Ottawa at the request of London and was similar to British legislation enacted a year earlier. Britain had been experiencing problems with leaks of State secrets. The most embarrassing of these leaks, and the one that is generally credited for being the catalyst for the Official Secrets Act, is the so-called Marvin incident which occurred in 1878.[28] A London newspaper, the *Globe,* published details of a secret agreement between Britain and Russia that had been prepared for the Congress of Berlin. Charles Marvin, a temporary Foreign Office clerk, had leaked the information for pay. A theft charge against Marvin—he was accused of stealing the paper on which the treaty was written—failed in court: Marvin had not stolen the paper; he had memorized the treaty details. In 1887, there was the Terry incident in which another government employee was set free by the courts although he had sold tracings of warships; Terry had used his own tracing paper. The law was too weak, hence the first British—and Canadian—Official Secrets Acts which made it an offence for civil servants to obtain information and communicate it against the interests of the State. The emphasis was on treason and sabotage and the legislation was sensitive to the difference between State secrets and those matters which government departments classify as secret for their convenience.[29]

---

28. For accounts of the legislative history of British Official Secrets Acts, see David G. T. Williams, *Not in the Public Interest,* London: Hutchinson, 1965, especially Chapter I; Jonathan Aitken, *Officially Secret* London: 1971; Civil Report of Departmental Committee on Section 2 of the Official Secrets Act 1911, Cmnd. 5104, London: 1922; (the Franks Report).
29. Donald Wraith, *Open and Closed Government*, London: The Royal Institute of Public Administration, 1977.

THE SECOND ACT

The Official Secrets Act lost its innocence in 1911 as Europe was headed for World War I. Germany was building a spy network in Britain. The first Official Secrets Act, then more than 20 years old, was inadequate to deal with the sophisticated techniques of German spies using cameras and radio-telegraph. Germans were "holidaying" in Britain where they were photographing strategic locations, including harbours, without fear of punishment.

The second Official Secrets Act (1911) was formidable legislation aimed at dealing with serious espionage problems. It introduced the concept, contrary to British legal principles, that the onus was on the accused to prove that the information had been collected innocently. The legislation also pioneered new ground in the leakage area: not only was it a crime to leak information but now the *receiver* of leaks was also guilty of an offence. The British parliament was given the impression that the leakage section, never mentioned in the parliamentary debates, was largely a fall-back position when it was too difficult to convict spies because of legal technicalities.

The international tensions—Germany had recently sent a gunboat into the Moroccan harbour at Agadir—assured swift passage in Parliament for the Official Secrets Act. The House of Lords where the legislation was first introduced, spent a half-hour on the Second Reading Debate. In the House of Commons, the bill passed through all stages in a half-hour. Considering the mood of the times, the Official Secrets Act appeared reasonable.

Evidence has since been uncovered that the 1911 Act was not nearly as innocent as had been assumed. The legislation had actually been in preparation for several years and was not at all a hasty response to a "crisis" situation. The leakage section was *intended* to extend the legislation beyond espionage and sabotage cases.[30]

The 1911 Official Secrets Act was made applicable to Canada and thus never scrutinized by Parliament in Ottawa. Britain further strengthened its Official Secrets Act in 1920 when there was again heightened national anxiety: there was the threat of civil war in Ireland; there were fears about the spread of communism and, there was concern about German "resurgence." Parliament at Westminster swiftly adopted the new legislation, without seriously examining its provisions. The 1920 changes did not apply to Canada for it was pointed out the Dominions were planning even stronger legislation. Canada waited 19 years.

THE CANADIAN OFFICIAL SECRETS ACT, 1939

Canada's present Official Secrets Act dates from 1939, the year that World War II broke out.[31] Bill 92, respecting official secrets, was passed by the Canadian House of Commons on May 30, 1939. Justice Minister Ernest Lapointe, who steered the bill through the Commons, said it "merely" consolidated the English

---

30. *Ibid.*
31. See *Proceedings,* House of Commons, May 30, 1939.

Acts of 1911 and 1920: "There is no difference except that [The British Official Secrets Acts] are made applicable to Canada and Canadian conditions." There was no debate or dissent in the House when the bill was given second reading or approval in principle. Clause-by-clause examination was given by the Committee of the Whole which reported the bill for third and final reading that same day. There were minor changes to correct typographical errors and there was an amendment to replace the words "an enemy" with "a foreign power," for it was pointed out that there is no enemy in time of peace. It would be another 100 days before the start of hostilities that brought Canada into World War II.

The honest confusion about "an enemy power" is a reflection of the mood of the times. Members of Parliament were not concerned about the provisions for secret trials nor were they interested in possible implications for freedom of the press. A strong Official Secrets Act to prevent German spies from operating in Canada was the main issue. As is so often the case in crisis situations, the threat of war meant a disregard of threats to civil liberties. The socialist CCF member for Winnipeg North, A. A. Heaps, noted that "in times such as the present every nation has the right to defend itself." He thought that the bill didn't go far enough and he quoted an article from the *New York Post* about Nazi spy ring activities in Montreal. Mr. Heaps wanted the government to root out wherever they possibly could the men who were carrying on espionage in this country. Another member of the House, Thomas Reid (Liberal, New Westminster), was not happy with Section 12 of the Act which provided that the Attorney General of Canada must give his consent for a prosecution, for Reid felt that nothing should stand in the way of swift police action. Denton Massey (Conservative, Greenwood) inquired as to whether the penalty in other countries for these types of crimes included death; he also noted that the Official Secrets Act did not mention deportation. Justice Minister Lapointe gave his assurances that an accused could be deported under the Criminal Code and that naturalized persons could have their citizenship certificates cancelled. The Social Credit member, René Antoine Pelletier (Peace River), called on the government to exercise a good deal of care in the choice of the people permitted to come to Canada.

The Justice Minister was a calming influence. He said "Ninety-five percent of our foreign population are opposed to the views which some people are trying to instill in them; they are loyal to Canada. . . . We believe in the necessity and the utility of freedom of speech and in the vigilant preservation of the institutions which make it possible. We cannot preserve democracy by throwing away the freedom of discussion."

For the most part, the sense of direction of the Official Secrets Act is unmistakable: it seeks to deal with espionage and related offences carried out on behalf of foreign countries against Canadian interests. But even Section 3, the espionage section, has been criticized for lacking clarity and precision. Professor Martin Friedland examines in detail the problem areas of the Official Secrets Act in *National Security: The Legal Dimensions,* a study prepared for the McDonald Commission Inquiry into the RCMP. The Commission has recommended new espionage legislation which would apply only to conduct which relates to the communication of information to a foreign power, including foreign groups, such as terrorist factions, that have not achieved recognition as a foreign state.[32]

THE LEAKAGE CONTROVERSY: SECTION 4 AND THE MEDIA

As far as the media are concerned, Section 4 of the Official Secrets Act, the leakage section, is of special importance. This is the most controversial part of the legislation because the sweeping language used here outlaws the unauthorized flow of information and lends itself to being applied to what are not genuine spy cases. Merely receiving secret (that is, classified) information, without even passing it on, constitutes a crime; the receiver of information is as guilty as the person leaking it. The media, as receivers of leaks, are subject to prosecution (under Section 4 (3)). If the media proceed to publish in print or broadcast form, they are liable to further prosecution for communicating information "obtained in contravention" of the Official Secrets Act. The *Toronto Sun* case, discussed below, is an example of the media caught in a double trap as receiver and communicator of classified information.

In the previous chapter, considerable importance was attached to the role of the leak in tempering the secret nature of the Canadian political system. Section 4, as it reads, is aimed at plugging leaks at the governmental level and preventing the dissemination of leaks by the mass media. It can be used to keep the lid down on politically embarrassing information on subjects far removed from security.

The "catch-all" nature of the leakage section appears to be all-embracing to protect the confidentiality of government information. There are no qualifications. There is no differentiation between true State secrets and politically motivated secrets. There are no degrees of seriousness of offences. The maximum penalty for leaking or receiving leaks is an outrageously high 14 years, the same as for espionage. Section 4 applies to leaks at both the federal and provincial level although it has never been used by a province. (Since the consent of the Attorney General of Canada is required for all prosecutions under the Act, a province would have to take the unpalatable step of asking permission from Ottawa.)

THE USE OF THE OFFICIAL SECRETS ACT

Canadian governments have usually shown restraint and good sense in invoking the Official Secrets Act. There have been 21 prosecutions up to 1981.[33] Of these, 13 resulted in convictions but four of the convictions were successfully appealed; this means that only nine cases have been upheld after appeal. (There were six

---

32. Commission of Inquiry Concerning Certain Activities of the Royal Canadian Mounted Police (McDonald Commission), First Report, Freedom and Security under the Law, 1979.
33. *Ibid.*

acquittals and in the two other cases the charges were dismissed at the preliminary inquiries.)

There has been a tendency in Canada to see the Official Secrets Act as a sort of an ultimate weapon, with penalties of up to 14 years in prison. It applies to everybody: Cabinet Ministers, parliamentarians, Public Service officials, members of the armed forces, the press and the public at large where there has been a serious breach of highly classified information.[34] There has been one instance when it has been applied in relation to a Member of the House of Commons in connection with espionage activities, as revealed in the Gouzenko Affair.

The Gouzenko trials, which account for well over half of the 21 prosecutions, provide the best illustrations of the use of the Official Secrets Act. Almost all of the prosecutions were under the espionage section of the Act; only one was based exclusively on the leakage section.

Igor Gouzenko, a cipher clerk in the Soviet Embassy in Ottawa, defected in September 1945 with numerous documents. The *Ottawa Journal* turned Gouzenko away when he showed up with his sensitive material and Canadian officials refused to take him seriously for two or three days, partly because his disclosures about a Soviet spy ring in Canada and other western countries were so sensational.[35] Furthermore, there was concern at the highest level of government that the Gouzenko affair could cause a serious rift in western relations with the Soviet Union that had been cemented during the wartime alliance. The Embassy documents named approximately 300 Canadians the Soviet Union attempted to recruit as spies. A Royal Commission appointed to examine the affair reported in 1946: "The most startling aspect is the uncanny success with which the Soviet agents were able to find Canadians willing to betray their country." It was not until October 1981—36 years later—that the federal government released the accounts of secret testimony to the Taschereau-Kellock Commission. British journalists, including Chapman Pincher and Anthony Boyle, have written fascinating accounts of some of the spying activities that came to light as a result of Gouzenko's revelations. Canadian journalists, for their part, remained largely silent for 36 years, testimony to Canada's attachment to secrecy and the hesitancy of the media to probe in "dangerous territory."

There have been only four prosecutions under the Official Secrets Act since the Gouzenko disclosures, although the government considered using the Act in at least another five or six cases. One of the prosecutions, the Featherstone case, is straightforward. In 1967, Bower Edward Featherstone, a lithographer in the

---

34. *Proceedings*, Standing Committee on Elections and Privileges, *op. cit.*, August 11, 1975, p. 69.

35. See C.E.S. Franks, *Parliament and Security Matters*, A Study for the McDonald Commission, Ottawa: Minister of Supply and Services, 1980 pp. 41-42. For an account of the use of the Act in the Gouzenko Trials, see Maxwell Cohen, "Secrecy and Policy: The Canadian Experience and International Relations," in Thomas Franck and Edward Weisband (ed.) *Secrecy and Foreign Policy*, New York: Oxford University Press, 1974, pp. 355-376.

federal resources department, stole two secret naval maps that he tried to pass to Soviet diplomats. The maps showed location of shipwrecks off the Newfoundland coast, information that would be useful for submarines that could hide near the wrecks to avoid detection. Featherstone was convicted under Section 3, the espionage section, and sentenced to a two-and-a-half year term at Kingston penitentiary. It is the only conviction that has stood up beyond appeal in more than 30 years. The other three "recent" prosecutions, *Biernacki* (1961), *Toronto Sun* (1978) and *Treu* (1978), are of special interest to the mass media.

Biernacki, 1961. The prosecution of Biernacki, a Polish immigrant, provides guidelines on the type of information covered by the Act. There are inconsistencies in the Canadian legislation, including a misplaced comma, translation errors in the French text, and the use of the words "secret" and "official" that are sometimes left out and at other times are included in reference to documents.

Biernacki was collecting information about Canadian residents of Polish background that might have been useful in setting up a spy ring. The case was dismissed under the espionage section of the Act at the preliminary inquiry because the information was not "official" and "secret"—it was in the public domain. The court interpretation suggests that the application of the Act in Canada is more difficult than in Britain.

Toronto Sun, 1978. The only Canadian prosecution under the Official Secrets Act that involves the press directly is the *Toronto Sun* case. A government document stamped TOP SECRET FOR CANADIAN EYES ONLY had come into the possession of the *Sun* and the mere receiving of such a document would appear to be a crime under the Official Secrets Act. The *Sun* published details of the document, making the contents available to friend and foe. The *Sun* and two senior executives were charged with receiving secret information [Section 4(3)] and with communicating information obtained in contravention of the Official Secrets Act [Section 4(1) (a)].

The *Sun* affair began February 9, 1978, when the Minister for External Affairs, Don Jamieson, announced in the House of Commons that 13 Soviet diplomats were being expelled for spy activities. Two of the diplomats had already left Canada and the other 11 left shortly afterwards. The disclosure of the spy ring was dramatic by Ottawa standards, for the Canadian government had made it a practice to expel spies quietly. The Minister for External Affairs went from the Commons to a news conference at which he praised the RCMP and displayed photographs of Soviet spy gadgets, including a cigarette pack with a secret compartment. The Ottawa disclosures, however, did not impress Conservative MP Thomas Cossitt. Making use of information that had been leaked to him, Mr. Cossitt alleged in the House of Commons that there was much more to the Soviet spying activities than the government had made public. Mr. Cossitt also commented on Soviet spying in interviews with reporters outside the House.

The nature of the comments by Mr. Cossitt and the kinds of questions he asked convinced the government that the Opposition member had in his possession a

Top Secret RCMP document approved on March 24, 1976. Mr. Cossitt on three occasions revealed information in the House from the 60-page document that contained a great deal of sensitive material. The government wanted the document returned and was anxious to find out who leaked it. The controversy surrounding Mr. Cossitt attracted front page headlines across the country and received widespread coverage on radio and television. The case became further complicated in that the CTV television network in a programme *Code Blue* in its *Inquiry* series broadcast nationally on February 12, 1978, made references to parts of the secret document.

On March 7, 1978, the *Toronto Sun* published a column written by editor-in-chief, Peter Worthington, under the heading: "What Secret Report Says." The column quotes from the same TOP SECRET document that the government had requested Mr. Cossitt to return. The Worthington column cited widespread Soviet spy activities in Canada and named names of KGB agents. It also reported Soviet attempts, some of them successful, to get Canadians to cooperate in intelligence activities. The *Sun* column said the secret document that it had in its possession was a virtual catalogue of Soviet crimes, or attempted crimes, against Canada and Canadians in business, academic, journalistic, military and political areas. Mr. Worthington indicated that his column and the disclosures from the RCMP document were a response to a statement by Prime Minister Trudeau at a news conference March 2, 1978, in which the Canadian leader differentiated between the KGB and the Soviet government. The Prime Minister had said the KGB was "an enemy of any country on which it is spying," but that he did not consider the Soviet Union to be an enemy. Mr. Worthington, who at one time was correspondent in Moscow for the now defunct *Toronto Telegram*, argued that one could not view separately the Soviet government from its intelligence and espionage forces and used the TOP SECRET document to make his points.

In the 10 days that followed the printing of the *Toronto Sun* column, there was high drama in Ottawa as the government demanded the return of the secret document from Mr. Cossitt and pondered what action to take against the *Toronto Sun*. On March 17, the Minister of Justice, Ronald Basford, announced the government's decision not to prosecute Mr. Cossitt because he had made his disclosures in the Commons and had elaborated on them only slightly outside the House. The privileges of Members of Parliament protected Mr. Cossitt. With regard to the Worthington column, the Justice Minister pointed out that the press and journalists did not have any special privileges and ordered the prosecution under the Official Secrets Act. As required, the Attorney-General of Canada authorized the *Sun* prosecutions, which were by indictment, meaning that they carried the possibility of 14-year prison terms. (If the Attorney-General decides the accused should be summarily prosecuted, the maximum penalty on conviction is a $500 fine and/or 12 months imprisonment.)

Questions were raised in the press and in Parliament as to why the Attorney-General had decided to allow prosecution of the *Toronto Sun* and not of Mr. Cossitt and the CTV network. This seemingly arbitrary action was interpreted in some quarters as an attempt by the government to deal harshly with a newspaper that had been highly critical of the Trudeau administration.[36]

It took just over one year from the time the *Sun* was charged until the completion of the preliminary hearings to find that there was no evidence to commit the newspaper and its two top executives. Judge Carl Waisberg found that the TOP SECRET document was no longer secret, if ever secret—substantial parts had been made public, in Parliament and on the CTV network, prior to the appearance of the *Sun* column. It also came out in the preliminary hearings that 67 copies of the document were distributed among governmental departments in March 1976, a full two years before the appearance of the Worthington column. Judge Waisberg found that these factors "have brought the document, now 'shopworn' and no longer secret, into the public domain." He also stated that since the Official Secrets Act is a restricting statute, and seeks to curb freedom, such as freedom of speech and the press, it should be given strict interpretation. He commented on the ambiguous and unwieldy provisions of the Act and thought a "complete redrafting seemed appropriate and necessary."

The outcome of the proceedings is more a criticism of the government's classification system as to what constitutes secrecy than an assertion of the right of the press to receive or publish secret materials.

The Treu Case, 1978. The *Toronto Sun* case came at a time when there was controversy over another prosecution under the leakage provisions of the Official Secrets Act. Peter Treu, an electronic expert specializing in air defence systems, was charged on two counts; first, for the illegal retention of documents [Section 4 (1) (c)] and second, for failure to take reasonable care of these documents [Section 4 (1) (d)]. Mr. Treu at one time worked for Northern Electric Company Limited (now Northern Telecom Canada Limited) on government contracts in air defence systems. When Northern Electric got out of the defence contract business, Mr. Treu set up his own consulting firm, Cantalin, with the apparent encouragement of his former employer. Deeply involved in North Atlantic Treaty Organization (NATO) defence work, he had top security clearance and held in his possession highly sensitive documents, some of which he himself had authored. In August, 1973, the Security Service learned that Mr. Treu was personally responsible for the tender via Hong Kong to the People's Republic of China of a prospectus which contained secret information relating to NATO's air defence communication and surveillance system. Mr. Treu's consulting firm also had contacts with India and Pakistan about air defence systems that these coun-

---

36. The McDonald Commission offered a different explanation: Mr. Cossitt was not prosecuted because he might be able to rely on the privileges he enjoys as a Member of Parliament. The Justice Department had divided the secret document into 16 different items and 12 of these were regarded as being in the public domain. The CTV programme did not release any of the still secret information. The Justice Department took a much more serious view of the *Toronto Sun* article. It was said to have "contained information which had not been published previously and which was considered to be prejudicial to security." McDonald Commission, *First Report on Freedom and Security under the Law*, 1979, p. 7.

tries wanted to build. Mr. Treu's secrecy clearance was cancelled in December 1973, but he was not informed and continued receiving secret information and documents from NATO.

In March 1974, the RCMP raided Mr. Treu's suburban Montreal home and carried away some 350 pounds of documents, files and boxes. Two years later, Mr. Treu was charged with the two offences under the leakage section of the Official Secrets Act. The trial, which began in April 1977, was closed to the press and public. (The Act allows for secret trials and defence lawyers had not objected.) Mr. Treu was convicted and sentenced to two years for illegal retention of documents and one year concurrent for failure to take reasonable care of the documents. The Quebec Court of Appeal on February 20, 1979, unanimously set aside conviction and extended an acquittal.[37]

The controversy surrounding Treu continues to this day. The McDonald Commission Inquiry suggests that Mr. Treu could have been charged under the espionage section of the Official Secrets Act but the Justice Department decided against this because certain key witnesses refused to testify. Mr. Treu has no way to defend himself against these allegations. This practice runs against the grain of Canadian justice. The media have described Mr. Treu's dilemma as a Catch-22 situation: a self-enclosed system of thwarting and tormenting.

Some Observations

If the leakage provisions of the Official Secrets Act were taken literally, then Cabinet Ministers and civil servants would be committing many thousands of offences every day.[38] Mark MacGuigan, the legal authority who later became Minister for External Affairs, observed in 1978 when he was chairman of the House of Commons Standing Committee on Justice and Legal Affairs that Section 4 is "so sweeping that it is almost difficult to conceive that in strict law any minister or public servant could lawfully communicate any significant information."[39] The silence in government would be deafening—government business would grind to a halt—if civil servants continuously required specific authorization when discussing important matters, and perhaps even matters of little significance, with each other, the public and consultants. Legal experts believe the courts would never support such an absurd application of the law, that the concept of authorization would be interpreted in an elastic form to incorporate the doctrine of implied authorization.[40] (The British governmental committee headed by Lord Franks in 1972 put forward this explanation when it examined the similar situation in that country.) It can then be argued that ministers are self-authorizing and can decide on their own what to reveal. Senior civil servants

---

37. *Ibid,* p. 5. The Quebec Court of Appeal felt there was reasonable doubt. It did not examine the secret material produced at the in-camera trial because "the contents were largely irrelevant. What mattered was the Appellant's state of mind, and not the technical data . . . "
38. Friedland, *National Security: The Legal Dimensions, op. cit.,* p. 56.
39. House of Commons, *Proceedings 1978,* p. 6251.
40. Friedland, *National Security: The Legal Dimensions, op. cit.,* p. 56.

have considerable discretion as to what is permissible to communicate, but this discretion diminishes along with descent in the civil service hierarchy.

There have been only the aforementioned two Canadian prosecutions under the leakage provision in more than 30 years, compared to about 35 cases in Britain. Both Canadian prosecutions failed (*Toronto Sun* at the preliminary hearings and *Treu* on appeal) and the government decided against appealing to higher courts. The Canadian experience suggests that the courts interpret the "catch-all" Section 4 in as limited a form as possible; the poor drafting of the legislation has provided a useful opening.

The indications are that largely because of the sledgehammer characteristics of its leakage section, the law itself has become discredited. Three royal commissions—the Taschereau-Kellock Commission set up in the wake of the Gouzenko disclosures, the MacKenzie Commission on national security and the McDonald Commission on RCMP wrongdoings—have criticized the legislation, though sometimes for different reasons. In Parliament, Gerald Baldwin (now retired) was the loudest and most outspoken critic. He said that the Act posed a great danger to civil liberties, calling it stupid, monstrous, ridiculous and silly, tyrannical and authoritarian. "A law like this," Mr. Baldwin declared, "deserves contempt and that's all I have for it."

The fact that the leakage section has been used only once against the media suggests (1) the government's hesitancy to use the draconian legislation and (2) the media have generally behaved so well that the use of the law has not been required. Equal emphasis should be placed on the "good behaviour" of the media, and on the government's reluctance to prosecute.

The Official Secrets Act gives the government a big stick to use on the press and the very existence of this "weapon" is a restraining influence. There is little doubt that the Official Secrets Act is important in the interaction of press and politics.

The failure of the government's prosecution against the *Toronto Sun* was due to the fact that Judge Waisberg regarded the secret information as "shopworn" and therefore in the public domain. The courts never suggested that the press was protected from prosecution for either receiving or publishing improperly leaked information. The *Toronto Sun* case did not clear muddy waters; it raised more questions than it answered. Professor Friedland makes the following observation: "The information (published in the *Sun*) had not been officially released and one wonders whether it is correct interpretation of the (leakage) section to give *carte blanche* to publish information because some of it has already been improperly leaked."[41] The uncertainty about the meaning of the leakage section remains.

If vagueness and uncertainty about the meaning of the law is one fundamental shortcoming, another is the unpredictable way the Act may be used. The prosecution of the *Toronto Sun* and the decision not to take similar action against the CTV Network and MP Tom Cossitt illustrates a capricious use of the Official Secrets Act.

---

41. *Ibid*, p. 57.

The Act helps to create an atmosphere of secrecy because of three basic flaws: (1) the extraordinary wide prohibitions on the flow of classified information, backed up by intimidating penalties, (2) the uncertainty of the meaning of the Act and (3) the arbitrary manner in which it can be applied.

The Official Secrets Act is a two-way restraint. "Journalists," says Albert Pickerell, "are deterred from probing and civil servants are over-cautious in disseminating information."[42] The British journalist, William Hardcastle, in writing about the effects of this kind of statute, says it "stiffens the secret spine of the bureaucrat and softens the vertebrae of the press."[43]

In simple language, the Official Secrets Act can be seen as a subtle but nevertheless effective instrument of censorship. It places the onus of self-censorship on journalists and media institutions. It is inconceivable, for example, that Canadian newspapers would publish the equivalent of the American Pentagon papers on the Vietnam war, as occurred in the United States. In such a situation in Canada, both the press and those involved in providing the documents to the press would be open to prosecution under the Official Secrets Act. Editors and publishers could be given long jail terms for this offence.

Self-censorship by the media is a particularly dangerous form of censorship. The public is unaware of its existence and there is the illusion that all is well in the democratic process.

The notion of censorship, while generally regarded as abhorrent in the Canadian political process under normal conditions, is not all that alien to us in times of severe stress. And it may be argued that crisis situations are a moment of truth for the political system and the social institutions, providing important clues about basic characteristics in our society. The last time Canada imposed censorship was in the course of the Front de Libération du Québec (FLQ) crisis in October 1970 which saw political kidnappings in Montreal and other traumatic developments, including the murder of a Quebec Cabinet Minister, Pierre Laporte. The invoking of the War Measures Act by the federal government, in effect declaring a state of emergency in Canada, limited the freedom of the press.[44] The regulations under the Act imposed censorship, prohibiting media publication of anything that threatened security or in any way gave a platform to statements or publications by the FLQ.[45]

The FLQ crisis marks the most dramatic use of censorship in Canadian peacetime. In Quebec province, the menace of the highly unpopular Padlock Law, "An Act to Protect Against Communistic Propaganda," which was operational for 20 years until the Supreme Court found it *ultra vires* in 1957, provides an unhappy story of a form of press censorship in Canada. The Alberta Press Act,

---

42. Albert Pickerell, "Official Secrets Acts, the D-Notice System and the British Press". Paper presented to Association for Education in Journalism, Ottawa, August 1975, p. 13.
43. *Ibid.* Mr. Hardcastle made his observations in *The Listener,* December 7, 1967.
44. For a detailed analysis of the interaction of the press and politics in the FLQ Crisis, see Arthur Siegel, "Canadian Newspaper coverage of the FLQ Crisis," Ph.D. thesis, McGill University, 1974.
45. Cohen, "Secrecy and Policy," *op. cit.,* p. 362.

disallowed by the federal government after referral to the courts, is yet another example of the authorities trying to exercise media control, using the argument that they were actually promoting freedom of the press. There had, of course, been censorship in this country in World War II under regulations of the War Measures Act as well as outside the Act for a limited period. Wartime censorship goes back to World War I. Before that, Canada's communications system was not regarded as an effective enough carrier of information that it could be seen as having adverse effects on Canadian involvement in such conflicts as the Crimean and Boer wars.

PARLIAMENTARY PRIVILEGE

We return to the Reid case, which involves a clash between two basic principles of Canadian democracy: freedom of Parliament and freedom of the press. The House of Commons Standing Committee on Privileges and Elections, reporting after its investigation of the Reid incident, said it was conscious that "a balance must be struck" between the principle that Parliament should be protected from improper obstruction of its functions and the principle of freedom of speech of the citizen to criticize the institution or membership of Parliament. In searching for such a balance when the press and Parliament are in conflict with one another, there is no turning to a third party, such as the courts, to adjudicate. Instead, Parliament becomes accuser, judge and jury. The procedure runs against the grain of justice and fair play.

Parliament is at the core of democratic practices and it must appear strange to suggest that parliamentary privilege is a legal restraint on political communications flow. Parliamentary privilege is aimed at ensuring that members of both Houses of Parliament are as free as possible from outside pressures and restraints in the transaction of public business.[46] The privileges and immunities of Members of Parliament developed in England in the first instance to protect legislators from meddling by the Monarch.

The evolution of privileges for parliamentarians has been an important aspect of ensuring a free Parliament with parliamentarians at liberty to present their views on the floor of the House. Thus, freedom of speech is ensured; no charge in court can be based on any statement made by a member in the House or Senate. This privilege appears to extend also to issuing a press release.[47] The assumption here is that the occasional abuse of the privilege of freedom of speech will be more than compensated for by the gain in complete frankness in discussion.[48] When Parliament is in session, a member is excused from jury duty and does not have to appear as a witness in court, nor can a member be arrested or imprisoned under civil process. There is no protection, however, for members who have committed criminal offences, but the Speaker has to be immediately informed.

---

46. Mallory, *The Structure of Canadian Government, op. cit.*, p. 274.
47. Friedland, *National Security: The Legal Dimensions, op. cit.*, p. 64.
48. MacGregor Dawson, *The Government of Canada, op. cit.*, p. 372.

In addition to the privileges of individual members, there are the collective privileges of the House. Some are designed to maintain order and discipline, others to protect the House from outside. A breach of the collective privileges is called contempt, and contempt of Parliament has somewhat similar implications as does contempt of court. If Parliament considers comments on its proceedings as libellous or scandalous, then the offender may be charged with contempt. An attack on a member of the House in his capacity as parliamentarian is regarded as an attack on the privileges of the House as a body.[49]

The impact of parliamentary privilege on the interaction of press and politics has not been adequately researched in Canada. In Britain, its use against newspapers is well-recorded. In the American colonies, parliamentary privilege was an important weapon used by the British authorities in attempts to still the revolutionary fervour of editors and journalists.[50] Its increasingly frequent use after the Zenger case in New York in 1734 (discussed in Chapter V) is of importance in evaluating the Canadian situation. Zenger was a milestone case in that it showed that juries could no longer be trusted in seditious libel trials, that they could turn their backs on legal procedures to take sides with journalists in conflicts involving the State and press. Professor Donald Pember writes that government strategy changed after Zenger. Rather than go the court route with libel charges, "the government hauled printers and editors before legislatures and state assemblies which were usually hostile to journalists. The charge was not sedition, but breach of parliamentary privilege, or contempt of the assembly."[51]

In British North America, seditious libel cases against journalists fared well before the courts until about 1833. In that year, the jury in the Joseph Howe trial (see Chapter V) disregarded the law to side with the editor of the *Novascotian*. It is safe to assume that the authorities appreciated the merits of using parliamentary privilege in dealing with difficult journalists and editors. The enormous official displeasure with the press is revealed clearly in many recorded statements including one by the Attorney-General of Upper Canada, John Beverley Robinson in 1833, who said: "It is one of the miserable consequences of the abuse of liberty, that a licentious press is permitted to poison the public mind with the most absurd and wicked misrepresentations, which the ill-disposed, without inquiry, receive and act upon as truth."[52]

The effects of parliamentary privilege on the media are far more important than would be indicated by the relatively few formal clashes that have taken place. The Reid case was only the fourth such public confrontation between press and Parliament since 1900. It is useful to look briefly at these four cases and a number of other relevant incidents.

---

49. See generally, J.P.J. Maingot, Proceedings of Committee on Privileges and Elections, August 8, 1975, *op. cit.,* pp. 18-64
50. Don R. Pember, *Mass Media Law*, 2nd edition, Dubuque, Iowa: W.C. Brown, 1981, p. 41.
51. *Ibid.*
52. Quoted in Paul Rutherford, *The Making of the Canadian Media*, Toronto: McGraw-Hill Ryerson Ltd., 1978, p. 1.

Reid, 1975. The legal principle on which the Reid complaint is based goes back more than 250 years to February 26, 1701, when the British House of Commons resolved that to print or publish any libellous comments reflecting on any member of the House for or relating to his service therein was a high violation of the rights and privileges of the House.[53] Mr. Reid's principal complaint was that he had been libelled in the *Gazette* article.

Mr. Reid embarked on two courses of action. He took his grievances before Parliament (a procedure available only to parliamentarians) and at the same time initiated legal action, much like any other citizen might do, by having his solicitors give formal notice, as required by law, that he intended to sue the *Gazette* and reporter Jacques Hamilton for damages for libel. There is precedent that the courts and Parliament in Canada can embark on legal-type proceedings at the same time because the two institutions are independent of each other.

The Standing Committee on Privileges and Elections reported after its investigation that there were errors in the *Gazette* story and that the Montreal daily fell short of the standards to be expected of a newspaper, but there was no evidence that the paper was acting with malice. The Report was not debated in the House because there were no specific recommendations for censure or imprisonment. The Committee's investigation—that is, taking evidence from witnesses—was open to the press and public, but the deliberations for drafting the Report took place behind closed doors.

As a test case of freedom of Parliament versus freedom of the press, the Reid incident did little more than reaffirm Parliament's right to censure the press. The Gazette, for its part, rejected Parliament's actions. It described the investigation as "a case of midsummer's madness," "a waste of the taxpayers' money," and "a waste of [the *Gazette*'s] time."[54] In an editorial, the *Gazette* questioned the fairness of it all: "A Member of Parliament, exercising his privilege of unlimited free speech, already had a powerful means at his disposal to attack what he believed to be unfairness on the part of the information media. He has a recourse to law that the media do not have against him."[55]

The Speaker's Bias Case and the Escapades of Travelling Parliamentarians' Case, 1962. There were two other occasions, both in 1962, when newspaper articles brought before the House of Commons were referred to committee for formal investigation. One of the cases involved an article in the November 1, 1962, issue of *Le Devoir* of Montreal. The story was based on an interview with a Social Credit MP, who complained that the Speaker of the House was biased against the Social Credit Party and was not allowing questions to be asked about bilingualism in the Question Period.

The second incident rose out of two articles in Montreal's *La Presse* on November 29, 1962: a news story and an editorial describing the escapades of

---

53. *Proceedings of Committee on Privileges and Elections*, August 8, 1975, *op. cit.*, p. 21.
54. *Gazette*, October 18, 1975.
55. *Gazette*, October 19, 1975. For interesting highlights of the Reid case see Dave Crowe, "Free Parliament versus Free Press," *Carleton Journalism Review*, Vol. 1, No. 1, Spring 1977.

travelling parliamentarians. *La Presse* said a Canadian parliamentary delegation attending a North Atlantic Treaty Organization conference in Europe was "never well-prepared, often without any interest and sometimes without any talent." *La Presse* also referred to the nighttime partying and daytime sleeping of the parliamentarians.

In both of the November 1962 cases, the Speaker of the Commons ruled that there was merit to the complaints (i.e., *prima facie* cases) and the House voted to refer them to the Standing Committee on Privileges and Elections. But the Committee never dealt with these cases because Parliament was soon dissolved for a general election.

Cinq-Mars, 1906. Outside the Reid case, the only other occasion this century when a question of privilege concerning a newspaper article went through the full process of investigation in the Ottawa Parliament was in 1906. A member of the House complained about an article in *La Presse* of Montreal in which reporter J.E.E. Cinq-Mars criticized Conservative MP George Foster for derogatory statements about the people of Quebec, French-Canadians and Catholicism.[56] Cinq-Mars said Foster's remarks in Parliament and in public speeches belonged to the school of falsehood, hypocrisy and cowardice.

It is interesting to note the procedure that was followed in the Cinq-Mars case. The clerk read the article, after which the House resolved that Mr. Cinq-Mars be summoned to appear before the Bar of the House the next day, "to be examined touching" the article.[57] Mr. Cinq-Mars appeared as requested and was granted a week's delay to obtain counsel. The following week, Mr. Cinq-Mars gave his reasons for writing the article, and expressed his belief that it did not misrepresent Foster's anti-Quebec views. There was a House debate while Mr. Cinq-Mars was standing at the Bar. Later that day, Mr. Speaker communicated to Mr. Cinq-Mars the resolution of the House, which was that the article passed the bounds of reasonable criticism and constituted a breach of privilege and that he had therefore incurred the censure of the House. It was the Prime Minister himself, Sir Wilfrid Laurier, who moved the motion of censure, although Sir Wilfrid allowed that he had some misgivings about the matter being raised before the House.[58] Parliament was the accuser, prosecutor, judge and jury in deciding what was fair criticism of the activities of parliamentarians.

Black Friday, 1956. The most sensational breach of privilege case that involves the press surfaced in the Canadian Parliament on May 21, 1956. The CCF member for Nanaimo-Cowichan-The Islands, Mr. Cameron, drew the attention of the Speaker to two letters-to-the-editor published on May 30 and 31 in the *Ottawa Journal* which were critical of the proceedings in Parliament and of Mr. Speaker specifically.[59] One of the letters (also published in the *Globe and*

---

56. *Ibid.*
57. Details of the Cinq-Mars procedure were outlined by Maingot, Proceedings of Committee on Privileges and Elections, August 8, 1975, *op. cit.*, p. 23.
58. *Ibid.*
59. Grant Dexter, "Politics, Pipeline and Parliament," *Queen's Quarterly*, Vol. 63, 1956, pp. 223-237.

Mail on May 31) was from the constitutional expert, Eugene Forsey, the then director of research for the Canadian Labour Congress who later became one of Canada's most distinguished senators. The Forsey letter was especially critical of the Speaker, René Beaudoin, with regard to the highly controversial gas-pipeline debate in which the government had curtailed debate by invoking closure. Mr. Forsey likened the Speaker to a ''hockey referee who asked, 'How long am I going to allow the visiting team to score goals? How many goals must I allow them to try before I let the home team have a chance?' '' Mr. Forsey suggested that the Speaker's actions implied that ''if the rules (of Parliament) get seriously in the way of doing something the government very much wants done, no reasonable person can expect the government to follow them, or the Speaker to enforce them, at any rate after a certain point.''

The CCF member for Nanaimo declared that the letters in the *Ottawa Journal* contained statements that were derogatory to the dignity of Parliament. Speaker Beaudoin accepted the motion; in fact, he even advised Mr. Cameron as to how to present it. Furthermore, the Speaker stressed the seriousness of the subject: ''more serious than are foreseen at this moment.'' The Speaker promptly permitted debate on the motion of censure on Thursday night. In doing so, the Speaker created an incredible hurdle to the government's tight timetable, operating under rules of closure, to bring about passage of the pipeline legislation.

The next day, Friday, June 1, in the most dramatic turnabout in Canadian parliamentary history, Speaker Beaudoin ruled that the motion of censure relating to the letters in the *Ottawa Journal* was out of order. The Speaker announced to the House that the letters he had found so outrageous only the previous evening were, in fact, fair comment.

There was a great outcry from the Opposition parties. John Diefenbaker (PC-Prince Albert) inquired, ''Why did you change overnight? . . . Are you afraid today?'' W. Earle Row (PC-Dufferin) wanted to know, ''What took place in the dark?'' The controversy precipitated by the Speaker's actions is referred to as ''Black Friday.'' The *Globe and Mail,* reporting on the events in Parliament that June 1st, 1956, declared in a bold page one headline spread across the full width of the paper: COMMONS IN STATE OF RIOT. The *Globe and Mail* said the police would have been called if the meeting had taken place in a public place instead of Parliament. The House of Commons was in a state of bedlam; members stood around the Speaker's mace (symbol of authority and democracy), pointed at the Speaker and shouted ''puppet,'' ''dictator'' and other abuses. The Leader of the Opposition, George Drew, put forward a motion of censure, the first-ever such motion of non-confidence in a Speaker of the Canadian Parliament.

The government majority enabled the Speaker to survive the censure motion. Mr. Beaudoin's effectiveness was, however, permanently damaged. He offered his resignation but it was refused by Prime Minister Louis St. Laurent. The Black Friday incident and other aspects of the gas-pipeline debate contributed to the defeat of the Liberal Party in the 1957 general election which brought John Diefenbaker to power.

Leaks. It is useful to refer yet to another question of privilege raised about newspaper articles. This next event occurred only a few days after Parliament's mild rebuke of the Montreal *Gazette* in the Reid case. In October 1975, Montreal's *Le Devoir* and the Toronto *Globe and Mail* were accused of breaching the privileges of Parliament by publishing a confidential preliminary draft report of the Senate-Commons Committee on immigration policy. A former labour minister, Martin O'Connell, the Commons co-chairman of the Committee, introduced the formal motion in the House that the matter be referred to the Standing Committee on Privileges and Elections. Mr. Speaker reserved his decision on the validity of the motion until he could examine the precedents. He later ruled against it.

*   *   *   *   *

What do these precedents, and others, in the Canadian Parliament tell us about the constraints on the media that flow from parliamentary privilege? Perhaps the most important point that can be made—and this can be seen as a redeeming feature—is that parliamentary privilege in relation to the media is rarely employed in Canada. From time to time, parliamentarians criticize broadcast programmes and articles in the print media, but hardly ever does Parliament embark on formal action that leads to censure of the offending journalists and editors. All the same, there are a number of troubling characteristics that can be observed in the Canadian experience. They include:

–Procedures contrary to the tradition of Canadian justice: Parliament is the accuser, prosecutor, judge and jury (e.g., Cinq-Mars, Reid).
–Parliamentary privilege incidents involving the press do little to enhance the prestige of the House. On the contrary, they often cause embarrassment.
–Parliamentarians sometimes find it necessary for the "sake of principle" to back up—sometimes to ridiculous lengths—their colleagues whose good sense or proper conduct has been questioned by the media.
–Parliamentary privilege lends itself to being used in a capricious manner.
–Vested party interests can become entwined in cases of parliamentary privilege, as occurred in the Black Friday incident.
–Parliamentarians have considered using the rules of privilege to stop leaks from documents which Parliament is not yet ready to make public.

In the context of this chapter, parliamentary privilege is defined as a legal restraint. The House of Commons, sitting as the High Court of Parliament, embarks on a legal process, and there are sanctions for the delict. Traditionally, Parliament censures the offender, but it can also imprison him for the life of the Parliament. It was observed in the committee proceedings on the Reid case that if someone were found in contempt of Parliament and there was a resolution that he be committed to the county jail in Ottawa, then he would go to jail. If the warrant called for imprisonment, without stating cause or reason, no judicial authority could get the offender out of jail: the writ of *habeas corpus* would not succeed.[60]

---

60. Committee on Privileges and Elections, August 8, 1975, *op. cit.*

Canadian Parliaments and provincial legislatures have ordered persons imprisoned for breaches of privilege.[61] The last time that this happened in Ottawa was in the Miller case in 1913 (discussed earlier). The fact that commitment has not been used by the Ottawa Parliament in 70 years indicates that the practice is probably obsolete, but the *power* to censure (and order imprisonment) is real.

Parliamentary privilege appears to be an even more vexing problem for journalists in provincial Legislatures than at the federal level.[62]

Parliamentary privilege is a more important restraint on the flow of political communications than would be indicated by the few cases that have occured during this century. Its impact is largely unseen, for it sets a framework of subtle and vague rules—hardly ever broken by the media, hardly ever formally enforced by Parliament—for the style of coverage of Parliament and its members. Furthermore, since most journalists writing about federal politics in Canada are members of the Parliamentary Press Gallery, parliamentary privilege undoubtedly has an effect on the institutional interaction between Parliament and the Gallery.

The Canadian experience shows that parliamentary privilege has been used in an unpredictable manner; few, if any, of the cases have much in common. Seymour-Ure, writing on the situation at Westminster, says that the mood of the House, the subject of the complaint and the political climate are major considerations.[63] The *Montreal Star,* in a strong attack on the raising of a question of privilege in relation to the leaks from the report of the parliamentary committee on immigration in October 1975, said that Parliament was abusing its privileges in such a way that "the power of Parliament becomes a threat to, rather than a protection of, our liberties."[64]

LIBEL

The professional interest of the media in news and information does not give them the right to unfairly damage the reputations of persons, whether they be public officials or private citizens. Persons who believe they have been libelled or defamed by the media can turn to the courts to seek compensation from the offenders for the harm done to their reputations or careers. The laws of civil libel, slander and defamation are under provincial jurisdiction and are not uniform across Canada.

Civil libel and defamation should not be confused with criminal libel, which falls under federal jurisdiction and includes sedition, blasphemy, obscenity and defamation. Seditious libel was a formidable weapon used in the eighteenth and nineteenth centuries to suppress media criticism of the authorities, but court interpretations (as in the Boucher case, 1950) have "effectively turned around (the law) to represent a protection of free speech, rather than a suppression of

61. Franks, *Parliament and Security Matters, op. cit.*, p. 78.
62. Kent Commission Report, *op. cit.* p. 49.
63. Seymour-Ure, *The Press, Politics and the Public, op. cit.*, p. 171.
64. *Montreal Star*, 23 October, 1975.

it.''[65] The Kent Commission on Newspapers regards seditious libel and blasphemy as falling into the realm of ''legal oblivion.'' The criminal law relating to obscenity is not likely to create problems in media coverage of politics. There have been very few prosecutions (only three in the past 40 years) involving the media for criminal defamation in Canada, and the Kent Commission notes there is little judicial guidance as to the full meaning of the criminal defamation provisions relating to the press. Criminal defamation proceedings are initiated by the government for the protection of the public interest and public safety.

It has been said that the nightmares of editors usually involve civil libel and defamation. Unlike the Official Secrets Act and parliamentary privilege, which are rarely activated, libel is a much more visible restraint; it is the most common legal problem that Canadian journalists and the owners of the print and electronic media have to deal with. Libel is a matter of daily concern, since the danger can arise in virtually every story that is printed or broadcast. The laws of libel, say the Kent Commission, have a pervasive influence on the way journalists may write, for ''they impose constant and drastic restraints.''[66]

A libel can be defined as a false statement about a man that is to his discredit. An expert in the field, who is a former parliamentarian and law professor, says, ''This definition would appear to apply to libels of practically all the forms of mass media in Canada: newspapers, magazines, reviews, books, broadcasts and telecasts. And with respect to newspapers in particular, virtually all parts of them are capable at some point of being libellous: cartoons, editorials, news reports, letters to the editor, photographs and even advertisements.''[67]

The laws of libel in the Canadian provinces are more strict than those in the United States.[68] In Canada, the media can get into libel difficulties for small, factual inaccuracies while in the United States there is some allowance for errors that occur in good faith. When U.S. public figures are concerned, the mistakes have to be deliberate or reckless.[69] There is, thus, greater opportunity in Canada to use libel suits as a device to frighten off unwelcome comment. Another cause for concern, overlooked until recently, is that the courts, at times, permit prior restraint. That is to say, the plaintiff in a libel suit can apply for an injunction to prevent the print or broadcast media from making public an alleged libellous comment.[70]

The strictness of Canadian libel laws would suggest that newspapers, magazines and broadcast stations would be involved in legal cases more frequently than their American counterparts. This is not the case. Libel cases in Canada are in fact relatively infrequent, for the media tend to be cautious. Many newspapers, for example, ''retain legal counsel to whom they routinely submit items prior to publication.''[71]

---

65. Kent Commission Report, *op. cit.,* p. 49.
66. *Ibid,* p. 51.
67. Atkey, ''The Law and the Press,'' *op. cit.,* p. 134.
68. Grant, ''The Legal Perspective,'' *op. cit.,* p. 12.
69. *New York Times* v. Sullivan.
70. Grant, ''The Legal Perspective,'' *op. cit.*
71. Kent Commission Report, *op. cit.,* p. 51.

The strictness of Canadian libel laws is offset in part by procedural practices that can be most helpful to the media. Nuisance and frivolous action suits are discouraged as the result of two practices: (1) if the person suing for libel loses, he may have to pay some of the defence costs and (2) lawyers cannot accept cases on a speculative basis where they are paid only if they win, with the lawyer's fees based on the size of the settlement.[72] The libel action has to be initiated within a certain time limit—six weeks in most provinces—after the offending article or broadcast came to the attention of the plaintiff.[73]

The person planning to sue a newspaper or broadcast station for libel must give formal notice of his intention. This provides an opportunity for the media to apologize. Such an apology does not absolve the defendant of guilt, but usually places limits on the amount of damages that have to be paid.[74] The apology must be sincere and straightforward. There are a number of examples (such as *Platt vs. Time International of Canada Limited*, 1964) where an inadequate apology resulted in punitive damages.[75]

Libel has its roots in the common law and is one of the most complex areas of law study. Media stories that may not be libellous in one province can be libellous in other provinces. The mood of the times is also an important element for it helps to set the values as to what kind of statement "tends to lower a person in the estimation of right-thinking men, or cause him to be shunned or avoided, or expose him to hatred, contempt or ridicule."[76]

Two recent cases, one involving a political cartoon and the other a letter to the editor, illustrate the complexities of libel laws. The cartoon case (*Vander Zalm vs. Times Publications et al*) centred around a drawing in June 1978 in the Victoria *Times* that showed the then British Columbia Minister of Human Resources, William Vander Zalm, plucking wings off flies. Mr. Vander Zalm argued successfully in the courts, where he was awarded $3,500 in damages, that the cartoon showed him up as a cruel and sadistic person who enjoyed torturing helpless people. The libel decision was overturned by the B.C. Court of Appeal, which noted that "the cartoonist makes his point indirectly by the use of symbolism, allegory or satire and, exaggeration."[77] The Appeal Court accepted the cartoonist's explanation that the drawing was aimed at the minister's public profile, not his private character.

The letter-to-the-editor case involved the Saskatoon *Star-Phoenix*. The Supreme Court of Canada agreed with a court ruling in Saskatchewan that a letter from two law students, who later left the province, libelled an alderman by implying he was racist. It came out in the trial that neither the editor nor pub-

72. Grant, "The Legal Perspective," *op. cit.*, pp. 10-11.
73. Atkey, "The Law and the Press," *op. cit.*, p. 141.
74. *Ibid.*
75. Wilfred H. Kesterton, *The Law and the Press in Canada*, Toronto: McClelland and Stewart, 1976.
76. Kent Commission Report, *op. cit.*, p. 51. This definition is attributed to Alexander Stark, "Dangerous Words." Paper delivered to the Managing Editors' Conference, Niagara Falls, Ontario, January 28, 1950.
77. *Newsletter*, Canadian Daily Newspaper Publishers Association, March/April 1980.

lisher of the *Star-Phoenix* agreed with the comments contained in the letter. The court ruling put newspapers in a near-impossible situation, for the letters to the editor are usually intended to provide an opportunity for a variety of viewpoints, many of which differ with the editorial policy of the paper. It is reassuring that the provinces have moved to amend their libel laws to provide more reasonable protection for newspapers on the letters' issue.

A reading of Kesterton's *The Law and the Press in Canada* suggests that, on the whole, the libel laws and practices in Canada provide a respectable attempt to safeguard both individual rights and the interests of a free media. The Kent Commission agrees with this assessment: generally speaking, a critical balance is being maintained "between the public interest in free speech, which includes the right of the press to publish without undue inhibitions, and the individual's right to his reputation."[78]

Libel suits can be costly, especially in situations where there are punitive damages. In 1978, for example, the Montreal *Gazette* was ordered to pay $135,000 as damages to city councillor Gerald Snyder for defaming him in a 1975 article.[79] In 1982, the CBC agreed to an $82,500 out-of-court settlement in an action brought by Alberta Premier Peter Lougheed. The CBC also lost a costly (more than $100,000) libel case in British Columbia.

More often the judgements for redress tend to be on the low side compared to the situation in Britain where libel is similarly defined. When Gouzenko, the former Soviet Embassy cipher clerk, took *Maclean's Magazine* to court over a September 5th, 1964, article that made 17 references which might have been construed as derogatory, damage was assessed at $1.[80]

The number of libel cases involving what could be considered public policy matters is low. The libel suits involving politicians, where a politician sues the media relating to coverage of his governmental or political party activities, are rare. One of the necessities of political life is a thick skin, an ability to live with criticism and even the inaccuracies that may be libellous. When a politician is confronted with derogatory remarks, he can hardly be considered defenceless. He has a number of ways to set the record straight: a statement in Parliament or Legislature, a press conference, public speeches, radio and television appearances and handouts to the media. The threat to sue for libel is heard from time to time, but as in the Reid case, these libel actions are more often than not quietly dropped.

Libel laws are not directly a major threat to freedom of expression; their impact is partly unseen. Libel difficulties can beset the media in unpredictable ways and consequently there is a trend, an overemphasis, on caution. It may be argued that Canada's strict libel laws reinforce an attitude held by the management of newspapers that investigative reporting is a luxury that does not lead to extra profits and, in fact, introduces legal and financial risk.

---

78. Kent Commission Report, *op. cit.*, p. 52.
79. *Globe and Mail*, March 9, 1978.
80. Atkey, "The Law and the Press," *op. cit.*, p. 134.

SUMMARY

The interaction of media, the law and politics brings into conflict at times basic principles of democratic practices and the political process in Canada. Our analysis of five legal restraints indicates that the free press principle has to accommodate the "higher interests" of free Parliament and the independent judiciary. The traditions of confidentiality in the Cabinet and bureaucracy are well protected by law.

Journalists attending the *Media and the Image of Justice* conference at Halifax in October 1980 expressed concern about an increase in the number of cases involving libel, revealing of sources, and police attempts to utilize the notes, tape recordings and films of reporters. These are the "visible" restraints that lend themselves to court battle and which, in the long term, help to clarify the meaning of the law of the press. Little attention has been given to the well-hidden characteristics of the Official Secrets Act, parliamentary privilege and libel that individually, and in combination, encourage self-censorship by the media.

In theory, the restraints on the media that stem from the characteristics of the political system (Chapter III) and the legal restraints discussed here appear to be formidable. The especially dangerous invisible restraints are, however, largely psychological and may not fare all that well when contested. The unpredictable way in which some legal restraints can be employed is a major factor contributing to the cautiousness of the media. It is a characteristic of the Canadian media to err on the side of caution in order to avoid legal confrontations. In effect, journalistic decisions are being made all too frequently for legal reasons.

In practice, governments and individual politicians personally have been most hesitant to become involved in legal confrontations with the media. The Canadian experience has been that the media have done extremely well before the courts in the relatively few cases where the rights of the press and freedom of the press are concerned.

In Canada, the press in this century has become largely depoliticized and shows a general lack of enterprise in dealing with politics and government. The structural arrangements of our political system make the House of Commons the main source of political news; media attention is channelled in the direction of situations that are normally under the control of the government. The Press Gallery in Ottawa is a vital link in the political communications flow from the federal level of government to the public. Professor Westell's writings about the shortcomings of this arrangement suggest that there is a rather shallow coverage of the nation's business and little scope for investigative reporting.[81] This situation encourages strong government but leaves much to be desired with regard to the role of the media in the Canadian political process. The emphasis in the Canadian political process is biased toward efficiency, not communications.

---

81. Anthony Westell, "Reporting the Nation's Business," in Adams (ed.), *Journalism, Communication and the Law, op. cit.,* pp. 54-69.

CHAPTER V

THE MASS MEDIA AND CANADIAN NATIONHOOD: AN HISTORIC PERSPECTIVE

This chapter focuses on the history of the Canadian mass media. It begins with the introduction of newspapers in North America around 1700 and follows through to the development of broadcasting 200 years later. Particular emphasis is given to the role of newspapers in the political process in the nineteenth century, their involvement in the emergence of political parties and their contribution to the Confederation process. At the end of the chapter there is a discussion of the special Canadian interest in electronic communications as a support structure for nation building.

HISTORIC OVERVIEW

It is necessary to look at the history of journalism in the broader North American setting to understand the development of newspapers in Canada and their role in politics. Perhaps most important is the fact that the United States (then the 13 colonies) had newspapers for a half-century before the first Canadian newspaper appeared. Newspapers didn't come from Britain to the British North American provinces (later to become the nucleus of Canada), but from the United States.

Nor in the days of French colonization of North America was there a French journalistic input. France didn't tolerate any printing presses, for fear that they might undermine political and religious interests. There is no record of any printing presses in New France during the entire French regime.[1] Britain, which also had considerable misgivings about the press, nevertheless felt that the advantages of print outweighed the disadvantages, and that British rule would be enhanced

---

1. Aegidius Fauteux, *Introduction of Printing into Canada*, Roland Paper Co., Montreal, 1940. See also A. Fauteaux, ''Les débuts de l'imprimerie au Canada,'' Les Cahiers des Dix., 16, 1951., and Kesterton, *A History of Journalism in Canada, op. cit.*, p. 2. The printing shops in France were producing the religious, administrative and other materials that were shipped to North America.

by the dissemination of laws, rules and regulations in printed form in British North America. The press was to be used as an aid to governing. Journalism was tolerated rather than encouraged. The press was to be closely controlled, and operated in the interests of the governors.

THE AMERICAN INFLUENCE

The press came to Canada from the United States. This is true for nearly all parts of the country. Virtually every newspaper published in the six eastern provinces between 1752 and 1807, the so-called pioneering period of Canadian journalism, was started by an American or by a printer trained by Americans. A century later, when newspapers were introduced in the west, the American influence was also strong. For example, the first western paper, the *Victoria Gazette and Anglo-American*, was founded on June 21, 1858, by two journalists from San Francisco and printed by two other Californians.[2] Newspapers, then, were transplanted from the United States to Canada (south to north) and were not an east-west or all-Canadian spread. The Canada-U.S. relationship in mass media had its roots in the very beginnings of journalism in Canada.

Journalism in the American colonies was influenced by the technological, social, political and religious practices in Western Europe, especially Britain. The settlers of the seventeenth century brought with them the ability to print, but the use of printing presses was strictly controlled, and printers who offended the authorities faced severe penalties (fines and/or imprisonment) and could lose their presses. Understandably, printers stuck to what was regarded as safe: bibles, a few books and almanacs. From time to time, news about especially important events was disseminated on broadsides, which were single sheets of paper printed on one or both sides. The broadsides were the forerunners of newspapers.

It wasn't until 1690 in Boston that the first meaningful attempt was made to publish a newspaper in North America: *Publick Occurences, Foreign and Domestick*. The printer was Benjamin Harris, who had fled to Boston after spending two years in a London jail for publishing a newspaper that was critical of the authorities. Boston, at the time, was the most important business centre and had the largest population in America.

Harris' small newspaper measured six by nine inches. It was a mere sheet of paper with printing on both sides that was folded to produce four pages. The last page was left blank; Harris wanted readers to insert their own observations before giving the paper to friends.[3] In the opening paragraph, Harris said that he planned to publish once a month, or more often if events warranted it. As things turned out, *Publick Occurences* appeared only once. Critical comments about the authorities enraged the governor of Massachussetts, who then declared the paper

---

2. Kesterton, *A History of Journalism in Canada, op. cit.*, p. 30.
3. Fred Fedler, *An Introduction to the Mass Media*, (New York: Harcourt Brace Janovich, Inc., 1978), p. 21.

could not be published without a licence.[4] Harris' record in England hardly made him a suitable candidate and he never applied.

The *Boston News-Letter* is generally regarded as the first real newspaper in America, for it appeared at regular weekly intervals. It was started on April 24, 1704, with government permission, by Postmaster John Campbell, who had until then been distributing a hand-written newsletter about developments in Boston. When this became too much to write out by hand, Campbell hired a printer to produce the *News-Letter*.[5] The post office was a social gathering-place and an excellent locale to collect information. Also, the postmaster had franking privileges and could send out mail (including his *News-Letter*) free of charge. Campbell's *News-Letter* contained no advertising and was filled with serious news, including reprints of stories from English newspapers, many weeks old because of the time required for the Atlantic crossing, but still of great interest in Boston. When a new postmaster was appointed in 1719, he established a second paper, the *Boston Gazette*.[6]

In the early 1720s, the Franklin brothers (James and Benjamin) introduced a third Boston paper, the *New England Courant*. The Franklin paper was different: it contained current news and numerous politically oriented essays, often critical of the Governor and constitutional authority. James Franklin landed in jail for a short period and was released after promising to mend his ways, a promise he didn't keep. In fact, the *New England Courant* is regarded as the first rebellious newspaper in America. Benjamin Franklin, who had been an apprentice at his brother's paper, moved on to Philadelphia where he acquired the *Pennsylvania Gazette* in 1729, and proceeded to prosper through political caution, advertising and government patronage. He was made the King's Printer and postmaster. Another source of profit for Benjamin Franklin was *Poor Richard's Almanac*. Franklin encouraged his apprentices to move on and invested in some of the newspapers and print shops they founded. He also invested in papermills. Franklin was America's first press magnate. (Benjamin Franklin's early political caution is in strong contrast to the daring exploits later in his journalism career, when the *Pennsylvania Gazette* became a powerful influence in the controversies between England and the colonies.)

Boston and Philadelphia became important print centres, ranking just behind London. The early newspapers focused largely on international news—especially news from Britain—business and commerce. There was news about the arrivals of ships and their cargoes, market information, trade developments and

---

4. George F. Mott and others, *New Survey of Journalism*, (New York: Barnes and Noble. Fourth Edition, 1969), p. 21. In England, Parliament refused to renew the Monarch's right to license newspapers in 1694. There is evidence, however, that the licence practice was maintained in the colonies some 30 years after it was abandoned in England.

5. Fedler, *An Introduction to the Mass Media, op. cit.*, p. 21.

6. Campell refused to hand over his *News-Letter* to William Brooker, who became postmaster in 1719. This led to Brooker's *Boston Gazette*, also published by authority. Both the *News-Letter* and the *Gazette* were cautious papers and gave much prominence to foreign news. Later in the century, the *News-Letter* was an influential voice in opposition to the colonial power.

advertising. Business news also led the printers into the politics that affected trade and commerce, and this in turn led to greater political involvement.

Criticizing the authorities was risky. The immediate suppression of *Publick Occurences* is one example, the jailing of James Franklin another. The *Boston News-Letter*, printed on government authority, was rebuked by the government on occasion and publication was suspended several times. The law was used effectively to control printers, for seditious libel was an especially serious charge. The legal threat, however, declined sharply as a result of the celebrated Peter Zenger case in New York City in 1734.

THE ZENGER CASE

Zenger, a small New York printer, was commissioned by a group of New Yorkers opposed to the colony's governor to start the *New York Weekly Journal* in November, 1733. Critical stories about the governor specifically, and the authorities generally, written by Zenger's financial backers appeared in the *Weekly Journal*. The paper attacked authoritarian practices and advocated freedom of the press. Zenger was arrested on November 17, 1734 and charged with publishing seditious libels.[7] Zenger spent nine months in prison awaiting his trial but his paper continued to appear.

Under the British law of the time, Zenger was certainly guilty even if he could prove that he was printing the truth—truth was no excuse. The jury's task was limited to deciding whether Zenger had published the critical articles. The judge, for his part, was to decide on whether the criticism had been libellous. But the judge never got the opportunity to decide on the question of libel because the jury, shutting its eyes to the obvious fact that Zenger had published the stories, brought in a verdict of "not guilty." In effect, the jury agreed with the arguments of the famed defence lawyer, Andrew Hamilton, that men had an inherent right to criticize their government. The Zenger experience was one of the factors that led to the freedom of the press provision in the first amendment of the U.S. constitution a half-century later.

CANADA

The early American development of newspapers is important to Canada, because the print shop apprentices of Boston and Philadelphia newspapers became the pioneer newspaper publishers in British North America. The link between the first American newspaper, the *Boston News-Letter*, and the first Canadian newspaper is very close.[8] Two years after the establishment of Halifax in 1749, the grandson of the first printer of the *Boston News-Letter* arrived in the community with a printing press, but died before he could set up a newspaper.[9] The press

---

7. Maurice R. Cullen, Jr., *Mass Media and the First Amendment*, (Dubuque, Iowa: William C. Brown Co., 1981), pp. 16-27. See also H.L. Nelson and D.L. Teeter, *Law of Mass Communications*, 2nd ed., (Minedo, N.Y.: The Foundation Press, 1973), pp. 23-24.
8. Kesterton, *A History of Journalism in Canada, op. cit.*, p. 2.
9. *Ibid.*

was used by another Boston printer, John Bushell, to produce the first edition of the *Halifax Gazette* on March 23, 1752. This marked the start of newspapers in Canada. Bushell was made the official King's Printer.

Professor Wilf Kesterton, in his remarkably detailed *A History of Journalism in Canada*, describes the spread of newspapers to the six eastern British North American provinces. It took just over 50 years. Two Philadelphia printers produced Quebec's first paper, the *Quebec Gazette*, in 1764. Two other American printers, one from Rhode Island and one from New York, were the founders of the *Royal St. John Gazette* in New Brunswick. A Boston-trained printer became Prince Edward Island's first newspaper owner in 1787 when he published the *Royal American Gazette and Weekly Intelligencer* in Charlottetown. The American connection in starting Canadian newspapers is consistent. An employee of the *Quebec Gazette* was brought in to start the first Ontario (Upper Canada) paper in 1793 in Newark (now Niagara-on-the-Lake) which was then the capital. The Rhode Island printer who helped found the first New Brunswick paper produced the first newspaper at St. John's, Newfoundland, in 1807, called the *Royal Gazette and Newfoundland Advertiser*.

There is a direct Philadelphia connection in the establishment of the first Montreal paper, *La Gazette du Commerce et Littéraire*.[10] The printer Fleury Mesplet, who was born in Lyons, France, had moved to Philadelphia to become an associate of Benjamin Franklin. Mesplet came to Montreal in 1776 as a printer for a special American commission, headed by Benjamin Franklin, that was to promote the cause of the American Revolution. The American mission failed to rally support in Montreal and Franklin fled when the British army approached. Mesplet stayed behind with his printing press. He was imprisoned for about a month and on his release became Montreal's first printer. He produced numerous books including religious works, school books, Latin books, literary works, military manuals, a medical work and an Iroquois primer. In 1778, Mesplet expanded from his "book and job" printing to launch *La Gazette du Commerce et Littéraire*. He soon ran into trouble with the authorities and after serving some time in prison, Mesplet produced the far less controversial English language *Montreal Gazette*.[11] The *Gazette* is Canada's oldest surviving paper and marked its 200th anniversary in 1978.

The first publisher in a province was usually also the official government printer, or King's Printer, as he was known. The papers kept within bounds of official favour; they criticized the governmental authorities more by accident than by intention. It was a controlled press, with the main source of income coming from government patronage such as contracts to print official announcements and regulations. Revenue from advertising and from the sale of papers was small because of the low state of development of business enterprises and the small circulation. With the bulk of his income coming from the government, the printer could be described as a quasi-civil servant.

---

10. E.A. Collard, *A Tradition Lives*, Montreal; The *Gazette*, 1953.
11. *Ibid.*

The *Halifax Gazette* started with a circulation of 72; some 50 years later, there were three weeklies in Halifax with a combined circulation of 2,000.[12] There were several reasons for the low circulation in the early days of journalism. Communities had small populations and the ability to read was limited. Also, the contents reflected élite interests, with a large part of the paper devoted to the revenue-producing government announcements, proclamations, orders and enactments. Some commercial news and advertising was also included. Foreign news, which came second in prominence to the "official information," probably attracted the widest interest although it was reprinted from old British papers. Local news was not important in the papers, because the communities were sufficiently small that gossip could spread much faster than the waiting period between newspapers (which appeared every week and in some cases every other week).

The press in Canada started in the authoritarian mold, and kept its place because the printers knew on which side their bread was buttered. There were no rebellious editors comparable to James Franklin of the *New England Courant* in British North America. Those who stepped out of line usually ended up in prison or had other disasters befall them. In some cases, the printer had to deposit sizable bonds to ensure good behaviour. Whether printed in English or French, the early newspapers were usually started by Americans who had moved from the crowded printing field in the United States to seek fame and fortune in Canada. The papers were the products of printers, not journalists. The emphasis was on earning a living, and the economic rules of the game at the time required compliance with the wishes of the authorities.

Canadians were much less demanding about the rights of the individual in relation to the authorities, rights that had already been achieved in Britain and the United States before Canada got its first newspaper. Demands for rights and freedoms came usually in the wake of economic achievements. Certainly, there was no press freedom in Canada before the newspaper editors could turn their backs on government patronage.

SOCIAL AND ECONOMIC DEVELOPMENT

The authoritarian practices in the press system held sway well into the nineteenth century, when enormous population growth, urbanization, and changing economic and social life styles brought new realities to the communications scene. In the early days of journalism, the population in what were to become the six eastern provinces was about 90,000.[13] By 1800, the population was 250,000. The growth pattern developed momentum and by mid-century, the population had increased almost tenfold to 2,385,000. The economy changed markedly,

---

12. Kesterton, *A History of Journalism in Canada, op. cit.*, p. 8.
13. The population figures cited here are based on the estimates of population published in 1876. See *Censuses of Canada: 1665-1871* (Ottawa: I.B. Taylor, 1876). This publication is Volume IV of the *Census of Canada: 1870-71*.

with manufacturing and the timber trade taking over from the earlier emphasis on fish and fur trading. Social patterns also changed as towns and villages established roots.

The social and economic change brought about a stable environment that was favourable to the development of newspapers, and they began to spring up almost like mushrooms. There were 20 papers in the six eastern British North American provinces in 1813; by mid-century, there were nearly 300.[14] The papers developed a local personality that related to the community of publication and they became disseminators of local news when gossip could no longer do the job efficiently.

In the decade between 1820 and 1830, the printer who was subservient to and dependent on the government gave way to the editor who operated a small business. His revenues came from selling subscriptions, some advertising and "book and job" work. The "book and job" earnings (from the printing of books, almanacs, religious material, public and commercial announcements, invitations, etc.) helped subsidize the newspaper operation. It was a precarious way to earn a living, but the many papers that folded were quickly replaced by an even larger number of newcomers. Newspapers were small operations where the owner often did his own reporting, editing, typesetting and printing.

The end of dependence on government patronage brought about dramatic changes in the attitudes of the editors. They lost their fear of the authorities. This new breed of editors virtually thumbed their noses at their previous benefactors. An element of boldness emerged with the rise of the private enterprise press system. No longer were political and social issues taboo and to be avoided; rather, they became the material for content on which the press thrived. The papers became involved in the major issues of the day. Politically, the great issues were the rebellions of 1837 and the move toward Responsible Government, which was achieved in the late 1840s.[15]

THE PRESS, THE POLITICAL PROCESS AND THE REBELLION OF 1837

The press in the 1820s and 1830s politicized the inhabitants of the British North American provinces by providing insights into the workings of government. The groundwork was being prepared for the creation of a more open society, and the press was deeply involved in the process of fostering new political practices. An important milestone was the Joseph Howe trial in 1835, which set a legal precedent about the right of the press to criticize the authorities. The Howe case had much in common with the Peter Zenger trial (discussed earlier); the spirit of press freedom that had developed in the American colonies was taking hold in British North America a century later.

---

14. For a discussion on the proliferation of newspapers, see Paul Rutherford, *The Making of The Canadian Media*, (Toronto: McGraw-Hill Ryerson Ltd., 1978), pp. 1-37.
15. Nova Scotia, the Province of Canada and New Brunswick attained Responsible Government in 1848, Prince Edward Island in 1851 and Newfoundland in 1855.

THE HOWE CASE

Joseph Howe was the son of a New England loyalist family that had settled in Halifax. The young Howe learned printing in his father's shop and in 1828, when he was 24 years old, became the owner of the *Novascotian*, a Halifax paper. He made it the most influential journal in the province. On January 1, 1835, the *Novascotian* carried a letter signed "The People" that alleged that magistrates and police were pocketing money. There were also critical comments about the Lieutenant-Governor. Howe was charged "as seditiously contriving, devising and intending to stir up and incite discontent and sedition. . . ." Although Howe's case appeared hopeless, the jury took only 10 minutes to acquit the accused editor. There was a landmark quality to the case, for Howe had made truth a defence against a libel charge. The case helped to define and expand the rights of the media in the political setting.[16]

The Howe trial revealed a new political reality: the press had become an important instrument of power "which officialdom could not easily silence nor effectively discipline. . . ."[17] The existing political power structure was under challenge through the polemics of the newly self-assertive press.

Another extremely influential journalist and political figure of this period was William Lyon Mackenzie of Upper Canada, who in 1824 established the *Colonial Advocate* in York. Mackenzie was a strong critic of the Family Compacts, the small group of establishment persons who controlled political offices, banks, education, land granting, etc. An organized gang of Family Compacts supporters broke his press and threw the type into Toronto Bay. Mackenzie collected damages and rebuilt his *Colonial Advocate*, which bolstered his political career in the Reform Party. In July of 1837, Mackenzie's paper was asking: "Will Canadians declare Independence and shoulder muskets?"[18] He became a leader in the Rebellion which broke out in Upper Canada later in the year.

At the time of the Rebellion, the press "had already undermined the hierarchical structure and the social harmony upon which the Tory authority relied."[19] The Attorney-General of Upper Canada, John Beverley Robinson, said in 1838 that a "licentious press is permitted to poison the public mind with the most absurd and wicked representations."[20] There was, however, no turning back of the clock. The movement toward democratic practices, in which the press played a major role, gained momentum.

---

16. A. Siegel, "The Canadian Mass Media and Politics: Legal and Constitutional Restraints," in *The Canadian Legal System*, (Toronto: Canadian Daily Newspaper Publishers Association-Canadian Institute for the Administration of Justice, 1978), pp. 109-139. For details of the Howe trial, see Kesterton, *A History of Journalism in Canada, op. cit.*, pp. 21-23.
17. Rutherford, *The Making of the Canadian Media, op. cit.*, p. 1.
18. Quoted in George W. Brown, *Building of the Canadian Nation*, Vol. I, 1492-1849, (Toronto: J.M. Dent for Macfadden-Bartell Books, 1952), p. 323.
19. Rutherford, *The Making of the Canadian Media, op. cit.*, p. 1.
20. *Ibid.* Mr. Robinson is quoted in Rutherford's book.

THE PRESS AND RESPONSIBLE GOVERNMENT

Responsible Government was a major stepping stone to democracy, home rule and eventual independence for British North America. The basic principle, fashioned on practices in Britain, is that Parliament controls the executive or Cabinet. The Cabinet must always have the confidence of the people's representatives, and is responsible to the House of Commons: hence the name "Responsible Government."

For years, the Reformers had been urging that the Executive Council which advised the Governor should have the confidence of the elected Assembly.[21] This, it was argued, would bring political harmony by ending the friction that had developed between the executive and the legislature in the course of the dynamic economic development in the first half of the nineteenth century. The political institutions in British North America did not reflect the economic and social realities.

A number of reasons have been put forward as to why Responsible Government was achieved in the late 1840s. Certainly, the Rebellion of 1837 was a catalyst; Lord Durham, who had come from Britain to lead an inquiry into the Rebellion, recommended the introduction of Responsible Government in his Report. Harold Innis suggests economic reasons: political autonomy was essential for mobilizing financial support for major industrial projects that were to be the catalyst for prosperity and development in the British North American provinces.[22]

The press played a major role in the public debate on Responsible Government. It became the theme to which editors gave their most sustained attention after the emergence of the free enterprise press between 1820 and 1830. Support for and opposition to Responsible Government led to polarization within the press: Reform and Anti-Reform papers.[23] The press was bringing politics to an ever-wider public. Thus, by indirectly involving people and by direct force of argument, newspapers were powerful weapons in the drive to contain the powers of the Crown and prime movers in the evolution of the political system.

THE PRESS AND THE CANADIAN UNION: CONFEDERATION

The press was a unifying force for Canadian nation building in the nineteenth century. This is not to suggest that newspapers and their editors worked uniformly for such a goal. In fact, the press set off contradictory forces for the establishment of one country.

Newspapers appeared first in the political and commercial centres in the provinces with some circulation in the countryside, and were thus early agents of metropolitanism.[24] This metropolitan influence was tempered later by the proli-

---

21. R. MacGregor Dawson, *The Government of Canada, op. cit.*, pp. 12-15.
22. Harold A. Innis, *Political Economy in the Modern State*, (Toronto: University of Toronto Press, 1946), p. 188.
23. Kesterton, *A History of Journalism in Canada, op. cit.*, p. 14.
24. Rutherford, *The Making of the Canadian Media, op. cit.*

feration of newspapers in the smaller communities, which reflected the local character. Furthermore, newspapers reflected specific political ideologies, religious outlooks and some advocated causes that were in themselves a growth industry. These differentiated ideological perspectives gave rise to a press that served and reinforced "limited identities."[25] It can thus be argued that the press was a fragmenting influence in society, a fragmentation that in itself was a precondition for the dynamic balance of unity and heterogeneity that gained momentum in the 1860s.

The many factors that are usually cited for helping to bring about the Canadian federal union include the threat of absorption by the United States, railway building, British colonial policy, economic problems and the politics of chaos in United Canada (Lower and Upper). The Maritimes and Canada knew relatively little about each other. Railway building created a national issue that was at once linked to intercolonial trade, defence strategies and an expanded British North American role in the British Empire trade routes. Later in the 1860s, Confederation became the dominant national issue. "British North American newspapers," says Peter Waite, "were the principal, if not the only means of intercolonial communication" on the railway and Confederation questions.[26]

It is significant that the 98 participants at the Charlottetown Conference in 1864, where the decision was taken to establish the union, included 23 journalists; most others had very close, if not direct, ties to newspapers. Influential journalists and journalist politicians, including the renowned Joseph Howe, also opposed Confederation. On balance, newspapers made a vital contribution to its evolution. As Professor Waite observes: Confederation "fired the imagination of many men, editors not least."[27]

THE PRESS AND POLITICAL PARTIES

Professor Pool has pointed out that the growth of political parties and the growth of the press went hand in hand in most countries of the world until recent decades.[28] Canada is an especially good illustration of this pattern. Newspapers politicized the population by reporting on the political arena, including detailed accounts of the Assembly proceedings. In putting the spotlight on the Assembly, the people's representatives gained political prominence and became an important counter-force to the all-powerful Governor and his Executive Council. This in turn fostered demands for reform in government, specifically the call for "Responsible Government." Their attitude on Responsible Government was the litmus paper test for labelling the political allegiance of newspapers. Other political factions surfaced, some with religious perspectives, others relating to specific

25. J.M. Careless, " 'Limited Identities' in Canada," *Canadian Historical Review*, 50, 1969, pp. 1-10.
26. Peter Waite, *The Life and Times of Confederation 1864-1867*, (Toronto: University of Toronto Press, 1962), p. 17.
27. *Ibid.*, p. 3.
28. I. de Sola Pool, "Communication: Political," *International Encyclopedia of the Social Sciences* (New York: The Macmillan Company and Free Press, 1968), p. 94.

local and provincial issues and yet others taking stands on such international questions as the Civil War. The British North American newspapers reflected the spectrum of the politics of factions that prevailed. The interdependence of press and politics was real and strong. There was a very direct relationship in that "it was almost impossible to be an editor without being a politician also."[29]

Jean-Louis Gagnon, in discussing the enormous impact of newspapers on the political development of Canada, says that the reason for this is simple: "At the beginning of Confederation, the editor-in-chief of a newspaper, whether a daily or a weekly, was always an *ex officio* politician, and was often an intellectual leader."[30] The list of politicians who were also editors—including George Brown of *The Globe*, Wilfrid Laurier (*L'Electeur*), Henri Bourassa (*Le Devoir*), Joseph Howe (*Novascotian*), Amor de Cosmos (*Victoria Colonist*), Hector Langevin (*Le Courrier*)—is long: "They are as much a part of the history of Canada as they are of the history of journalism."[31]

Equally important to the self-serving interests of the editor/politician were financial considerations. The key to the relationship between newspapers and politicians was patronage in one form or another. This money flowing from the political sector to the press led to the establishment of many newspapers and made some of the owners rich. The fortunes of the newspapers depended in large part on the political fortunes of the causes that they championed. Peter Waite's *The Life and Times of Confederation* provides a fascinating account of the integral role newspapers played in the developmental stages of party politics.

Financial support provided by political factions, and later by political parties, to newspapers shaped in large part the contents of the press. Information was distorted to suit the political interests, causes were taken up and dropped on the basis of cash flow, and information that favoured opponents was conveniently left out. However, the large number of newspapers, on the whole were reflective of political viewpoints in British North America, resulted in a dynamic marketplace of ideas. At the same time, a body of press law was developing that established parameters of legal operations of newspapers, and the authoritarian practices of an earlier period were pushed aside. A libertarian press system emerged. But there were qualifications. It was not an autonomous press because of the subsidies flowing from the political parties and factions.

NEWSPAPERS FOR THE MASSES: THE PENNY PRESS AND THE DAILIES

Newspapers became the first modern mass communications medium with messages reaching many people at about the same time. The press, however, had

---

29. G.M. Grant, *Joseph Howe*, Halifax, 1906. Quoted in Waite, *Life and Times of Confederation*, *op. cit.*, p. 8. See also George V. Ferguson, and Frank Underhill, *Press and Party in Canada: Issues of Freedom*. (Toronto: The Ryerson Press, 1955).
30. Jean-Louis Gagnon, "Community, Identity, Unity." York University, Gerstein Conference on Mass Communication and Canadian Nationhood, April 10, 1981.
31. *Ibid.*

anything but a mass audience in its early days. Many people were illiterate, and many others could not afford newspapers—not that they were particularly interested in the contents. The early circulation figures, even allowing for small populations, fade into insignificance when compared to newspaper distribution today. A major inducement for people to buy papers was that they were made very affordable. In the United States, the penny papers—sold on the streets for a penny—appeared about 1830. Within a short time, their circulation climbed dramatically. The *New York Herald* and the *New York Tribune* were penny newspapers of quality that concerned themselves with major issues of the day and gained international prominence.

In British North America, newspaper development was well behind the innovative trends of the United States and Britain. Dailies came late; they did not dominate Canadian journalism until the second half of the nineteenth century. At the time of Confederation, there were fewer than 30 dailies; in 1881, there were 61; by 1900, the number of dailies had climbed to 121.

The first British North American penny paper was the *Morning News* in Saint John, New Brunswick, in 1839. It started as a tri-weekly and became the first daily in the Maritimes two years later.[32] The affordable newspaper was a catalyst for the emergence of the daily press. The first mass daily was George Brown's Toronto *Globe*, joined soon afterward by the Montreal *Witness*. Technological developments were bringing major changes: the linotype invented in the 1880s made it possible to set type mechanically, and now whole lines could be cast instead of each letter being set by hand, one at a time. The telegraph and the telephone were beginning to have a major impact on news collection toward the end of the nineteenth century. High-speed presses made mass production of newspapers possible. Canada was moving into a new era of mass communication.

THE ELECTRONIC ERA AND CANADIAN NATIONHOOD

The changes in the newspaper system in the twentieth century must be seen in the broader context of a technological revolution that brought electronic communications into the mass media sphere: radio in the 1920s, television in the 1950s.

What stands out in the Canadian preoccupation with communications, and especially our achievements in technology, is the emphasis that has been placed on the electronic media. There are good reasons for this. Canadians have to "think big" in the communications sphere, whether it be physical communications as in the case of road, rail and airplane transportation, or the articulate communications of information, ideas and images. The inland waterways were the first highways to the interior. The very formation of Canada was facilitated by the building of a transcontinental railway. The ability to move goods and people across the country—of critical importance in economic development and defensive capability—was in itself not enough; there was also a need for a rapid and reliable messages transmission system to link the big Canadian entity.

---

32. Kesterton, *A History of Journalism in Canada, op. cit.*, p. 25.

Electronic communications stirred the imagination of Canadians. In 1846, two years after Samuel Morse invented the telegraph in the United States, the first commercial telegraph system began operations in Canada, linking Toronto to Niagara. Thirty years later, the invention of the telephone by Alexander Graham Bell (at Brantford, Ontario) created new communications opportunities and set Canada almost immediately on the path of developing one of the world's most highly advanced telephone systems. Canada became a proving ground for the new communications technologies.

The railways, the telegraph and the telephone created an east-west lifeline of communications. They provided the communications infrastructure for managing and governing a newly formed political community that quickly expanded, from a union of four provinces stretching only two thousand miles, to one that spanned the continent from the Atlantic to the Pacific. "Communications was to be the adhesive," writes Robert Fortner, "that would allow Canadians to defy all handicaps in search of the projected national destiny."[33]

The institutions that created the political community in 1867 were the nucleus of nationhood. The British North America Act, the main constitutional document for 115 years, provided the legal framework within which, Eugene Forsey notes, Canada could "adapt, adjust, manoeuvre, innovate, compromise and arrange."[34] The constitution, the powers of government and legislatures, the division of powers between the federal and provincial levels of government and the institutions of the economy were the matters of immediate concern.

The creation of the federal union was a beginning step in nation building, not the achievement of nationhood. It brought with it the challenge to create a sense of "we feeling" among a small population of diverse religious and linguistic backgrounds spread across a continent where different natural resources and physical/geographic characteristics would nurture differing regional interests. Newspapers, as was noted earlier, played an important role in the "confederation process." But the printed word is handicapped in transportation; news is a perishable item and consequently newspapers do not travel well. Newspapers thrived in the local setting and could only have a limited impact in helping to create a national understanding. The development of a mass communications system that could conquer space and distance and domesticate centrifugal pulls by placing them in a national context remained elusive. As recently as 1936, Prime Minister Mackenzie King observed in Parliament: "If some countries have too much history, we have too much geography."[35] In 1977, the Inquiry into Broadcasting (the Boyle Committee) noted that "the airplane in the physical sphere, and radio and television in the articulate one, are the technological devel-

33. Robert Fortner, "Communication and Canadian National Destiny," *Canadian Journal of Communication*, Vol. 6, No. 2, Fall 1979, p. 43.
34. Eugene Forsey, *How Canadians Govern Themselves*, (Canada: Supply and Services, 1980), p. 12.
35. *Debates*, House of Commons, June 1936. Quoted in Warner Troyer, *The Sound and the Fury*, (Toronto: John Wiley and Sons, 1980), p. 11.

opments that can finally make sense of the country and cross the immense gaps in communications within it."[36]

The notion of bigness is basic to the word "broadcasting" which has an agricultural origin: spreading seeds broadly. In contrast to the localism of newspapers in Canada, broadcasting can reach out beyond the local or regional area and be truly national. At the same time, broadcasting provides links to an international communications system that could help Canada balance her over-developed communications interaction with the United States by reaching out for the long-sought connection with Europe and other world regions.

Radio and television made it possible to reach millions of Canadians simultaneously and were thus perceived as powerful instruments in shaping societal values. By providing a window through which Canadians could see themselves, the broadcast media were seen as instruments that would promote national culture and a sense of identity. Canadians could get to know each other and share their experiences; they would find out what makes them Canadians and develop Canadian reference points for perceptions of the world at large.

The realities of Canadian broadcasting do not meet the expectations. Broadcasting, it will be argued later, has failed to provide either a cultural highway of national self-expression or Canadian reference points for viewing the world. Instead, it has served as a roadway for American influence. The challenge today, as CRTC chairman John Meisel has noted, is the attainment of something considered impossible: "the retrieval and consolidation on our airwaves of a substantial and genuine element of Canadian content."[37]

36. *Report.* Committee of Inquiry into the National Broadcasting Service, (Ottawa: C.R.T.C. 1977), p. 15.
37. John Meisel, "Five Steps to Survival," York University, Gerstein Conference on Mass Communications and Canadian Nationhood, April 10, 1981.

CHAPTER VI

THE NEWSPAPER INDUSTRY: ECONOMICS AND POLITICS

The Charter of Rights and Freedoms in the new Canadian Constitution guarantees "freedom of the press and other media of communication." The press is listed first, but the Charter guarantees are a reminder—if any were needed—that newspapers no longer reign supreme in the mass communications field as was the case in the nineteenth century. The press today competes for audiences and advertising revenues with radio, television and other media that are products of new communication technology. However, because of greater emphasis on their journalistic functions, newspapers are important in collecting information that flows through all the mass media.

Canada's newspaper system is one of the most advanced in the world. It thrives on modern technology: computers, laser-beam scanning, satellite transmission and offset printing. This sophistication and related financial success are in stark contrast to the humble beginnings of the industry 230 years ago.

The *Halifax Gazette* appeared in 1752 with 72 subscribers; it published for 14 years until it was suspended for political reasons. Publishing a paper was often a difficult way for a printer to earn a living in the eighteenth and nineteenth centuries. The economics of the newspaper industry, sometimes related to political and ideological issues, account for the large number of papers that emerged and disappeared. For more than 100 years, papers appearing at weekly intervals dominated the press scene, with the daily newspaper coming comparatively late to Canada. It was not until well into the second half of the nineteenth century that daily newspapers began to replace the weeklies as the most important channel of mass communication focusing on domestic and foreign news. Weeklies, for their part, moved into a supplemental position and largely fostered a community orientation; hence, they are referred to as community papers.

In 1982, there were 117 daily newspapers and nearly 1,100 community papers of less-than-daily frequency. Newspaper receipts from advertising, subscriptions and street sales amounted to $1.7 billion in 1981, with the daily newspapers accounting for 85 per cent of those revenues. This chapter focuses on Canada's 117 general interest dailies (106 published in English and 11 in French) which play a central role in national news collection. There will be an examination of the economics of the daily newspaper industry and an evaluation of how economic factors have affected the political role of the press.

REVENUES: ADVERTISING AND SALES

The daily newspaper industry is big by almost any standards of measurement: readership, employees and revenues. It is estimated that about 14 million Canadians regularly read daily newspapers, an average of just under three readers for each copy of a paper. The industry has combined revenues of just under $1.5 billion. Some $400 million come from the sale of 1.7 billion copies (the annual circulation rate) of newspapers; the income from subscription and street sales covers the cost of newsprint and ink consumed by the industry. The biggest source of revenue is advertising: $1 billion. Advertising revenues pay for capital investments, labour costs and other expenses, and provide the profits.

Canadian newspapers generate the bulk of their income at the local level, the city of publication (see Chart VI.1). Local retail advertising, classified advertising and the money spent on the purchase of newspapers provide, on average, 85 per cent of a newspaper's revenues; the remainder comes from national adver-

CHART VI.1. Newspaper Income in Canada, by Sources of Revenue, 1981

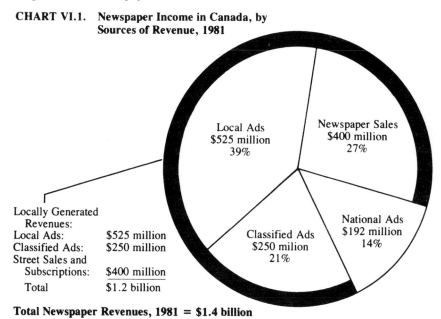

Locally Generated
Revenues:
Local Ads: $525 million
Classified Ads: $250 million
Street Sales and
Subscriptions: $400 million
Total $1.2 billion

Total Newspaper Revenues, 1981 = $1.4 billion

Sources: Maclean-Hunter Research Bureau
Statistics Canada
J. Walter Thompson Company Ltd.

tising. The economic dependence of a newspaper on the city of publication is a major factor in shaping the local character of Canadian dailies.

CIRCULATION

Daily newspaper circulation in 1981 reached an all-time high of 5.5 million. In the 20-year period from 1961-1981, newspaper circulation climbed by 42 per cent, compared to a 32-per cent population growth. There was a temporary circulation decline in the 1979-80 period as a result of the closing of three large dailies: The *Winnipeg Tribune, Ottawa Journal* and *Montreal Star*. However, surviving dailies in Winnipeg and in the English-language market in Ottawa and Montreal have had strong circulation increases after the disappearance of the competition. In the long term, total circulation is only marginally affected.

Canadians in 1981 purchased nine times as many papers as they did in 1900. One obvious reason for more newspaper consumption is that there are more people living in Canada today (450 per cent more) than at the turn of the century. The rate of circulation increase, however, has been about double the rate of population growth. Circulation appears to be tied closely to the distribution of population between town and country: people living in cities buy more newspapers than those living in farming communities. Urban growth, then, has been a major factor in shaping circulation patterns: 76 per cent of today's population is classified as urban, compared with 37 per cent in 1900. Language, too, is important: English-speaking Canadians on average buy more newspapers than the French-speaking population, and immigrants whose mother tongue is neither French nor English buy comparatively few papers. Circulation of the mass press is also sensitive to other social and economic factors, including education, age, kind of work performed, how one commutes to the job, the structure of the family, household earnings, vacation patterns and leisure time. All of the above considerations contribute to variations in newspaper consumption in different regions of Canada (Table VI.1).

Canada has not experienced the stagnation in circulation that has been observed in several other industrial nations. In the United States, for example, circulation is well below the peak reached in 1973. At the same time, Canada has never experienced the high per capita circulation figures observed in such countries as Japan, Britain and the United States. Consequently, there appears to be a growth potential for Canadian newspaper circulation and this has given rise to new market strategies in the industry. A detailed examination of circulation figures for individual newspapers suggests there is a growth pattern underway in 1982 that is ahead of population growth.

READERS: PROFILE

Statistics from the newspaper industry usually focus on circulation figures to which advertising rates are closely tied. But the newspaper influence in society, and even its value to the advertiser, is usually linked more closely to readership

Table VI.1 Daily Newspaper Circulation In Canadian Provinces, by Population and Households (March 31, 1981)

PROVINCE	NUMBER OF NEWSPAPERS	CIRCULATION	POPULATION	CIRCULATION PER 1,000 POPULATION	HOUSEHOLDS	CIRCULATION PER 100 HOUSEHOLDS
Newfoundland	3	56,587	584,500	97	148,800	38
Prince Edward Island	3	34,405	124,200	277	38,100	90
Nova Scotia	8	194,095	856,600	227	274,500	71
New Brunswick	6	150,317	709,600	213	219,700	69
Quebec	11	1,158,378	6,334,700	183	2,129,500	54
Ontario	43	2,339,665	8,614,200	260	3,031,800	74
Manitoba	9	273,736	1,028,800	266	368,000	74
Saskatchewan	5	144,619	977,400	148	328,700	44
Alberta	9	527,363	2,153,200	245	717,000	77
British Columbia	20	607,991	2,701,900	225	954,600	64
Yukon	1	4,800	21,800	220	8,200	58
Northwest Territories	0	—	43,100	—	13,800	—
Total Canada	118	5,491,956	24,150,000	227	8,232,700	67

Sources: Canadian Daily Newspaper Publishers Association
Audit Bureau of Circulation
Statistics Canada

patterns and the characteristics of these readers. A 1978 survey carried out by Statistics Canada of a sample of 20,000 Canadians aged 15 and over provides the following findings:[1]

Population: 14 million Canadians, or 83 per cent of the population (aged 15 and over), read newspapers and spend an average of 42 minutes a day on this activity.

Geographic Distribution: Canadians living in Quebec and the Atlantic Provinces (except Prince Edward Island) read less than those living in Ontario and the western provinces. The Quebec-Ontario border appears to be the dividing line; 80 per cent east of the line read newspapers compared with 85 per cent west of the line. Few Canadians read newspapers from other provinces or countries.

Sex: Men, on average, are slightly heavier newspaper readers than women (84 per cent vs. 82 per cent) and spend about 44 minutes a day on this activity, compared to an average of 40 minutes for women.

Education: Persons with a higher education are heavier newspaper readers than those with less schooling. (The profile of those who say they read newspapers is as follows: university degree—94 per cent, secondary school—90 per cent, one to eight years of school—70 per cent, 'others'—36 per cent.)

Age: Fewer young people read newspapers compared with their elders. Furthermore, the "young" spend about half-an-hour reading a newspaper compared to about an hour for "older" readers. The dividing line between young and old readers appears to be around age 35.

Marital Status: Married people are generally heavier newspaper readers than singles.

Language: Anglophones are heavier newspaper readers than Francophones. Eighty-seven per cent of Anglophones are newspaper readers compared to 77 per cent of the Francophone population. Anglophones hardly read French dailies except in Quebec where 10 per cent of the English-speaking population reads French papers. Francophone reading patterns of English-language newspapers depends on which province they live in. Very few French-speaking Quebecers (3 per cent) say they read English papers; outside of Quebec where French-language daily newspapers are not published (except Ottawa and Moncton, N.B.), 42 per cent of the Francophone population read English

---

1. Yvon Ferland, "The Canadian and His Newspaper," *Canadian Statistical Review*, July 1979. The survey was conducted within the framework of Statistics Canada's monthly Labour Force Survey.

newspapers. Only 11 per cent of French-speaking Canadians living outside of Quebec read a Quebec newspaper.

* * * * * * *

PROFITS

As Senator Keith Davey likes to point out, his Senate Committee on the Mass Media (1970) destroyed once and for all the myth of media poverty.[2] The profit margin for newspapers is among the highest in the industrial sector. The Kent Commission (1981) noted that in 1978 (not a good profit year because of large capital expenditures, labour disputes and the real losses of newspapers about to close down), the newspaper industry, nevertheless, achieved a 25 per cent return on net assets.[3] Only the private broadcasters and the beverage industries showed similar levels of profitability. Such industries as metal fabricating had 9 per cent returns as net assets, food had 10 per cent and textile mills, 7 per cent.

It is useful to look at the profit pattern over the seven-year period from 1973-80, which includes both good and lean years. The average return on net assets was 30 per cent, with a whopping 37 per cent return in 1974-75.[4] It is obvious that newspapers are highly profitable. The Kent Commission thought that in terms of economic survival, the Canadian newspaper industry is "the Queen Elizabeth of life rafts."[5]

Ten years earlier, the Davey Senate Committee arrived at similar conclusions about the excellent profits in the newspaper industry. It observed: "Owning a newspaper . . . can be almost twice as profitable as owning a paper-box factory or a department store."[6]

With 22,000 employees, the daily newspaper industry is one of Canada's leading employers. In fact, one out of every 500 persons in the labour force works for a newspaper. It is significant that the industry showed excellent profit growth in the 1970s when the Canadian economy in general was troubled by both inflation and recession. The earning performance of Thomson Newspapers Ltd. has been especially impressive: in 1978, net profit margins were 18.4 per cent; in 1979, 19.3 per cent; the company achieved record profits in 1981 ($1.96 per share), and even higher profits have been projected for 1982.[7]

While the Thomson earnings have been the best for the newspaper companies, they are at the same time reflective of the high profits in the industry. Thomson, Southam and the Toronto Sun Publishing Corporation reported exceptionally good profit gains in 1981, with earnings at least 25 per cent better than in the previous year. Market conditions, and especially the general absence of competi-

2. The Special Senate Committee on Mass Media. *Report*. (Ottawa: Queen's Printer, 1970).
3. Royal Commission on Newspapers. *op. cit.*, pp. 82-85.
4. *Ibid.*, p. 84.
5. *Ibid.*, p. 85.
6. Senate Committee on Mass Media, *op. cit.*, Vol. I, p. 47.
7. *Globe and Mail*, May 22, 1982, p. B7.

tion, give the owners considerable flexibility in setting both advertising rates and the price that the consumer pays for a copy of the newspaper. Higher newsprint costs have been readily passed on. While wages have increased in line with the wage explosion fuelled by inflationary pressures in the 1970s, productivity in the newspaper industry has increased even faster, so much so that labour costs have decreased every year in the past seven years as a proportion of total expenses. Salaries in 1980 accounted for 44 per cent of expenditures, compared to 48 per cent in 1974.[8] The trend to lower labour costs is expected to continue into the mid-1980s as the benefits of new technology, including offset printing, are harvested.

The Senate Study on the Mass Media quotes the late Roy Thomson's classic observation that a television broadcast permit is "like having a licence to print your own money" and goes on to say that ownership of a daily newspaper in Canada often amounts to the same thing, except you don't need a licence.[9]

THE PRESS SYSTEM TODAY

The politically active press of the nineteenth century, when newspapers catered to readers who shared the political persuasion of the respective editors, has given way to a press system that thrives on mass audiences of all political viewpoints. The largest newspaper today, the *Toronto Star*, has a circulation that nearly equals the combined circulation of all of Canada's 121 dailies at the turn of the century. There are fewer newspapers in 1983 than there were in 1900, although the circulation has increased from 600,000 to 5.5 million.

The economic interests of the owners, not their politics, ideology or religion, are in nearly all cases the main motivation for a daily newspaper's existence. Three French-language dailies are the principal exceptions to this approach. Moncton's *L'Evangeline* is dedicated to Acadian survival in New Brunswick, Ottawa's *Le Droit* is owned by a religious order of nuns and dedicated to the interests of Francophones, and Montreal's *Le Devoir* operates on a unique trusteeship formula and has at times been called the conscience of Quebec. These three papers have a combined circulation of 105,000, or less than two per cent of Canadian newspaper circulation. The circulation figures, however, do not necessarily reflect their influence. *Le Devoir*, in particular, ranks among the most important newspapers in Canada.

The economic factors shaping the newspaper industry have, of course, major political and social implications. In discussing this subject, it is useful to examine the characteristics of the newspaper system. These characteristics are: the non-competitive nature; the concentration of ownership; localism and regionalism; the predominance of small circulation dailies; the increasing importance of morning and all-day papers; and the increasing importance of tabloid papers.

---

8. Royal Commission on Newspapers, *op. cit.,* p. 78.
9. Senate Committee on the Mass Media, *op. cit.,* vol. I, p. 47.

THE NON-COMPETITIVE NATURE

Canada's 117 dailies are published in 97 cities. In 15 cities there are two or more dailies, but in three of the cities—Moncton, New Brunswick; Sherbrooke, Quebec; and Ottawa, Ontario—the two papers appear in different languages. New tabloids, the Halifax *Daily News* and the *Winnipeg Sun*, were introduced in 1981, but these papers have not yet reached circulation levels to be regarded as viable competition. In five cities—Halifax, Charlottetown, Saint John, Thunder Bay and Vancouver—the two major dailies are owned by the same publishers and are therefore not in competition with each other. This leaves only six cities with any meaningful newspaper competition: St. John's, Quebec City, Montreal, Toronto, Calgary and Edmonton. (See Chart VI.2).

English-language Competition

In the English-language newspaper market, there are four cities with meaningful competition.

TORONTO. The most dynamic English-language newspaper city in Canada, Toronto has three profitable dailies: the morning *Globe and Mail,* the all-day *Toronto Star* and the morning tabloid, *Toronto Sun.* Toronto had three daily newspapers for many years but appeared to be headed for a decline in competition when the *Telegram* discontinued publishing on October 31, 1971. The next day, the *Toronto Sun* was born.

CALGARY. There are two dailies: The *Herald* (established in 1885) and the *Calgary Sun,* which replaced the *Calgary Albertan* in 1980. The *Sun* venture is an attempt by the owners of the *Toronto Sun* to apply their successful Toronto formula in this Alberta city.

EDMONTON. This city is unique among Canadian newspaper cities because there is a reversal of the trend toward monopolies. The *Edmonton Journal* (established in 1903) had been the only newspaper in the city since the folding of the *Edmonton Bulletin* in 1950. New competition was introduced in 1978 with the creation of the *Edmonton Sun.* The *Journal,* for its part, launched a morning edition in September 1980, to compete with the *Sun.* Both the *Journal* and the *Sun* are showing circulation increases, a sign that they are seeking out new readership rather than taking away each other's customers. (Alberta's booming economy is creating suitable conditions for newspaper growth in Edmonton and Calgary.)

ST. JOHN'S, Nfld. St. John's is an anomaly by Canadian newspaper standards: the morning *Daily News* with a circulation of 11,000 remains in a market that is dominated by the evening *Telegram,* which has a circulation of 36,000. The Davey Senate Committee suggested that this situation ''will not necessarily continue indefinitely.''

WINNIPEG AND HALIFAX. Reference has already been made to the new tabloids that entered these markets in 1981. The circulation for the *Winnipeg Sun* (not related to the *Sun* chain) has been fluctuating between 30,000 and

CHART VI.2. Daily Newspaper Competition in Canadian Cities, French and English, 1982*

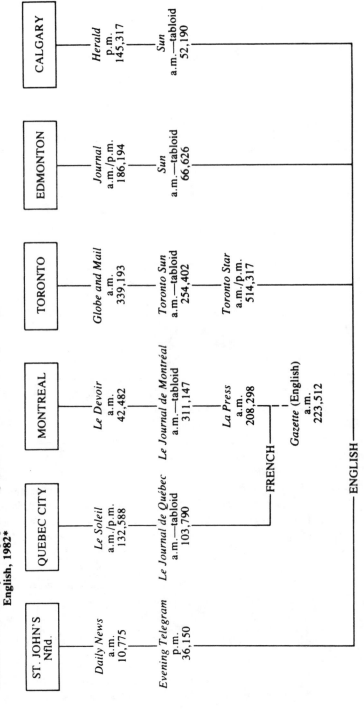

CALGARY	*Herald* p.m. 145,317	*Sun* a.m.—tabloid 52,190			
EDMONTON	*Journal* a.m./p.m. 186,194	*Sun* a.m.—tabloid 66,626			
TORONTO	*Globe and Mail* a.m. 339,193	*Toronto Sun* a.m.—tabloid 254,402	*Toronto Star* a.m./p.m. 514,317		
MONTREAL	*Le Devoir* a.m. 42,482	*Le Journal de Montréal* a.m.—tabloid 311,147	*La Press* a.m. 208,298	*Gazette* (English) a.m. 223,512	
QUEBEC CITY	*Le Soleil* a.m./p.m. 132,588	*Le Journal de Québec* a.m.—tabloid 103,790			
ST. JOHN'S Nfld.	*Daily News* a.m. 10,775	*Evening Telegram* p.m. 36,150			

FRENCH

ENGLISH

*Circulation figures are for 1981.

40,000, compared to the nearly 200,000 circulation figure for the *Winnipeg Free Press.* The Halifax *Daily News* has a circulation of about 10,000, or less than eight per cent of the combined 129,000 circulation of the *Chronicle-Herald* and *Mail-Star* (owned by the Dennis family). In realistic terms, there is as yet no competition in Winnipeg and Halifax.

French-language Competition

In the french-language newspaper market, there is competition only in Montreal and Quebec City.

MONTREAL. There are four Montreal dailies: three French, one English. Three of the dailies are owned by newspaper groups and the fourth, the fiercely independent *Le Devoir* has not always shown a profit, and at times has resorted to fund-raising campaigns. *Le Devoir,* profitable in recent years, plays a special role in French-Canadian journalism: it addresses itself to an intellectual élite. Its circulation of 42,000 is comparatively small when taken in the context of the Montreal market.

Until the 1970s, *La Presse* was the largest French-language daily outside of Paris. It has fallen from this pivotal position for a number of reasons, including labour strikes and disagreements among members of the family that previously owned the daily. *Le Journal de Montréal,* a tabloid established in 1964, has a circulation of 311,000, making it the largest French daily and the second largest newspaper in Canada.

The fourth daily, the *Montreal Gazette*—Canada's oldest newspaper—has done extremely well in the monopoly situation that it attained in the English-language market with the closing of the *Montreal Star* in 1979.

All four Montreal newspapers publish in the morning; 10 years earlier, afternoon dailies dominated the market.

QUEBEC CITY. *Le Soleil,* with a circulation of 133,000, is the largest daily. The tabloid *Le Journal de Québec,* a sister paper of *Le Journal de Montréal,* has a circulation of 103,000. Two newspapers folded in Quebec City in the last 10 years: the English-language *Chronicle Telegraph,* owned by Thomson, and *L'Action,* a small French-language daily that had been subsidized by the Roman Catholic Church.

In 1970, when there was newspaper competition in eight cities, the Davey Senate Committee concluded that there was "genuine competition" in only five. Similar criteria would suggest that "genuine competition," where newspapers are competing for the same market segments, is limited to three cities in 1982. Using less-demanding standards, six out of Canada's 97 newspaper cities have competing dailies. (see Chart VI.2). There are only two cities, Montreal and Toronto, that have more than two dailies. This is in sharp contrast to the situation in 1900, when 35 cities had "genuine competition" with 18 of them having three or more newspapers.[10]

---

10. Kesterton, *A History of Canadian Journalism, op. cit.,* p. 73.

The end of competition in Ottawa, Winnipeg and Vancouver on August 27, 1980 (discussed in the following chapter) reflects a trend that has been in evidence for many decades. Intra-city rivalry in the newspaper field is virtually dead. The predominant situation is the single-newspaper city: one newspaper with a monopoly in the community.

Competition

The first element of press rivalry in Canada dates to 1769 when the unofficial *Nova Scotia Chronicle and Weekly Advertiser* began competing with the official *Nova Scotia Gazette*. By 1786, Halifax had three dailies, all of them politically uninvolved and enjoying good relations with the provincial establishment which provided the printing patronage that kept the papers in business.

Meaningful press competition—in economic, political and journalistic terms—developed from about 1813 onward and was flourishing in the 1830s.

The politicization of the press and dynamic competition became possible because of the changing economic support structure. Advertising, larger subscriptions and printing, ("book and job" work) made editors independent of government patronage.

The political involvement of newspapers attracted another source of income: financial backers, who had a specific viewpoint on public affairs. To convey competing political, religious and social causes to the public, newspapers sprang into existence in nearly all communities that were big enough to support them. Halifax was among the most competitive markets: in 1864, there were eight competing papers presenting a broad spectrum of political orientations.[11]

Today, Halifax has no meaningful newspaper competition. The city's two main dailies, *The Chronicle-Herald* (circulation 72,000) and *The Mail-Star* (circulation 57,000), are owned by the same publisher and are essentially morning and evening editions of the same newspaper. They have a virtual monopoly on print communication in Halifax and account for 73 per cent of all daily newspapers circulated in Nova Scotia.

The Halifax papers shun controversy and the taking of partisan positions. Publisher Graham Dennis told the Kent Commission that "it is our duty, in so far as possible, to avoid aggravation of our political conflicts." The Commission did not comment on the merits of this benign journalistic approach to politics, but did point out that the Halifax papers spend below the national average—less than 15 per cent of their revenues—on editorial expenses.

The Senate Study on the Mass Media found a sad state of affairs in the Halifax newspaper field in 1970: "There is no large Canadian city that is so badly served by its newspapers."[12] The Halifax papers are highly profitable and "had for years been guilty of uncaring, lazy journalism" with the publisher indifferent to the needs of the readers. The Senate Committee also noted the intimate and

---

11. Rutherford, *The Making of the Canadian Media, op. cit.*, p. 30.
12. Senate Committee on the Mass Media, *op. cit.*, Vol. I., p. 89.

uncritical relationship of the Halifax papers with the Nova Scotia power structure during the premierships of Robert Stanfield and Henry Hicks. The findings of the Senate Committee suggest that Halifax, Canada's first newspaper city and the one which fostered the start of dynamic newspaper competition, had fallen on hard times in journalistic terms.

Halifax is not a unique example of the decline of competition, for many of today's single-newspaper cities had several papers in the 1860s. At the same time, Halifax is not necessarily typical of the effects of newspaper monopoly. Publishers have argued that the emergence of one economically strong daily in a community has resulted in newspapers with the financial means to bolster their editorial content. It is generally argued that the press needs a strong economic base to preserve its political independence, although Montreal's *Le Devoir* is an example of a newspaper that faced economic problems for some years without compromising its independence.

Why the competition disappeared

There are at least five reasons for the decline in competition: changing politics, new technology, economics of print, interests of the advertisers and the difficulties of starting a daily in a community where one already exists.

Changing Politics. At the high point of competition, newspapers were seeking out their own special interest audiences rather than competing for the same readership. The heterogeneous British North American society gave rise to numerous political and ideological factions that were willing to support newspapers that carried their respective messages to the public. When political factions internalized their differences in the process of forming political parties, fewer newspapers were needed. In other words, once a political cause faltered or was absorbed by another group, its media outlet closed.

New Technology. The waning interest of political factions in subsidizing the press came at a time when technological changes created new economic realities for newspapers in Canada. The presses that came into widespread use in Canada late in the nineteenth century produced thousands of newspapers per hour. There was a plentiful supply of cheap newsprint made from woodpulp (instead of hard-to-get linen rags). The railways made it possible to distribute newspapers swiftly over a wider area. The telephone and telegraph—intimately linked to the development of transportation in Canada—expanded the area of news coverage: news dispatches could be phoned or telegraphed from outlying communities to the newspaper. The expanded area of news coverage and the expanded territory of newspaper distribution brought increased readership. Instead of serving "limited audiences," newspapers sought a mass audience by catering to broadly defined general interests.

Economics. In newspaper production, bringing out the first copy is the largest cost. The salaries of reporters, editors and support staff, and the cost of printing presses and typesetting are essential expenses whether the press run is 20,000 or 40,000. Salaries are the biggest cost in newspaper production, accounting for 44 per cent (compared to 50 per cent 10 years earlier). Paper and ink cost about 27 per cent and are largely covered by the selling price of the dailies. When circulation increases, the cost of the additional output is marginal and paid for by the consumer.

Increased circulation benefits the advertiser and the publisher. It is cheaper for an advertiser to buy space in one daily than to advertise in two or three dailies that, through combined circulation, reach the same audience. Major department stores, for example, spend less money on newspaper advertising in single-newspaper cities than in cities where there are competing dailies.[13] The publisher, for his part, can charge more for advertising, since advertising rates are tied to circulation. The ideal situation for the publisher and advertiser is one newspaper in a community—in other words, a monopoly.

• *Monopolies.*   Once a monopoly has been achieved in a newspaper market, it is extremely difficult to introduce new competition. Starting a new paper has been likened to economic suicide. (The only exceptions are tabloids in large markets, which will be discussed later.) Raising capital is one obstacle to starting a new competitive newspaper; lack of industry support is another. This lack of industry support is exemplified in the membership practices of the Canadian Press news agency, the "wholesale distributor" of news copy. Canadian newspapers have no trouble in becoming CP members, but they must pay the going rate. Furthermore, until 1970, new members had to pay surcharges for the first five years. For a new newspaper, the membership assessment is based on the circulation projected for advertising rates. Peter Worthington, one of the founders in 1971 of the spectacularly successful *Toronto Sun,* recalls that his new paper was basing its advertising rates on a circulation of 50,000 but had sought, unsuccessfully, to acquire CP membership at the 25,000 circulation rate. He says: "CP is not interested in helping to bring about newspaper competition."[14] The *Sun* worked out "a deal" with United Press International (UPI) and eventually became the principal owner of United Press Canada (linked to UPI). Canadian Press has a conservative approach to new membership in competitive markets in that the applicant has to show financial viability by paying the first-year assessment in advance—a heavy financial burden for a new venture.

CONCENTRATION OF OWNERSHIP

Just before the First World War, there were 138 daily newspapers in Canada with 135 publishers. In 1982, 12 publishing groups produced 88 of Canada's 117 newspapers. In other words, 75 per cent of the daily newspapers are involved in some form of common or concentrated ownership. The two biggest publishers are Thomson, with 40 newspapers, and Southam, with 14. The ownership pattern of Canadian newspapers is shown in Table VI.2, Table VI.3 and Table VI.4.

The extent of concentrated ownership appears even more pronounced when

---

13. Royal Commission on Newspapers, *op. cit.,* p. 71.
14. Information provided by Mr. Worthington.

examined on the basis of circulation. The six largest publishing companies, all of them chains or conglomerates, account for more than 80 per cent of the circulation of 5.5 million newspapers. Nearly 90 per cent of the circulation comes from the 10 largest newspaper publishers (Table VI.5).

• Canada has a higher concentration of ownership in the daily newspaper field than any other developed country. This concentration of ownership exists at all levels: there is national, English-language, French-language and provincial concentration.

The degree of national concentration has been summarized and is illustrated in Table VI.5. An important characteristic of chains, excluding the tabloid chains that cater to a specialized market segment, is that they do not compete with each other. The two largest chains, Thomson and Southam, do not compete in any of the 51 newspaper cities where they publish.

English Papers: Concentration of Ownership

In the English-language newspaper market, Thomson and Southam account for six out of every 10 newspapers sold. As shown in Chart VI.3, four Canadian publishers produce 78 per cent of the country's English-language newspaper circulation. Only 13 per cent comes from independent newspaper owners.

Table VI.2. English-language Daily Newspapers Owned by Chains and/or Media Conglomerates by Number of Papers and Circulation (1982)

SOUTHAM NEWSPAPERS INC.—14 Dailies

Circ.

223,512	*The Gazette,* Montreal, P.Q.
32,213	*The Expositor,* Brantford, Ont.
149,828	*The Spectator,* Hamilton, Ont.
24,236	*North Bay Nugget,* North Bay, Ont.
178,725	*The Citizen,* Ottawa, Ont.
20,327	*The Sun Times,* Owen Sound, Ont.
25,945	*The Sault Star,* Sault Ste. Marie, Ont.
92,244	*The Windsor Star,* Windsor, Ont.
145,317	*The Calgary Herald,* Calgary, Alta.
186,194	*Edmonton Journal,* Edmonton, Alta.
13,946	*The Medicine Hat News,* Medicine Hat, Alta.
22,838	*The Prince George Citizen,* Prince George, B.C.
379,017	*The Vancouver Province* and *The Vancouver Sun,* Vancouver, B.C. (2)
1,494,342	27.4% of Total Canadian Circulation (French and English) 5,450,529

THOMSON NEWSPAPERS—40 Dailies

9,662	*The Western Star,* Corner Brook, Nfld.
36,150	*The Evening Telegram,* St. John's, Nfld.
22,987	*Charlottetown Guardian* and *Evening Patriot,* Charlottetown, P.E.I. (2)
11,951	*The Evening News,* New Glasgow, N.S.

31,437	*The Cape Breton Post,* Sydney, N.S.
8,432	*Truro Daily News,* Truro, N.S.
11,314	*The Barrie Examiner,* Barrie, Ont.
17,300	*The Intelligencer,* Belleville, Ont.
8,709	*The Brampton Daily Times,* Brampton, Ont.
13,481	*Cambridge Daily Reporter,* Cambridge, Ont.
14,688	*Chatham Daily News,* Chatham, Ont.
17,263	*The Daily Standard-Freeholder,* Cornwall, Ont.
17,301	*The Guelph Daily Mercury,* Guelph, Ont.
5,852	*The Northern Daily News,* Kirkland Lake, Ont.
20,817	*Niagara Falls Review,* Niagara Falls, Ont.
9,170	*The Daily Packet and Times,* Orillia, Ont.
22,991	*The Times,* Oshawa, Ont.
7,339	*The Observer,* Pembroke, Ont.
23,240	*The Peterborough Examiner,* Peterborough, Ont.
10,128	*The St. Thomas Times-Journal,* St. Thomas, Ont.
22,673	*Sarnia Observer,* Sarnia, Ont.
9,838	*Simcoe Reformer,* Simcoe, Ont.
30,082	*The Sudbury Daily Star,* Sudbury, Ont.
34,943	*The Times-News* and *The Chronicle-Journal,* Thunder Bay, Ont. (2)
12,871	*The Daily Press,* Timmins, Ont.
339,193	*The Globe and Mail,* Toronto, Ont.
18,599	*Welland-Port Colborne Evening Tribune,* Welland, Ont.
9,347	*The Daily Sentinel Review,* Woodstock, Ont.
196,065	*Winnipeg Free Press,* Winnipeg, Man.
10,053	*Moose Jaw Times-Herald,* Moose Jaw, Sask.
10,014	*The Daily Herald,* Prince Albert, Sask.
28,594	*The Lethbridge Herald,* Lethbridge, B.C.
10,951	*The Daily Sentinel,* Kamloops, B.C.
15,412	*Kelowna Courier,* Kelowna, B.C.
9,487	*The Daily Free Press,* Nanaimo, B.C.
8,336	*Penticton Herald,* Penticton, B.C.
9,125	*Vernon Daily News,* Vernon, B.C.
79,404	*Victoria Times-Colonist,* Victoria, B.C.
1,175,199	21.6% of Total Canadian Circulation

TORSTAR—1 Daily, numerous Weeklies and other Media interests.

Circ.	
514,317	*Toronto Star,* Toronto, Ont.
514,317	9% of Total Canadian Circulation

MACLEAN-HUNTER/SUN PUBLISHING CORPORATION—3 Dailies

254,402	*The Toronto Sun,* Toronto, Ont.
52,190	*The Calgary Sun,* Calgary, Alta.
66,626	*The Edmonton Sun,* Edmonton, Alta.
373,218	6.8% of Total Canadian Circulation

IRVING NEWSPAPERS—5 Dailies

24,578 *The Daily Gleaner*, Fredericton, N.B.
45,610 *The Moncton Times* and *The Moncton Transcript*, Moncton, N.B. (2)
63,286 *The Telegraph-Journal* and *The Evening Times-Globe*, Saint John, N.B. (2)
133,474 2.4% of Total Canadian Circulation

ARMADALE COMPANY LIMITED—2 Dailies

69,078 *The Leader-Post*, Regina, Sask.
55,001 *The Star-Phoenix*, Saskatoon, Sask.
124,079 2.3% of Total Canadian Circulation

STERLING PUBLICATIONS—10 Dailies

11,418 *Summerside Journal-Pioneer*, Summerside, P.E.I.
473 *Lloydminster Daily Times*, Lloydminster, Sask.
4,228 *Cranbrook Daily Townsman*, Cranbrook, B.C.
3,993 *The Alaska Highway News*, Fort St. John, B.C.
2,410 *Kimberley Daily Bulletin*, Kimberley, B.C.
7,620 *Nelson Daily News*, Nelson, B.C.
7,838 *Alberni Valley Times*, Port Alberni, B.C.
4,092 *The Daily News*, Prince Rupert, B.C.
4,343 *The Terrace Herald*, Terrace, B.C.
6,605 *Trail Times*, Trail, B.C.
53,020 1.0% of Total Canadian Circulation

BOWES PUBLISHERS LIMITED—3 Dailies

4,483 *The Kenora Miner and News*, Kenora, Ont.
6,379 *Fort McMurray Today*, Fort McMurray, Alta.
8,628 *The Daily Herald-Tribune*, Grande Prairie, Alta.
19,490 0.4% of Total Canadian Circulation

JOHNSTON (NORTHUMBERLAND PUBLISHING LTD.)—2 Dailies

4,865 *The Cobourg Daily Star*, Cobourg, Ont.
3,251 *The Evening Guide*, Port Hope, Ont.
8,116 0.1% of Total Canadian Circulation
Total English Chain and Conglomerate Circulation: 3,895,255
Total Number of English Newspapers Chain- or Conglomerate-Owned: 80

*Circulation figures are for 1981.
Sources: Canadian Daily Newspaper Publishers Association
Audit Bureau of Circulation

French Papers: Concentration of Ownership

Until about 15 years ago, French-language newspapers were mostly independently owned. Today, concentration of ownership is just as strong in the French press as it is in the English press. The only French-language daily in Quebec province not controlled by newspaper chains is Montreal's *Le Devoir*. Two other French-language dailies, *L'Evangeline* in Moncton, New Brunswick and *Le Droit* in Ottawa, are also independently owned. In terms of circulation, 90 per cent of French-language dailies in Canada come from three newspaper chains (see Chart VI.4).

TABLE VI.3 French-language Dailies Owned by Chains and/or Media Conglomerates by Number of Papers and Circulation (1982)

PÉLADEAU GROUP—2 Dailies

Circ.
311,147   *Le Journal de Montréal*, Montreal, P.Q.
103,790   *Le Journal de Québec*, Quebec City, P.Q.
414,937   7.6% of Total Canadian Circulation

TRANS-CANADA NEWSPAPERS—4 Dailies

11,620   *La Voix de l'Est*, Granby, P.Q.
208,298   *La Presse*, Montreal, P.Q.
41,618   *La Tribune*, Sherbrooke, P.Q.
52,968   *Le Nouvelliste*, Trois Rivières, P.Q.
314,504   5.8% of Total Canadian Circulation

UNIMÉDIA INC.—2 Dailies

23,030   *Le Quotidien du Saguenay*, Lac St. Jean, Chicoutimi, P.Q.
132,588   *Le Soleil*, Quebec City, P.Q.
155,618   2.8% of Total Canadian Circulation

Total French Chain and Conglomerate Circulation: 885,059

Total Number of French Newspapers Chain- or Conglomerate-Owned: 8

CHART VI.3. **Ownership Profile of English-language Dailies in Canada, by Circulation**

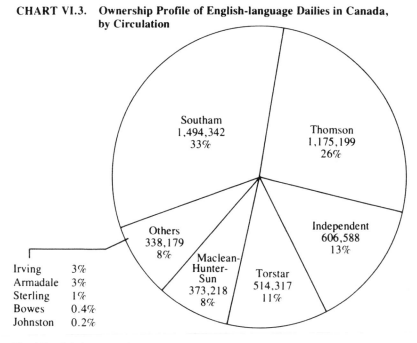

Irving 3%
Armadale 3%
Sterling 1%
Bowes 0.4%
Johnston 0.2%

Total English-language Circulation: 4,504,843

Two chains control 59 per cent of English-language market in Canada.
Four publishers control 78 per cent of English-language market in Canada.
Chains and conglomerates control 87 per cent of English-language market in Canada.
Independent publishers account for 13 per cent of English-language market in Canada.

TABLE VI.4 French and English Daily Newspapers Independently Owned by Circulation (1982)

Circ.	
10,775	*The Daily News*, St. John's, Nfld.
3,775	*Amherst Daily News*, Amherst, N.S.
129,216	*The Chronicle-Herald* and *The Mail-Star*, Halifax, N.S. (2)
9,284	*Daily News*, Halifax, N.S.
16,843	*L'Evangeline*, Moncton, N.B.
42,482	*Le Devoir*, Montreal, P.Q.
7,325	*The Sherbrooke Record*, Sherbrooke, P.Q.
14,233	*The Recorder and Times*, Brockville, Ont.
35,467	*The Whig-Standard*, Kingston, Ont.
71,577	*Kitchener-Waterloo Record*, Kitchener, Ont.
4,655	*The Lindsay Daily Post*, Lindsay, Ont.
128,266	*The London Free Press*, London, Ont.

46,129	*Le Droit,* Ottawa, Ont.
43,455	*The Standard,* St. Catharines, Ont.
1,000	*Sioux Lookout Daily Bulletin,* Sioux Lookout, Ont.
12,908	*The Beacon Herald,* Stratford, Ont.
	[*The Toronto Star,* Toronto, Ont. (listed as a conglomorate, circ. 514,317)]
19,007	*The Brandon Sun,* Brandon, Man.
2,987	*Dauphin Daily Bulletin,* Dauphin, Manitoba
3,800	*Flin Flon Reminder,* Flin Flon, Man.
4,563	*The Daily Graphic,* Portage La Prairie, Man.
2,200	*Roblin Daily News,* Roblin, Man.
700	*Swan River Report,* Swan River, Man.
2,987	*Thompson Citizen,* Thompson, Man.
41,427	*Winnipeg Sun,* Winnipeg, Man. (established as a Daily, April 27, 1981)
19,489	*The Red Deer Advocate,* Red Deer, Alta.
3,650	*Peace River Block News,* Dawson Creek, B.C.
28,642	*The Columbian,* New Westminster, B.C.
4,800	*The Whitehorse Star,* Whitehorse, YT
711,642	12.9% of Total Canadian Circulation

Total Number of Independently owned Dailies: 29

CHART VI.4.   Ownership Profile of French-language Dailies in Canada, by Circulation

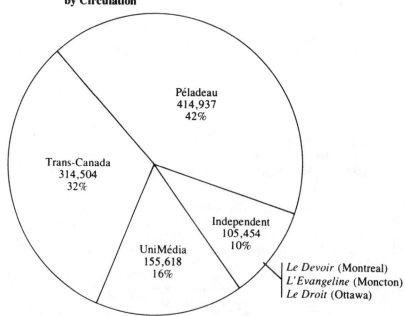

Péladeau
414,937
42%

Trans-Canada
314,504
32%

Independent
105,454
10%

UniMédia
155,618
16%

Le Devoir (Montreal)
L'Evangeline (Moncton)
Le Droit (Ottawa)

Total French-language Circulation: 990,513

Three chains control 90 per cent of French-language market in Canada.
Three chains control 95 per cent of French-language market in Quebec.

TABLE VI.5 Group, Conglomerate and Independent Ownership of Daily
Newspapers (1982),* by Number of Newspapers and Circulation

	PUBLISHER	NO. OF NEWSPAPERS	CIRCULATION	SHARE OF TOTAL CIRCULATION
	Southam	14	1,494,342	27.4%
	Thomson	40	1,175,199	21.6%
	Torstar (Media Conglomerate)	1	514,317	9.4%
	Péladeau	2	414,937	7.6%
	Maclean-Hunter—Sun Publishing	3	373,218	6.8%
	Trans-Canada	4	314,504	5.8%
	UniMédia	2	155,618	2.8%
	Irving	5	133,474	2.4%
	Armadale	2	124,079	2.3%
	Sterling	10	53,020	1.0%
	Bowes	3	19,490	.4%
	Johnston	2	8,116	.1%
	Sub-total	88	4,780,314	87.6%
	Independent	29	711,642	12.9%
	TOTAL CANADA	117	5,491,956	(100.5)

(left margin label: CHAIN AND CONGLOMERATE DAILIES)

*Circulation figures are for 1981.
Sources: Canadian Daily Newspaper Publishers Association
        Audit Bureau of Circulation

Regional Concentration of Ownership

We now move from concentration of ownership by language to publishing dominance on a geographic basis. As shown in Table VI.6 in eight of Canada's ten
provinces, one publisher controls at least 65 per cent of newspaper circulation.
The provincial concentration of ownership is almost total in New Brunswick,
where the Irving family owns all five English-language dailies. The Thomson
chain controls more than 80 per cent of newspaper circulation in Newfoundland
and Manitoba, 68 per cent in Prince Edward Island and 65 per cent in Alberta.
Armadale (Michael Sifton) controls 86 per cent of newspaper circulation in Saskatchewan. With more than 65 per cent circulation control, Southam is the dominant publisher in Alberta and British Columbia. The Dennis family (Halifax
Herald Ltd.) is the dominant publisher in Nova Scotia with 73 per cent of total
provincial circulation. Quebec and Ontario are the only provinces where there is
a significant distribution of circulation control among several publishers. The
analysis shows that a publisher with only a small share of overall Canadian circulation may be the dominant—or even the exclusive—publisher in a particular
province. This situation has important political implications because of the
regionalism and localism of Canadian newspapers.

TABLE VI.6 Provincial Newspaper Circulation, by Dominant Publishers and Group Ownership

Province/Circulation	Dominant Publisher*: Circulation Share	Other Major Publishers (Chains & Conglomerates)	Independent Publishers: Circulation Share	Chains & Conglomerates: Total Circulation Share	Observations
Newfoundland 56,587	Thomson—84%		16%	84%	
Nova Scotia 194,095	Halifax Herald Ltd.—73%	Thomson—27%	(73%)	27%	
Prince Edward Island 34,405	Thomson—68%	Sterling—32%	—	100%	
New Brunswick 150,317	Irving—91%		9% (French)	91%	Irving family owns all five English-language papers.
Quebec 1,158,378	Péladeau—40%	Trans-Canada—25% Southam—19% (English) UniMédia—13%	4%	96%	
Ontario 2,339,665	Thomson—27%	Torstar—22% Southam—22% Maclean Hunter-Sun—11%	18%	82%	Torstar, which publishes the *Toronto Star*, is a media conglomerate involved in publishing 27 community papers, books and magazines. The *Toronto Star* revenues are less than 38% of Torstar's total revenues.
Manitoba 273,736	Thomson—87%		13%	87%	
Saskatchewan 144,619	Armadale—86%	Thomson—14%	—	100%	
Alberta 527,305	Southam—65%	Maclean Hunter-Sun—23% Others—8%	4%	96%	
British Columbia 607,991	Southam—66%	Thomson—22% Sterling—6%	5%	94%	

* Dominance is based on circulation share in province and is not necessarily tied to influence or metropolitan market penetration.

Concentration of ownership has grown a great deal since 1970, when the Senate Study on the Mass Media drew attention to what was then regarded as an almost alarming situation. The number of papers owned by chains increased, there was a consolidation of groups, and the group- and conglomerate-controlled circulation climbed from 77 per cent of total circulation to nearly 90 per cent. Competition between chain newspapers in such major markets as Ottawa, Montreal (English market), Winnipeg and Vancouver disappeared.

The discussion here is confined largely to daily newspapers but reference must also be made to related problems: interlocking ownership within the print media—dailies, weeklies and magazines—and interlocking ownership between the printed press and the electronic media, including radio, television and cable companies. Torstar Corporation, for example, in addition to publishing the *Toronto Star*, controls 27 community newspapers within 40 kilometres of Toronto; is a major book publisher (Harlequin); is involved in a partnership with Southam in Infomart (an electronic information delivery system); publishes consumer magazines; and is involved in numerous other enterprises in the communication field. Southam has major holdings in newspaper, broadcasting and other communications sectors. The media conglomerate Maclean Hunter moved into the daily newspaper field in 1982. The Irving family owns all of the English dailies in New Brunswick as well as radio and television stations in the province. Michael Sifton, the dominant publisher in Saskatchewan, owns broadcast stations in that province and elsewhere. The Blackburn family publishes the *London Free Press* and has broadcast holdings (radio and TV) in the same city.

Group Ownership

The desire to own groups of newspapers and publish in more than one city is not new to Canada. In the 1860s, John Dougall, publisher of Montreal's successful *Daily Witness*, and George Brown of the Toronto *Globe* were expanding their publishing interests to include other communities. Dougall felt he had a calling from God to promote his religious beliefs, while the politically involved Brown launched the *Globe*'s drive to add readership and holdings (e.g. *Western Globe* in London, Ontario) beyond Toronto.[15]

Dougall and Brown, however, were exceptions for their times. Newspaper chains in the modern sense of the word came to Canada long after they had started in the United States. Among the earliest American owners of groups of newspapers was W.E. Scripps in the 1880s. At the start of the century, there were eight major U.S. newspaper chains including Hearst, Pulitzer, Booth and Scripps-McCrea. Today there are 167 newspaper groups in the United States with the top firms including Knight-Ridder, Gannett, Newhouse, Thomson, Hearst and Dow Jones. What is different about Canadian and U.S. chains is the greater dilution of ownership in the United States. This is especially revealing in an examination of circulation figures. The largest American chain, Knight-Rid-

15. Rutherford, *The Making of the Canadian Media, op. cit.*, pp. 10-14.

der, accounts for just over six per cent of total U.S. newspaper circulation, compared to Southam's nearly 30 per cent in Canada. The 10 largest American chains account for less than 40 per cent of the daily circulation in contrast to the 80 per cent controlled by the six largest publishers in Canada. The degree of concentration that exists in Canada would not be permitted under anti-trust laws in the United States, where there have been demands in Congress for laws to limit group ownership.

The growth of newspaper chains in Canada reflects, in large part, a pragmatic approach to an economic problem: how to redeploy profits. Successful newspapers are great cash producers, for the industry is neither capital-intensive nor does it have large capital requirements. Because it is difficult to find equally good returns on investments in other industries, newspaper companies intensively pursue acquisitions within the industry. Different models of newspaper chains have evolved in Canada. They include Southam, Thomson and the Tabloid Model.

Southam.   The oldest newspaper chain in Canada, Southam Inc. had humble beginnings in 1877 when William Southam, a printer who had worked for the *London Free Press*, acquired a half-interest in the Hamilton *Spectator*. Twenty years later, in 1897, the Ottawa *Citizen* came under Southam control and became the nucleus of the chain. Over the years, other newspapers were absorbed: the *Calgary Herald* in 1908, the *Edmonton Journal* in 1912, the *Winnipeg Tribune* in 1920 and the *Vancouver Province* in 1923 (Table VI.7). In the early period of chain development, Southam also became an important printing company.

After World War II, Southam began a new round of acquisitions. Since 1960, the company has branched out beyond newspapers and printing into other sectors of the broadly defined communications/information industry.[16] There are two major reasons for this diversification: first, concern that new technology could come along to erode the relative position of daily newspapers in the total marketplace and second, the need to deploy profits in a meaningful way.

Table VI.7. Southam Daily Newspaper Acquisitions

YEAR ACQUIRED	WHOLLY OWNED DAILIES
1877	Hamilton *Spectator*
1897	*Ottawa Citizen*
1908	*Calgary Herald*
1912	*Edmonton Journal*
1920	*Winnipeg Tribune* (ceased publication August 27, 1979)
1923	*Vancouver Province*
1948	*Medicine Hat News*
1956	*North Bay Nugget*
1969	Montreal *Gazette*
	Owen Sound *Sun Times*
	Prince George Citizen

16. For analyses of Southam holdings, see Lea B. Hansen, "Southam Inc." Dominion Securities, 1979 and Anthony Arrell, "Southam Press Ltd.," Gardiner Watson Ltd., 1978.

1971	*Windsor Star*
	Brantford *Expositor*
1975	*Sault Star*
1979	*Vancouver Sun*
	PARTIALLY OWNED DAILIES
1953	*Kitchener-Waterloo Record* (48%)
1967	*Brandon Sun* (49%)

Southam's major holdings can be summarized as follows:

—Newspapers: 14 fully owned dailies, two partly owned dailies and the nationally distributed weekly business newspaper, *Financial Times of Canada.*

—Printing: 10 printing plants. One of the country's most important printing companies with the largest share of printing revenues coming from catalogues, magazines and booklets.

—Business Publications: Southam entered this field in 1960. Owns 75 business and professional publications serving such industries as construction, pulp and paper, forestry, mining, petroleum, medicine.

—Trade Shows: Produces 53 trade shows and exhibitions.

—Book Retailing. In 1978, Southam acquired Coles Book Stores, the largest chain of retail book stores in Canada. Coles also owns book stores in the United States.

—Electronic Media: Southam owns about 30 per cent of Selkirk, a broadly diversified broadcasting conglomerate. Selkirk owns or has major interests in five TV stations and 11 radio stations in Canada. Selkirk is also involved in Cable TV in Canada and the United States, movie making, radio stations in Britain, and computer-controlled communications systems.

Newspapers remain, by far, Southam's most important holdings. Based on circulation figures, Southam is the largest newspaper chain in Canada. Its 14 dailies in markets from Montreal to Vancouver have a combined circulation of 1.5 million compared to the one million circulation of 40 Thomson papers. Southam specializes in large city newspapers: it owns seven of the 12 English-language dailies that have a circulation above 100,000. Until the late 1970s, Southam papers faced competition in such markets as Montreal, Ottawa, Winnipeg, Calgary and Vancouver. Today, the only competition for Southam dailies is in Calgary and Edmonton, where the tabloid *Sun* papers have become new entrants in the newspaper market.

Thomson. The incredibly successful international economic Thomson empire had its start with a $200 downpayment on a Timmins, Ontario newspaper in 1934. That was all that Roy Thomson could afford when he purchased *The Timmins Daily Press* for $6,000, with $5,800 in promissory notes.[17] Thomson's rise to riches, power and honours—he was later to become Lord Thomson of

17. Russell Braddon, *Roy Thomson of Fleet Street,* (New York: Walker and Company, 1965). See also Lord Thomson of Fleet, *After I was Sixty,* (Don Mills, Ont., Thomas Nelson and Comp., 1975).

Fleet—is one of the most spectacular success stories of the twentieth century. He died a billionaire in 1976. His son Kenneth S. Thomson, who now heads the vast global enterprises says, "Everything that my family has today, and in terms of opportunities for the future, goes back to our newspaper organization."[18]

Thomson was a late bloomer in the newspaper field; he was already 40 when he bought the Timmins daily. Some of his previous business ventures were unsuccessful and he found it difficult to obtain credit, for the newsprint deliveries from Abitibi Pulp and Paper were on a strictly cash basis. Thomson was also active in operating radio stations in Northern Ontario. (An early partner in the broadcast ventures, Jack Kent Cooke, also went on to amass a fortune in the mass media.) In 1944, Thomson decided that his expansion would be in the newspaper field and purchased dailies in four Southern Ontario cities—Galt, Sarnia, Welland and Woodstock—for $888,000. (Southam thought the price was too high and had turned down the deal before it was offered to Thomson.) Over the next 10 years, Thomson added 10 more Canadian papers to his chain. In the late 1950s, the acquisition drive gained momentum and has since continued unabated. In 1982, Thomson Newspapers Ltd. owned 40 dailies and 12 weeklies in Canada, and 71 dailies and five weeklies in the United States.

The newspaper operations in Canada provided the cash flow for expansion into the U.S. market and for later diversification into numerous other enterprises: broadcasting, newspapers and weeklies in Britain, travel companies; real estate; North Sea oil rights; oil and gas holdings in the United States; high-technology communication; insurance, and giant retail holdings in Canada's Hudson's Bay Company, Simpsons, Simpson-Sears and Zellers. (When Thomson outbid George Weston Ltd. in the $640 million offer for control of Hudson's Bay, the country's largest retailer, the bidding was dubbed "Store Wars.")

Thomson's newspapers are outstanding profit-makers. In 1979, for example, the returns on net assets, before interest and income taxes, was just under 78 per cent. Thomson started small and grew big by continuing to think small. A key principle was to buy newspapers in small-town monopoly situations and turn them into efficient money-makers. Weeklies were changed to dailies when the communities grew big enough. He brought in the best printing equipment, emphasized automation, insisted on budgets and compared economic performance among the papers he owned. When Thomson bought his first newspaper in Timmins, he immediately sought ways to cut costs and asked the Canadian Press news agency for a special deal. When this didn't materialize, Thomson negotiated a discount rate with the telegraph company that was bringing the Canadian Press wire copy from North Bay to Timmins.

Getting the best possible deal, trimming expenses to the minimum, and bringing frugal but sound business practices to the newspaper business were catalysts in the dynamic growth pattern of the Thomson newspaper chain. Cheap small-town papers are no longer readily available in Canada but newspaper acquisition has continued. In 1980, Thomson absorbed the giant F.P. newspaper group for

18. Royal Commission on Newspapers, *op. cit.*, p. 91.

$165 million in what resembled, after bids and counter-bids by would-be buyers, an incredible poker game. As Kesterton has observed: "Originally you had newspapers swallowing newspapers; then you had chains swallowing newspapers and now you have chains swallowing chains."

The eight newspaper F.P. chain included such big city dailies as the Toronto *Globe and Mail*, the *Ottawa Journal*, the Winnipeg *Free Press* and the *Vancouver Sun*, a departure from the Thomson formula. The money-losing *Ottawa Journal* was closed down eight months later, the *Vancouver Sun* was sold to Southam and in Victoria, British Columbia, the morning and afternoon dailies were consolidated into one all-day paper. The financially troubled F.P. chain became highly profitable under Thomson ownership. In 1982, Thomson's Canadian newspaper holdings included two big dailies (in Toronto and Winnipeg), one of medium size (in Victoria) and 37 small circulation papers.

The Thomson chain has been frequently criticized, most recently by the Kent Commission, for its emphasis on profits, possibly at the expense of editorial quality. Except for the newly absorbed big dailies, the Thomson papers are on average considerably thinner than other newspapers of similar circulation, and they have a comparatively high ratio of advertising to "newshole" (all non-advertising) space.[19] But there is also evidence that Thomson has revitalized faltering dailies and, in changing weeklies to dailies, has contributed to the growth of the newspaper system. New printing presses and better layout have made many small Canadian dailies more readable and more profitable in a process that has generally been completed within 18 months.

There is some evidence that, after being purchased by Thomson, a small-city paper often becomes a little thinner and the share of advertising increases as a percentage of the newspaper's total space. Cost-cutting measures are frequently introduced. (At the *Cape Breton Post* in Sydney, Nova Scotia, for example, the paper discontinued its link with the *New York Times* news agency.) But the overall profile of content undergoes little change and, most important, there appears to be no decline in local news coverage. Thomson editors carefully count the number of local stories and there is an emphasis on maintaining and encouraging the ties of the individual papers to their respective cities of publication. Thomson has stated that in editorial matters there is no interference from corporate headquarters in Toronto: local autonomy is stressed.

Chain ownership has given Thomson considerable advantage in its relations with unions. At the *Peterborough Examiner* in 1968, for example, the paper continued publishing, although sharply reducing its local coverage, when editorial personnel belonging to the Newspaper Guild went on strike. There were reports that the paper's editorial staff was augmented by journalists brought in from other Thomson papers. At any rate, strikes have far more serious long-term implications for newspapers in competitive markets (for example, the defunct *Montreal Star*) than in monopoly situations.

---

19. Royal Commission on Newspapers, *op. cit.*, p. 69, especially Table 4.

The Tabloid Model.   Canada has two tabloid chains—one French, one English—and both are spectacularly successful. The newest tabloid chain has its origins in the *Toronto Sun,* which began publishing on November 1, 1971, the day after the closing of the 95-year-old *Toronto Telegram.* In fact, 68 of the *Sun's* original staff of 69 came from the *Telegram.* The *Sun* was started with a mere $375,000 of subscribed capital raised mainly by the well-known Toronto lawyer, Eddie Goodman.[20] Observers of the Canadian newspaper scene, including Lord Thomson and the then president of Southam, St. Clair Balfour, predicted that the *Sun* would not last long. To their surprise the *Toronto Sun's* performance has been outstanding. It has become a dynamic major force in the Toronto newspaper market with a daily circulation in 1981 of 255,000 (400,000 on Sundays), making it Canada's fourth-largest English daily. The *Sun* became a public corporation through stock offerings in 1978, the same year that it became a chain by starting publication of the *Edmonton Sun* (April 2nd, 1978). In the summer of 1980, the *Sun* chain expanded to Calgary, where it replaced the Thomson-owned *Calgary Albertan* (previously owned by F.P.). In 1982, Maclean Hunter purchased a 50 per cent interest in the *Sun* chain for $54 million.

The *Toronto Sun* company is non-unionized and has the latest in photocomposition, direct-entry terminals and offset printing technology. Labour costs at the *Sun* are an incredibly low 27 per cent of revenue compared with 38 per cent at the *Toronto Star.*[21]

In 1980, the Sun Corporation's consolidated revenues amounted to close to $60 million, an increase from $4.5 million only seven years earlier. The company has branched out into other fields: a general news service (United Press Canada, 80 per cent ownership); a business news service called UNIBIZ; commercial printing, Image Bank (a colour-photograph service for advertising agencies and publications), and manufacturing of newspaper boxes.

The *Sun* tabloid chain has its counterpart in the French press: *Le Journal de Montréal* (established in 1964) and *Le Journal de Québec* (established in 1967), controlled by Pierre Péladeau (Quebecor Inc.). The Péladeau company's diversified holdings in 1981 included five popular weeklies, 21 regional weeklies, the English-language Montreal weekly *Sunday Express,* printing plants, book publishing, record distribution and photo-film processing. Péladeau was also in the U.S. newspaper market where he established the Philadelphia *Journal* in 1977. It closed at the end of 1981.

The five tabloid papers of the Sun and Péladeau companies have a combined circulation of 788,000, or 14 per cent of the Canadian newspaper market.

REGIONALISM AND LOCALISM

A basic characteristic of the press in Canada is regionalism with a local emphasis.

---

20. H. Anthony Arrell, ''The Toronto Sun Publishing Corporation,'' a study prepared in 1978 by Gardiner Watson Limited (Toronto), Stockbroker.
21. *Ibid.*

This regional quality in the press has long been observed. Wilfrid Eggleston, one of the most noted students of the Canadian communications system, said in a brief to the Royal Commission on National Development in the Arts and Letters and Sciences in 1951:

An examination of the newspapers published at, say, Halifax, Quebec City, Toronto, Winnipeg and Vancouver will show that while a few subjects of national interest are covered in a common way and with much the same comments, there are striking regional and local interests which commonly transcend and crowd out the news in every regional centre.[22]

More recently, the Senate Study on the Mass Media said that Canadian newspapers "bear the stamp of regional disparity: quite aside from local content, a prairie newspaper is distinguishable from a paper published on the Atlantic coast, and to read the *Vancouver Sun* is a different experience from reading the Montreal *Gazette*."[23]

The Fragmented Press System

Studies on the press system in Canada have been vague about the implications of regionalism,[24] although the importance of this factor may be inferred from the absence of national newspapers that are widely read across the country and the astonishing number of Canadian cities—about 100—which have daily newspapers providing local, national and international news. Each of these 100 cities, with its immediate distribution area, might be considered a newspaper region. Certainly, one can conclude that the Canadian newspaper system is highly fragmented. No other country, except perhaps the United States, approaches this degree of fragmentation. This may be accounted for as follows: the local newspaper habit, the political system, and economic and social factors.

The Local Newspaper Habit

New communications technology has removed the physical difficulties of publishing national newspapers in an enormously big country. But the dominant pattern of Canadians buying their home-town daily is likely to continue in the foreseeable future.

Ottawa is the most important market for out-of-town dailies; influential Montreal and Toronto papers are bound to be of considerable interest in the federal capital. The penetration of the out-of-town dailies, however, is small compared to the circulation of the Ottawa *Citizen* in the English market and *Le Droit* in the

22. Wilfrid Eggleston, "The Press in Canada," Royal Commission Studies—A Selection of Essays prepared for The Royal Commission on National Development in the Arts, Letters and Sciences (Ottawa: King's Printer, 1951), p. 49.
23. Senate Committee on Mass Media, *op. cit.,* Vol. III, p. 187.
24. For a discussion of different approaches for classifying regions in Canada, see Paul Fox, "Regionalism and Confederation," in Mason Wade (ed.) *Regionalism in the Canadian Community, 1867-1967* (Toronto: University of Toronto Press, 1969), pp. 3-29. See also J.E. Hodgetts, "Regional Interests and Policy in a Federal Structure," *Canadian Journal of Economics and Political Science,* Vol. XXXII, No. 1, February 1966, p. 10.

French market. In virtually no major market do outside papers have a comparable circulation to the local daily.

On a circulation basis, there are no national newspapers in Canada, although the *Globe and Mail* has taken far-reaching steps to achieve this goal. In the fall of 1980, the Toronto daily introduced a "national edition" in two cities. In 1982, the "national" was being printed simultaneously in five cities: Moncton, Ottawa, Winnipeg, Calgary and Vancouver. Stripped of news stories and advertising that is of local (Toronto) interest only, the much thinner "national edition" is made up of two parts: a 24-page news section and the financial section *Report on Business*.

The *Globe and Mail* is the only paper available across the country on the day of publication and may have a special appeal to persons in business, government and the media. Also, it has news bureaus in Halifax, Quebec City, Montreal, Ottawa, Winnipeg, Calgary, Edmonton and Vancouver. The infrastructure for a national newspaper, in terms of news coverage and distribution, is now in place.

The facsimile transmission system used by the *Globe and Mail* is the most advanced in the world. Laser beams at the Toronto headquarters of the *Globe and Mail* scan the newspages, which have been prepared on thin pieces of cardboard, and electronic signals are transmitted from an earth station on the paper's parking lot via the Anik A-3 satellite some 36,000 kilometres above the equator to receiving stations at the printing plants. This is all performed at the rate of one page a minute. The electronic signals are converted by facsimile receivers to photographic negatives the size of newspaper pages and used to make printing plates for the presses that produce 700 papers per minute.

The *Globe and Mail*'s national venture is in line with the paper's efforts before the turn of the century to reach an audience beyond Toronto, and in this century to extend its circulation beyond Ontario. As noted earlier, the *Globe* published in London, Ontario in the 1860s. In 1887, the paper had its own high-speed train for deliveries to London and other Ontario points. In 1938, the *Globe and Mail* was experimenting with printing outside of Toronto and achieved a number of technological breakthroughs that were passed on to the allied governments in World War II. In the 1960s, the *Globe and Mail* experiments showed that a "national daily" was technically possible by transmitting pictures of newspages via the telephone company's microwave links. But surveys indicated that, in economic terms, and especially in attracting advertisers, such a paper would face staggering problems.

Today, the satellite transmission system is faster and less expensive than the telephone hook-up of the 1960s. Furthermore, projections indicate a growth market in such specialized areas as business, finance and travel for national advertising in newspapers. In 1975, national advertising amounted to $60,000,000; by 1980, it had climbed to $106,000,000. Although television is by far the most important medium for national advertising, a number of problems—including limits to the amount of advertising that can be sold on TV, high advertising rates and increasing fragmentation of TV audiences—are making national newspaper advertising more competitive.

In November 1981, the circulation of the *Globe and Mail* outside of Ontario was about 75,000, compared to 20,000 before the start of the satellite network a year earlier. But 35,000 of this new circulation is made up of former subscribers to *Report on Business*—previously sold separately outside Ontario—who automatically received the news section of the "national edition" at no extra charge. The circulation growth of the "national" in the first year was moderate, but may develop momentum with the expansion of printing facilities to five cities.

Globe and Mail circulation accounts for six per cent of all newspapers sold in Canada. The circulation profile, as illustrated in Chart VI.5, shows that 80 per

CHART VI.5. Globe and Mail Circulation Distribution

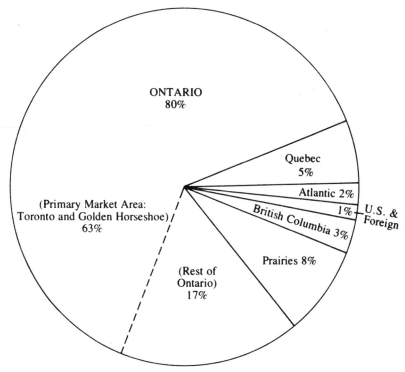

Total Circulation, March 31, 1981— 334,193
(Sept. 30, 1981—   355,762)

cent of distribution in 1981 was in Ontario, five per cent in Alberta, five per cent in Quebec and the rest of the country accounted for about eight per cent. Another way to examine the *Globe and Mail* circulation figures is on the basis of the provincial penetration rate per 100 households, as shown in Chart VI.6. Nine per cent of Ontario households receive the *Globe and Mail*, 2.6 per cent in Alberta,

1.5 per cent in Manitoba and about one per cent, or less, in the other provinces. In comparing these findings with the general Canadian circulation and penetration figures in Table VI.1, it is clear that *Globe and Mail*'s share of the newspaper market is very small outside of Ontario. In most cases the "national edition" is a second newspaper with readers also buying the local daily. The paper remains some distance from having a readership that would reflect a wide and deep appeal across the country, as in the case of national newspapers published in Tokyo, London and Paris.

The Political System

While federalism requires good internal communications on a national basis, it also discourages the establishment of national newspapers. Canada's federal system makes each provincial capital an important centre for decision making for many of the matters that vitally affect people at the local or most immediate level. Numerous facets of political, economic and social activities are under the jurisdiction of provincial legislatures and governments which also control the local and municipal level of government. At the community level, where there is considerable interaction between the population and the provincial authorities, there may well be much interest in localized or regional news coverage which has little appeal to readers beyond the provincial or regional boundaries, if not at the city limits. This form of political system tends to encourage regional containment of the press. No national newspaper could possibly relate intimately to the local

CHART VI.6.   Globe and Mail Circulation in Canadian Provinces in Proportion to Households:Penetration per 100 Households

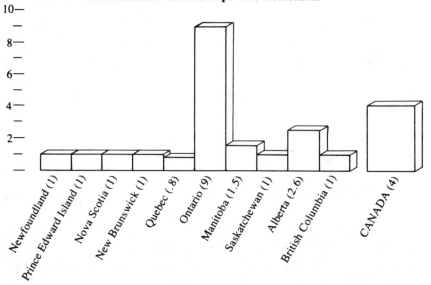

September 30, 1981

citizen on matters under provincial and municipal jurisdiction that affect his personal life and career and remain of considerable interest to him.[25]

The local and regional orientation of Canadian dailies was observed in an examination of Canadian newspaper coverage of the FLQ crisis in 1970 and in research studies looking at newspaper content in less troubled times. Content analysis studies of a number of medium-sized newspapers showed that far more space is devoted to local news than to Canadian national news. These studies also confirmed the provincial-regional containment of newspaper content. In some cases, fully two-thirds of all space devoted to Canadian news focused on the city and the province of publication. There is accumulating evidence that news from the "rest of Canada," except for national stories from Ottawa, receives little attention. This has serious implications for interregional communications interaction.

Economic and Social Factors

Localism in Canadian newspapers also appears to be related to the spending pattern of the Canadian population. The average household in Canada in 1981 spent about $11,500 at the retail level.[26] Mass spending power, studies have shown, provides enough spending decisions to support advertising as a major economic activity.[27] Canadian data[28] appear to bear out this conclusion. In 1981, gross advertising revenue reached $4.3 billion, or 1.32 per cent of the Gross National Product. The importance of advertising for Canadian journalism can be traced to the pioneering days of newspapers in British North America. In strict economic terms, the media exist as a message bearer for people who want to sell something to the readers. The readers are apparently satisfied with this arrangement, as a recent study in Quebec on the diffusion of information claims.[29] Statistics Canada figures show that the bulk of family spending takes place in the home community. Canadians spend well over 50 per cent of their earnings at retail outlets. To attract this vast amount of money—$95 billion in 1981[30]—advertisers must go to the local media, and this provides the economic base for the large number of dailies in Canada. Advertising, then, as it exists, supports and reinforces the local press.

---

25. In the United States, where there is also a federal system and the large size of country is a factor, localism in news institutions is also very pronounced. See Bagdikian, *The Information Machines, op. cit.*, p. 72.

26. Total retail sales in Canada amounted to $94,500,000,000 in 1981. See Statistics Canada Catalogue 63-005 (1981). There were 8,233,000 households in 1981.

27. Bagdikian, *The Information Machines, op. cit.*, p. 73.

28. For details of the growth pattern of retail markets in Canada, see Statistics Canada, *Family Expenditures in Canada*, (Ottawa: Supply and Services, 1980).

29. Québec, Assemblée Nationale, Enquête Sur La Diffusion de L'Information Au Québec, 2ième partie: "Sondage Auprès du Public," La Commission Parlementaire Spéciale sur les Problèmes de la Liberté de Presse, mars 1973, Vol. V, pp. 25-47.

30. Total wages and salaries in 1981 amounted to $184,752,000,000. Statistics Canada Catalogue 13-001.

THE PREDOMINANCE OF SMALL CIRCULATION DAILIES

Related to the localism of newspapers is the circulation spread in the press system. In 1981, there was one daily, the *Toronto Star*, with a circulation of a half-million. In all, there were 10 dailies—three in Montreal, three in Toronto, one each in Ottawa, Winnipeg, Edmonton and Vancouver—with circulations above 150,000. Seven papers had circulation figures between 100,000 and 150,000. The average circulation is 47,000, with 88 dailies, or 75 per cent, having circulations below this figure. Well over half of the dailies have circulations of less than 25,000. (See Table VI.8).

TABLE VI.8. Circulation Profile of Canadian Dailies

CIRCULATION	NUMBER OF DAILIES	GROUP- AND CONGLOMERATE- OWNED	INDEPENDENTLY OWNED
150,000 & over	10	10	0
100,000-150,000	7	5	2
50,000-100,000	12	10	2
25,000-50,000	18	12	6
10,000-25,000	31	26	5
Under 10,000	39	25	14

THE SHIFT FROM AFTERNOON TO MORNING AND ALL-DAY PAPERS

A revolution is taking place in newspaper reading habits, reflecting changes in lifestyles. Canadians, especially in large cities, are reading their newspapers earlier in the day and a number of afternoon dailies have switched to the morning market.

In 1981, four of the country's major evening newspapers—the *Toronto Star*, Quebec's *Le Soleil*, the *Edmonton Journal* and the Ottawa *Citizen*—started publishing morning editions, thus becoming all-day papers. The *London Free Press,* previously published in the morning and afternoon, switched to morning only.

The trend to morning and all-day papers is clearly shown by circulation figures (Chart VI.7). In 1981, the morning and all-day papers accounted for 56 per cent of the total Canadian newspaper market, compared to 24 per cent in 1970. Today, only three of 16 papers with circulations above 100,000 are afternoon dailies.

Afternoon newspaper circulation, including the p.m. share of all-day papers, has declined moderately since 1970; all the increase in newspaper circulation has been in the morning market. Furthermore, there has been a dramatic increase in Sunday circulation. In 1970, one daily published on Sunday with a circulation of

45,000; in 1981, there were nine dailies publishing on Sunday with a combined circulation of about 1.5 million. (The *Globe and Mail* and the Winnipeg *Free Press* have indicated that they plan to publish on Sundays.)

CHART VI.7. **Circulation Changes of Morning and All-Day, Afternoon and Sunday Newspapers, 1970-1981**

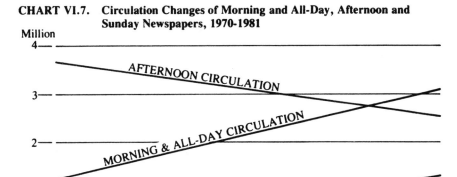

INCREASING IMPORTANCE OF TABLOID PAPERS

The circulation of tabloids has climbed from virtually zero to over 900,000 in the past 20 years. The tabloid phenomenon is partly a response to the newspaper needs of young people brought up with television: "they are used to a brief presentation of news." In Quebec province, where television has an especially strong appeal, tabloids account for 47 per cent of French-language newspaper circulation. In the English-language press, the tabloid explosion started later—in 1971—with the tabloids in 1981 accounting for 10 per cent of circulation.

The world's first newspapers had small, book-sized pages. Ben Bagdikian points out that oversize pages have their origin in the tax stamp which was introduced in Britain in 1712 and later spread to Europe and the British colonies and provinces in North America.[31] The tax was paid on each newspaper page. In switching to the oversize pages, the newspapers could carry the same content as fuller papers, and save on tax. By the time the "tax on knowledge" was rescinded, press technology was geared to large pages and, equally important, public habits favouring the large pages had taken hold.

Today, when many newspapers are read in such public places as crowded buses, planes and subways, the small-format tabloid papers make sense. But tabloids are not just big papers cut down in size. Many have a sensational orienta-

---

31. Bagdikian, *The Information Machines, op. cit.*

tion: attention-grabbing headlines, crisp stories and plenty of big pictures. Senator Keith Davey has referred to them as "that remarkable invention, newspapers for people who cannot read."[32]

The "bouncy irreverence" of the content has wide appeal, especially to the young. There is a tendency to overlook the political and social importance of tabloids; they present a broad spectrum of viewpoints through opinion pieces written by columnists. It is noteworthy that the tabloid *Toronto Sun,* through its daring publication of the contents of a secret government document, is the only Canadian newspaper ever prosecuted under the Official Secrets Act.

H. Anthony Arrell, an astute observer of the economics of the newspaper industry, has listed some major reasons for the success of the tabloids:[33]

—content appeal
—convenient for readers using public transportation
—one edition (compared to five for the *Toronto Star*) that is easily distributed to newsstands and coin boxes in the early morning hours
—circulation that is largely city-core, making it attractive to advertisers
—advertising rates (per thousand readers) that are lower than the costs of competing papers.

The tabloids have created a market for themselves in big cities among people who previously did not read newspapers. In 1981, Winnipeg and Halifax were added to the list of cities where tabloids were attempting to introduce competition in monopoly markets. The competitive aspect of tabloids is an important development in the newspaper system.

SUMMARY AND OBSERVATIONS

Our analysis shows that a combination of political, technological, economic and social factors gives rise to the distinctive characteristics of the Canadian press system. The cutting of the umbilical economic tie between newspapers and politics, accompanied by technological changes (fast presses, cheap paper, telephone and telegraph) unleashed market forces early this century that led to a restructuring of the press system. The editor/politician gave way to the businessman/publisher. The growth of the mass market was staggering; per capita newspaper consumption doubled between 1901 and 1911. By 1920, the outline of the modern press era was clearly visible: newspaper competition was on the decline and the first chain (Southam) was entrenched in five important markets. Economic pragmatism had become the main motivating force in the evolution of the press.

The shift in emphasis from newspapers as journals of opinion with a strong political orientation to newspapers that provide largely news and information

32. *Globe and Mail,* September 16, 1981. p. 7.
33. Arrell, "The Toronto Sun Publishing Corporation," *op. cit.*

accelerated in the 1920s and 1930s. Newspapers generally continued to support their favourite political party until World War II, but the editors-in-chief no longer played any real political role: "They had become spokesmen rather than intellectuals in the vanguard of ideas and policies of their respective parties."[34] Today, the party link is almost nonexistent.

The financial success of the newspaper industry can be attributed to several factors, including the absence of competition, the phenomenal growth of the Canadian economy since World War II (advertising revenues are closely tied to the GNP) and increased productivity through automation. Chains have numerous advantages over independent publishers: they have resources to modernize and automate, they are in a better position to absorb temporary losses due to strikes or other economic problems and they provide financial and administrative skills that are often in short supply in small publishing enterprises. Individual newspaper publishers, for their part, have sold to chains to harvest profits (chains offer high prices, often in the form of cash and stock), to resolve family disputes and to avoid crippling succession duties.

Canadian tax policies (sections 19 and 20 of the Income Tax Act) provide a sheltered market for newspapers by protecting them from foreign competition. Furthermore, newspaper companies find it profitable to borrow money to expand their holdings inside and outside the communications sector, at home and abroad. In this way, Canadian policies aimed at assuring Canadian ownership of the media and stimulating the economy have facilitated concentration of ownership and the growth of conglomerates.

The consolidation and concentration of newspaper ownership, including the rise of national chains, is divorced from the fragmentation of newspaper audiences (as evidenced by the circulation spread) and the patterns of messages flow (local and regional containment). The readership profile provides further support of fragmentation based on language and province of residence. French-speaking Canadians in Quebec and English-speaking Canadians do not read each other's paper; Canadians in one province do not read newspapers from another province.

In accounting for the fragmentation of the Canadian newspaper system, it was noted that the economics of publishing as well as political structure tend to steer newspaper interest in the local and regional direction. Newspapers in Canada are intimately related to the city of publication; thus, the intercity relationship in a regional and national context is of great importance. Cities in the Canadian setting have an economic, political, cultural and social relationship with the region in which they are located. The tie between cities and region is so intimate, argues Mildred Schwartz, that eventually regions may be seen as structural emanations of cities.[35] Professor Schwartz has pointed out that the growth of cities in Canada

---

34. Jean-Louis Gagnon, "Communication, Identity, Unity," Gerstein lecture, *op. cit.*
35. Mildred A. Schwartz, *Politics and Territory: The Sociology of Regional Persistence in Canada* (Montreal: McGill-Queen's University Press, 1974), p. 315.

has not taken place in such a way as to create national bonds cutting across regions.[36] In her view, there is no metropolitan dominance that links various parts of the country and the channelling effect appears to reinforce pre-existing barriers of a political, physical and cultural nature.[37] The fragmentation of the communications flow and the structural fragmentation of the press system observed here reflect and reinforce problems related to the unity aspect of Canadian federalism.

36. *Ibid.*, p. 318.
37. *Ibid.* See also J. Ross Mackay, "The Interactive Hypothesis and Boundaries in Canada: A Preliminary Study," *The Canadian Geographer*, Vol. 11, 1958, pp. 1-8.

CHAPTER VII

NEWSPAPERS AND GOVERNMENT IN CANADA: THE KENT COMMISSION REPORT

August 27, 1980, was a traumatic day in Canadian newspaper history. The *Toronto Star* declared in a red-ink headline story on page one: "Two more great newspapers died, the worst day in the worst year that Canadian journalism has ever suffered." The 94-year-old *Ottawa Journal*, owned by the Thomson newspaper chain, and the 90-year-old *Winnipeg Tribune*, part of the Southam chain, had ceased publication. The lights were being switched off and 800 employees were out of work. August 27, 1980, may have been a bad day for Canadian journalism but on the Toronto Stock Exchange newspaper stocks were having one of their best days ever: Thomson shares were trading at $20.75, their highest price up to that day in 1980, and Southam climbed a dramatic $1.12, closing at $38 a share.

The closings of the *Ottawa Journal* and *Winnipeg Tribune* were the direct result of economic expediency. The papers were certainly not beyond the means of their owners: Thomson and Southam have been among the most profitable of Canadian companies. With the two papers out of the way, even higher profits were in the offing and, in fact, have materialized. The demise of the *Ottawa Journal* gave Southam's *Citizen* a monopoly in the federal capital, while Thomson obtained a prized monopoly situation for his *Winnipeg Free Press* with the disappearance of the *Tribune*.

The Thomson and Southam companies insisted that they had arrived at their decisions to close their respective dailies in Ottawa and Winnipeg independently, and that there were no trade-offs. But there were other developments on August 27, involving the two newspaper chains, in Vancouver and Montreal. Thomson sold the *Vancouver Sun* and its 30 per cent interest in the Montreal *Gazette* to Southam for $57,250,000, giving Southam two other monopoly markets. It was an important date in carving up Canada's newspaper markets between the profitable giants.

Media critics and government officials declared that the demise of the *Ottawa Journal* and *Winnipeg Tribune,* both of which were respected newspapers dating back to the early years of Canadian confederation, was bad for democracy. The leader of the Opposition party in Parliament, Joseph Clark, said the situation was "alarming" and called for a parliamentary inquiry. A spokesman for the socialist New Democratic Party alleged there was "corporate collusion." Within a week, the Liberal government of Prime Minister Pierre Trudeau appointed a Royal Commission into newspaper ownership and control which would examine social, economic and political aspects of the newspaper industry, including their impact on local communities, on national unity and politics generally. The Royal Commission, headed by Professor Thomas Kent of Dalhousie University, was asked to make recommendations on how to overcome the bad effects of newspaper concentration. At the same time, government officials in Ottawa who were concerned with monopoly aspects of Canadian business began to examine whether the Thomson-Southam dealings were in violation of the Combines Investigation Act. In the following weeks, teams of Anti-Combines investigators raided the Toronto headquarters of the Thomson and Southam chains. Criminal charges, still before the courts, were laid against the Southam and Thomson companies. These developments amount to the biggest-ever investigation of Canada's newspaper industry and carry with them the possibility of governmental intervention.

GOVERNMENT INTERVENTION: GENERAL OBSERVATIONS

Government intervention in the printed press sector in Canada is highly controversial. The most important reason for concern is the implication for freedom of speech and expression; governmental control of this kind is abhorrent. The trend in Canada has been toward "open Government" (see Chapter III) and overcoming some of the constitutional and legal restraining influences on political communications flow. Any policies that would be interpreted as a reversal of this trend would be quickly discredited.

A second reason for viewing government intervention with concern is that in Canada there is a strong belief in the commercial ownership of the mass media, especially the printed press, operating in a competitive marketplace. Commercial media are apparently associated with having a monopoly on democratic principles. This view is partly based on American outlooks and practices. "Free" media systems are associated with "commercial control," while "totalitarian" systems are seen as those where there is "political control" of the media. Government intrusion in the mass media sphere, and particularly in the printed press sector, is labelled by critics as undesirable paternalism and a threat to press freedom. This ideological perspective is bolstered by Canada's historical experience in the printed press sector: privately owned newspapers played a major role in fostering democratic practices and in nation building. A third argument against government intervention is the limited federal jurisdiction in the newspaper field.

Although newspapers and magazines in Canada are owned mostly by companies that have national, and sometimes international, media interests, they are generally regarded as local enterprises in the city of publication and, under the British North America Act, the provinces have jurisdiction over the property interests. This situation complicates but does not preclude federal activity in the "national interest." Ottawa can assert itself in a number of ways, including:

—Blocking provincial actions that may interfere with the free flow of communications. The Ottawa record here is ambivalent and appears at times to be motivated by political interests. In 1937, the federal government sent the Alberta Press Act to the Supreme Court for a ruling on the constitutionality of the legislation that would have enabled the Social Credit government in Alberta to severely limit press freedoms.[1] The courts found the legislation unconstitutional (*ultra vires*) and the bill was disallowed, thus effectively blocking provincial censorship. In contrast, however, Ottawa did not resort to the courts to abort the so-called Padlock Law of the Maurice Duplessis government in Quebec province in 1939, although the legislation was effectively used to limit freedom of speech and the press.[2] It was left to private parties to absorb the costs for the many years of litigation, litigation which resulted in a ruling that the law was unconstitutional.

—Canadian ownership requirements. This requirement has existed in the newspaper industry since January 1, 1966. A Canadian newspaper is deemed owned by a Canadian if at least 75 per cent of the voting shares are owned by Canadian citizens. The only papers exempted from the "Canadian nationality" requirements are *The Red Deer Advocate* of Red Deer, Alberta, and four weeklies that have been owned for some years by a British publisher (*The Liverpool Post and Echo*). The citizenship provisions protect Canadian newspaper owners from foreign takeovers. The newspaper industry is thus a protected species and derives a number of benefits from this status. Potential competition financed by investors from abroad is effectively blocked. With their home market protected, Canadian communications companies can be less cautious when they make stock offerings to

1. The Alberta Press Act was entitled: "Act to Ensure the Publication of Accurate News and Information." The Lieutenant-Governor of Alberta did not give the bill the required royal assent; he reserved it for the "signification of the Governor-General's pleasure." The Federal Prime Minister, Mr. Mackenzie King, announced on November 3, 1937 the government's decision to refer the press legislation, two other Alberta Social Credit bills and the question of the constitutionality of the Crown exercising the royal prerogatives of reservation and disallowances to the Supreme Court. The Supreme Court judgement was rendered March 4, 1938. *Reference re: Alberta Statutes [1938] S.C.R. 100.* See G. Stuart Adam, "The Sovereignty of the Publicity System: A Case Study of the Alberta Press Act," in G. S. Adam (ed.), *Journalism, Communication and the Law*, Toronto: Prentice-Hall, 1976, pp. 154-171. See also W. H. Kesterton, *The Law and the Press in Canada*, Toronto: McClelland and Stewart, 1976.

2. *Switzman v. Elbling and A. G. for Quebec, [1957] S.C.R. 285.* The notorious Padlock Act was entitled "An Act to Protect the Province Against Communist Propaganda." There was no definition of communism and the law was effectively used to stifle freedom of discussion. For some details of the use of the Padlock Law against newspapers, see Kesterton, *A History of Journalism in Canada, op. cit.,* pp. 234-238. See also F.R. Scott, *Civil Liberties and Canadian Federalism*, Toronto: University of Toronto Press, 1959.

raise funds for increasing their media holdings. Canadian companies have acquired significant media interests in other countries, especially Britain and the United States.

—Taxation policies. There is considerable scope for federal intervention through taxes on individuals and corporations. In fact, the Canadian ownership requirements discussed above are embodied in the income tax bill passed by Parliament on June 28, 1965.[3] There can be no income tax deductions for advertising in newspapers that are not owned by Canadians, thus making it impossible for the papers to be economically viable. Taxation policy was used in 1976 in Bill C-58 in order to provide a suitable climate for *Maclean's* to emerge as Canada's first newsmagazine. Related to tax policies are economic measures that may be initiated in various departments of government. The Post Office rates for newspaper distribution, for example, are important for the economics of the industry. Taxes on promotional inserts in newspapers provide another example of using financial measures in the newspaper sphere. Taxation measures of this kind often generate great controversy, in that they have implications far beyond the economic structure of the newspaper industry. Advertising duties, excise duties and stamp duty—labelled by critics as "taxes on knowledge"—have been part of the print media experience in Canada.

—The Combines Investigation Act. Under this legislation, the federal government views certain monopolistic practices as criminal offences, subject to punishment under the Criminal Code, an area of exclusive federal jurisdiction.[4] Ottawa used this route in its unsuccessful attempt to dismantle the Irving monopoly of all English-language newspapers in New Brunswick. The conviction was overthrown on appeal, precisely because of the difficult demands on the prosecution in criminal offences. Changes in the Combines Investigation Act would be required if the government selected this approach for dealing with monopoly problems in newspapers.

—Import controls and duties. Newspapers are not significantly affected, as Canada is self-sufficient in newsprint production and indeed is one of the world's leading suppliers.[5] Ottawa has used import controls and duties on several occasions to enhance the economic environment for Canada's periodical industry. The experience has generally been unsatisfactory, partly because of inconsistencies in policies associated with change in government.

—The federal spending power. There are no constitutional restrictions on federal spending power and Ottawa could intervene here to foster competition in the newspaper industry. In the early days of Canadian journalism, gov-

3. Canadian Income Tax Act Revised, Part I (Div. B.) S 19, 1981.
4. Revised Statutes of Canada 1970, Chapter C-23. Parliament is now considering more stringent legislation.
5. Controls and duties on newsprint imports have been used in a number of countries to stifle press criticism of the government. This is essentially a practice associated with totalitarian governments.

ernment financial support for newspapers was the rule. The unfortunate consequences of financial dependence on government were discussed in Chapter V.

THE KENT COMMISSION: MAIN FINDINGS

The Royal Commission on Newspapers submitted its report to the Cabinet on July 1, 1981.[6] It painted a dreary picture of Canada's daily newspaper industry in which, it said, quality was being sacrificed for profits. The report upholds the principle of freedom of the press—that the press must be free of undue government interference—but concludes that government remedial action was indeed required to free the press from extraneous interest, specifically newspaper chains, that limit this freedom.[7] The details for the proposed structural changes in the newspaper business are outlined later in this chapter.

ABSENCE OF COMPETITION

The Commission noted that newspaper competition is virtually nonexistent in Canada. The economics of advertising created an overwhelming thrust towards newspaper monopolies: for advertisers, one newspaper for a community is more cost-efficient than two. Owning a monopoly newspaper is a highly profitable business venture.

The disappearance of head-on competition was the culmination of a long process and was not directly caused by concentration of ownership.[8] The monopoly situation appears to be irreversible and the Commission did not put forward recommendations to revive competition.

In voicing its concern about the absence of competition, the Kent Commission rejected the argument that competing media voices are supplied by radio and television. Newspapers, the Commission said, (i) are media of record, (ii) are principal collectors of news and (iii) supply through their news feeds to Canadian Press much of the news used by the broadcast media.[9] Tradition is yet another factor that, in the Commission's opinion, makes newspapers the principal internal influence on setting the agenda of public affairs. In the absence of competition, the reader is deprived of choice and the Kent Commission argues that "the special responsibilities of the monopoly newspapers are awesome."[10]

CONCENTRATION OF OWNERSHIP

The Kent Commission conclusions dealt in the main part with concentration of newspaper ownership in chains. This, it says, is "bad" and should not have been

6. The Report was made public August 18, 1981. The research studies on which the Report was partly based were released some months later.
7. The Royal Commission on Newspapers (1981), *Report, op. cit.*, p. 237.
8. *Ibid.*, p. 215.
9. *Ibid.*, p. 216.
10. *Ibid.*, p. 217.

permitted. The process of "monstrous concentration" has a momentum that is likely to grow unless something is done about it. The Commission had a dire warning: "Under existing law and policy, the process of concentration will continue to a bitter end: company will take over company, agglomeration will proceed, until all Canadian newspapers are divisions of one or two great conglomerates."[11]

The Commission found the present state of concentration "entirely unacceptable" for a democratic society. "Too much power is put in too few hands, and it is power without accountability."[12]

The Commission makes some distinction between good chains and bad chains and expressed concern that the bad would eventually absorb the good. Specifically, the Commission thought that Southam—"it spends millions of dollars a year providing better newspapers than any hard-nosed business calculation requires"—was ripe for a takeover by a conglomerate such as Thomson, which could produce greater profits by eliminating "extra costs" (in other words, reducing editorial expenditures). The Commission was also concerned that some of the remaining "independently owned" newspapers might be absorbed by chains. Time and again, the Commission speaks of the need to raise the quality of editorial standards above the level provided by the Thomson organization.[13]

The Commission asserts that, in the fulfillment of the newspaper's professional reponsibility to the community, editorial judgements "should be free from outside financial interests."[14]

The way the Commission sees it, the conglomerates should be kept out of the newsrooms. In a stinging indictment, the Commission notes that the conglomerates claim that they are not in the newsroom now, that "they have the power but they abstain." "Every reasonable person knows," says the Commission, "that it is far from the whole truth," and that is why newspapers do not stand high in public esteem.[15] The chain of command from the corporate structure ensures that their trusted agents keep the papers in line.

The Commission attached particular importance to its ranking of newspapers on the basis of how much they spend on editorial content as a percentage of revenue. It found that, on average, newspapers spent 15 per cent of revenues on editorial expenses. It drew up a table of 82 dailies: 34 of them spent above that average and 48 spent below. This table was used to make qualitative assertions about newspapers.

SUGGESTIONS TO THE NEWSPAPER INDUSTRY: VOLUNTARY MEASURES

The Report offers a few suggestions to the newspaper industry that would improve the situation. These can be divided into two groups. The first set of pro-

---

11. *Ibid.*, p. 220.
12. *Ibid.*
13. *Ibid.*
14. *Ibid.*, p. 233.
15. *Ibid.*, p. 233.

posals is aimed at raising the educational standards of journalists and it is the belief of the Commission that the newspaper industry should provide funds for this. The Commission did not think highly of journalism schools—at least not at the undergraduate level—and expressed the hope that persons educated in political science, economics, languages, business and history, among other fields, could seek careers in journalism. Specifically, the Commission suggested the establishment of a national training foundation or institute that could help provide journalists with ''the range, the expertise, the professionalism they need.''[16] Newspapers were also urged to provide in-house training programs devoted not only to reporting problems but also to bringing about better relations among management, the unions and editorial people.

The second set of suggestions constitutes a self-policing process. Newspapers, said the Commission, should become enthusiastically involved in press councils. ''Those who fail to do so are extremely short-sighted.''[17] The Davey Senate Committee had made strong recommendations for press councils a dozen years earlier but they have not caught on widely in Canada. At present only three provinces—Quebec, Ontario and Alberta—have press councils. Quebec's is the most dynamic and has some of the characteristics envisaged in the Davey Report. In Ontario, relatively few papers belong to the press council, diminishing its usefulness. Alberta's press council, according to the Kent Commission, is, at most, ''a pale imitation of the model.''[18] A major aspect of press councils is that they provide a forum for the public to lodge complaints against newspapers.

The Commission also urged the newspapers to appoint ombudsmen, who would serve as their own most severe critics. Four dailies presently have ombudsmen: The *Toronto Star* (which pioneered the practice in Canada), the Edmonton *Journal,* the Montreal *Gazette* and *Le Soleil* of Quebec City.

These suggestions are voluntary steps proposed to the newspaper industry. The Commission's recommendations urge remedial action by the federal government.

THE KENT COMMISSION: MAIN RECOMMENDATIONS

The Commission concluded that much of the press in Canada ''is not dedicated exclusively to the purposes of the press, to the discharge of its public responsibilities.''[19] Freedom of the press, argues the Commission, is undermined by the high degree of concentration of ownership and control of newspapers by interests whose business concerns extend far beyond their particular newspapers. Serious questions are raised as to whether the outside business interests of newspaper publishing companies are taking priority over efforts toward journalistic excellence.

The Commission recommends a legislative approach, in the form of a Canadian Newspaper Act, to ''secure for the press the freedom that is essential to a

---

16. *Ibid.,* p. 225.
17. *Ibid.*
18. Ibid.
19. *Ibid.,* p. 237.

democratic society from coast to coast.''[20] The proposed legislation, described as modest in the Royal Commission Report, could lead to far-reaching governmental intervention in the press sector. The recommendations can be divided into three areas: ownership restraints, financial incentives and journalistic independence.

OWNERSHIP RESTRAINTS

These restraints are aimed at blocking further concentration of ownership and cross-media ownership and to ''correct the very worst cases of concentration that now exist.'' The restraints include the following features:

On national newspapers:

No ownership of a national newspaper by a company that owns other newspapers.

(i) Thomson would have to sell its prestigious *Globe and Mail* or divest itself of its 39 lesser papers.

On regional ownership dominance:

Extreme geographic concentration would be prohibited and some newspapers would have to be sold.

(i) In New Brunswick, the Irving family—owner of all English-language dailies in the province—would have to sell its newspaper holdings either in Moncton or Saint John.

(ii) In Saskatchewan, the Armadale company (controlled by Michael Sifton) would have to sell its newspapers either in Regina or Saskatoon.

On the limits of chain growth:

Limitations on the future growth of group ownership based on the *number* of newspapers, *circulation* and *geographic proximity*. These restraints can be summarized as the *rule of five*. The maximum size of an evolving chain would be *five* newspapers, provided their combined circulation does not exceed *five* per cent of the total Canadian newspaper circulation and the papers in the chain are *five* hundred kilometres apart (or at least not in the same geographic region.)

---

20. *Ibid.*.

On cross-media ownership:

No ownership of a daily newspaper and broadcast outlet in the same community.

(i) Southam would have to sell its holdings in Selkirk, a major broadcasting company. At present, Southam newspapers and Selkirk broadcasting stations exist side by side in several cities, including Hamilton, Edmonton, Calgary and Vancouver.

(ii) In Saint John, New Brunswick, Irving would have to sell either its broadcast or newspaper holdings.

(iii) In London, Ontario, the Blackburn family would have to sell either the *Free Press* or its broadcast stations.

A daily newspaper could not be the dominant owner of community newspapers (e.g., a weekly) in its area of circulation. (However, Torstar, which is the publisher of the *Toronto Star* and virtually all community papers in the metropolitan Toronto area, would not be required to divest itself of the community papers.)

Newspapers would not be allowed to own videotax carriage systems. They could, however, become providers of content for such electronic information operations.

On the starting and closing of newspapers:

There would be no restraints on starting a "truly new" newspaper.

Sixty days' public notice would be required before a newspaper could be closed.

On preventing conglomerate control:

There could be no purchase of a newspaper by a person or company whose net assets outside the newspaper industry were greater than the assets of the newspaper being sought.

FINANCIAL INCENTIVES

The financial measures are aimed at improving editorial quality and encouraging local private investment in newspapers.

On increasing spendings on editorial content:

An editorial spending equalization formula. This would include tax credits for newspapers that spend more than the industry's average on editorial expenses (as a percentage of total newspaper revenue), and tax surcharges for those spending less. The monies in tax credit would presumably equal those in tax surcharges. Thus, the scheme could be seen as an editorial spendings transfer plan, with the low spenders subsidizing the high spenders.

On stimulating local private-capital investment in newspapers:

Tax haven provisions, similar to those used to encourage film production in Canada, that would make it financially attractive for persons to buy into the ownership—up to five per cent—of their local daily. This measure is designed to help raise local capital to maintain local ownership of any dailies that might be for sale.

On improving news agencies:

Grants to the Canadian Press news agency, and other Canadian wire services that may qualify, to encourage more intensive national and international coverage. The incentives would be in the form of matching grants: increased expenditures by the news agency to improve or expand editorial services would be matched by grants from the Federal Treasury. This would revive government subsidies to news agencies, a practice that was discontinued nearly 60 years ago in 1924, partly because of concern that press freedom might be compromised by government grants.

JOURNALISTIC INDEPENDENCE

The Kent Commission's most controversial recommendations are aimed at "freeing the press" from editorial interference that may flow from the vested interests of chains and conglomerate ownership. A key assertion of the Report is that when proprietors have extensive financial operations beyond an individual newspaper, freedom of the press must not be their freedom; it has to be the freedom of an editor protected from his owners. In contrast, freedom of the press for an "individual proprietor" will continue to mean freedom for that person to do what he likes with his newspaper provided that the newspaper is his principal property. (Newspapers owned by political parties and non-profit organizations qualify as individual newspapers.)

The editorial autonomy or "journalistic independence" provisions provide an insulation system from interference by the owners through affirmative action of law. There would be supervision and control practices directly affecting most newspapers in the country and indirectly affecting all of them. The "editorial autonomy'' protection mechanism provides for a complex process of accountability, starting from ''an editor-in-charge'' who would report to a local editorial advisory committee, which would answer to a national Press Rights Panel which would, in turn, report to Parliament.

The main features of the ''editorial autonomy'' protection mechanism are:

On accountability of persons owning a single newspaper:

None, if newspaper is principal property in business concerns.

On insulation of editorial operations from interference by chain and conglomerate owners:

Publishers with assets that exceed the value of the newspaper itself wiil be required to appoint an ''editor-in-chief'' under written contract.
The contract will specify the publisher's intention to devote adequate budgets to inform readers ''accurately'' and will outline the ''editor-in-chief's'' full responsibility for editorial content and conduct.

The ''editor-in-chief'' will make a yearly report (not later than January 31) to be published in the newspaper on the performance of the newspaper measured against the standards set out in his/her contract.

On local accountability and supervision of newspapers:

Establishment of an Editorial Advisory Committee at all newspapers not classified as ''individually owned.'' The committee will have seven members— two representing the publisher, two elected by the journalistic staff and three others selected from the local community. (The process of selecting and electing members of the Editorial Advisory Committee includes supervision by the Chief Justice of the Province and Press Councils, where they exist.)

The Editorial Advisory Committee would receive the annual Report of the ''editor-in-chief'' and participate in discussions on the objectives of the paper.

The Editorial Advisory Committee would itself report annually to a national Press Rights Panel.

On national accountability and supervision:

Establishment of a national Press Rights Panel within the Human Rights Commission.

The three-member panel—a chairman and two others—would be appointed by the Cabinet in Ottawa.

The Press Rights Panel would have broad functions, outlined in 15 separate points in the Kent Report, including regular reviews of ownership concentration. The Panel would have the power to order further divestments of media holdings by chains and conglomerates.

The Press Rights Panel would monitor and report on newspaper performance in Canada and would make recommendations to the government for financial incentives for the newspaper industry.

The Press Rights Panel would have the powers of a Superior Court of Record on relevant matters.

On accountability to Parliament:

The Press Rights Panel would report to Parliament through the Minister of Justice.

THE KENT REPORT: AN EVALUATION

The Kent Report is one of the most controversial reports ever presented by a Canadian Royal Commission. Although it dealt with an incredibly complex subject and made recommendations that touch on fundamental aspects of Canadian democracy, the Report was produced in haste at the request of the government.

The Commission embarked on an extensive research program including a national opinion survey of a sample 3,500 persons, held public hearings over a period of 19 weeks across the country (in 12 cities in seven provinces) at which 353 people gave evidence, examined 246 written submissions and 270 letters, deliberated on its findings and presented its recommendations in less than 10 months. In contrast, it took a British Royal Commission three years (1974 to 1977) to carry out a similar study of the press. The British Commission, which also carried out public opinion surveys, spent 10 months preparing, testing and fine-tuning the questionnaires to a point where the Commission knew it was asking meaningful questions in a meaningful way.[21]

The Kent Report was released several months before the publication of the research on which the recommendations were based. Consequently, much of the public debate precipitated by the Report was taking place in the absence of relevant information.

When the research was released, it did not provide meaningful evidence for two major assertions of the report; specifically, that concentration of newspaper

---

21. Lord McGregor of Duris, "How Kent Findings Differed from UK," *Globe and Mail,* October 28, 1981.

ownership and press ownership by conglomerates had resulted in a decline in the quality of Canadian newspapers or that it had resulted in restraints on the free flow of information. Lord McGregor, who headed the British Royal Commission on the Press (1977) and is one of the strongest critics of the Kent Report, notes that the British Commission "was unable to find evidence that concentration had led to the evils feared. On the contrary . . . chains were at pains to ensure that their editors were free of central direction."[22]

The evidence at the Kent Commission hearings (and 12 years earlier at the Senate Committee inquiry) suggests that Canadian chains have a hands-off policy in the editorial affairs of the papers they control, or at least, so they say.[23] The Kent Commission argues that the chain owners are not to be believed. (The Commission, which was aware of the findings of the British inquiry, decided not to conduct research on the most critical issue of central editorial direction and abuse of power that may have its roots in the extraneous interests of the owners.)

The Commission had an extremely broad mandate which included an examination of "the consequences of the present situation of the newspaper industry for the political, economic, social and intellectual vitality and cohesion of the nation as a whole."[24] The three-member Commission was too small to deal with the numerous dimensions of the inquiry. The Chairman, Mr. Kent, and Borden Spears were former journalists and Laurent Picard is a former president of the CBC.[25] This previous media involvement may explain why the Commission was able to deliberate on its findings and write a Report, without dissent, so quickly. But hardly was the Report made public when disagreements surfaced in comments that respective commissioners made to the press.

There are a number of contradictions in the Report. We will focus on two: (i) Canadians' perceptions of their daily newspapers and (ii) the Commission's views that concentration of ownership of English-language newspapers is bad, while even greater concentration in the French press is acceptable.

The Report notes in Chapter II that the Commission's research, based on a national survey of 3,500 Canadians, showed that "two out of three Canadians think their daily is doing a good or an excellent job in fulfilling its responsibilities to the public."[26] But later in the Report, the Commission disregards this documented finding and without providing any evidence declares: "Through its own research, public hearings and letters from newspaper readers across the country, the Commission has become aware of a national consensus on the quality of

---

22. *Ibid.*
23. See submissions by newspaper companies to the Davey Senate Committee and the Royal Commission on Newspapers. Kenneth Thomson, the head of the Thomson chain, for example, has long been on record as saying that he would never interfere in newsroom policies or decisions. He told the *New York Times,* "We provide the kind of support to give the professional the platform and strength to operate." *N.Y. Times,* January 18, 1980., p. D6.
24. Order-in-Council P.C. 1980-2343, Approval by Governor-General on September 3, 1980.
25. The British Royal Commission on the Press had 14 members.
26. Royal Commission on Newspapers. *Report. op. cit.,* p. 34.

political journalism. There is a belief that it has lost its vitality, and with this has come a decline in regard for the newspaper as an institution.''[27]

This contradiction illustrates one of the basic flaws of the Kent Report. It seeks to set standards for newspaper operations—especially their editorial quality—based on an élitist perception of what the press should be like.[28]

The Commission's different perceptions of the dangers of concentration in the French and English press are also not satisfactorily explained. Our analysis in the previous chapter (Table VI.1) showed that Quebec ranks eighth among the ten provinces in daily newspaper circulation per capita. Quebec has only 11 dailies, two of them in English, compared to 43 in Ontario. The mortality rate of daily newspapers in the past decade has been highest in Quebec. Furthermore, Quebec had an astoundingly high rate of concentration in the past dozen years. In fact, concentration has virtually reached saturation levels: three chains account for more than 95 per cent of French-language newspaper circulation in the province (Chart VI.2), and *Le Devoir* is Quebec's only independently owned daily. This situation is in strong contrast to Quebec's proud history of a dynamic press system.

The Commission's argument that weeklies play a significant role in Quebec society is important but in no way lessens the problem of newspaper closings or concentration. The Commission speaks of the need of newspapers to express vigorous views and of editorial pages to provide authoritative analysis. Yet, one of every two copies—46 per cent, to be exact—of French-language papers circulating in Quebec province is a tabloid without an editorial page or an editorial perspective. The Commission argues that *Le Devoir*, with a circulation of 40,000, is a "national" daily in the French language but provides little evidence for this, except to note the paper's élite readership and its historic influence. Furthermore, the Commission declares that Quebec papers (presumably French-language) "tend to spend more editorially than English-language papers.''[29] This conclusion is not borne out in the table of ranking of editorial expenditures: Quebec's two largest dailies, Montreal's *La Presse* and *Le Journal de Montréal*, are below average spenders for editorial operations; in Sherbrooke, Quebec, the English-language *Record* is above average, the French-language *La Tribune* is below; the Montreal *Gazette* ranks higher in editorial spendings as a percentage of revenues than *Le Journal de Québec*.

---

27. *Ibid.*, p. 135.
28. The Chairman of the Commission, Mr. Kent, did not hold the Canadian media in high regard even before the Royal Commission inquiry. At a conference at Dalhousie University in April 1979, Mr. Kent declared, "We can only envy the media standards that are possible in older and more densely populated countries." At the same time he did not think that Canada should be resigned "to the degree of sloppiness that now characterizes most of both the print and electronic media in this country." Mr. Kent proposed intervention by a "genuine ombudsman." He said further that he was not afraid of "hollow cries about freedom of the press." Tom Kent, "Parliamentary Government and Citizen Involvement" in H.V. Kroeker *Sovereign People or Sovereign Government,* (Montreal: The Institute for Research on Public Policy, 1981), p. 38.
29. Royal Commission on Newspapers. *Report. op. cit.,* p. 221.

If the principle of extensive concentration is bad, then concentration is as undesirable in the French as in the English press. Further, there can be no distinction between "good" chains and "bad" chains, a distinction made by the Commission in its evaluation of the English press.

The Commission's praise for Southam newspapers—although it did single out the Ottawa *Citizen* for criticism—includes such observations as "journalistic conscience" and an "inherited sense of *noblesse oblige.*" Southam's news service was described as the Cadillac of press services.

The Commission's strongest criticism was directed at the Thomson chain, although the *Globe and Mail,* a relatively new Thomson acquisition, was singled out for excellence. (The *Globe and Mail* is reported to be about twice as profitable as it was under the previous F.P. ownership.) The Commission suggested that Canada's largest chain often treated its dailies as "cash cows" whose earnings could be used to increase media holdings or finance unrelated ventures. As Kenneth Thomson told the Commission, "Everything my family has today, and in terms of opportunities for the future, goes back to our newspaper organization."[30]

Peter Desbarats, the Dean of Journalism at the University of Western Ontario, who served as a senior consultant to the Commission, suggests that the real reason for the Commission's existence was "not a high-minded concern for freedom of the press or the values of journalism."[31] Rather, it was the worrisome problem of the Thomson organization's latent power over public opinion. "No previous Government in Ottawa," says Professor Desbarats, "has faced that combination and concentration of power; any Government would be worried about the mere possibility of confronting it at some point in the future." He goes on to suggest that the "instinct of self-preservation on the part of the Government is at the root of Ottawa's desire to curb Thomson."[32]

This would explain one of the Commission's most important and controversial recommendations which calls for the Thomson organization to divest itself of either the *Globe and Mail* or the other 39 papers that it owns.

It would appear that the battle over freedom of the press, with both the Kent Commission and the newspaper organizations claiming that this is their primary concern, is in actuality a conflict over power between big business and big government.[33]

The recommendation for government subsidies to the Canadian Press news agency, a highly efficient organization, is neither necessary nor desirable. The profitable newspaper industry certainly has the means to provide more funds for cost-sharing news collection in Canada or abroad.

The Commission's suggestions to the newspaper industry to take voluntary steps to improve their product and to police newspaper activities, particularly

---

30. *Ibid.,* p. 4.
31. Peter Desbarats, "Power Is the Real Kent Issue," *Globe and Mail,* February 15, 1982, p. 5.
32. *Ibid.*
33. *Ibid.*

through participation in press councils, are extremely useful and were predictable.

The Commission has performed a laudable service in focusing public attention on the extent of concentration of ownership, cross-media ownership, the involvement of conglomerates in media operations and the possible societal implications of this pattern of ownership in the mass communication industry. Concentration of ownership and cross-media ownership are growing and thus presenting increasingly difficult problems, even if seen only in the more limited perspective of monopoly practices.

There is no doubt that newspaper concentration has reached intolerable levels in Canada. The process of consolidation of the press accelerated in the wake of the Senate Study on the Mass Media 12 years ago, partly out of concern by media conglomerates that government intervention may eventually be in the offing. These activities have not abated. Multi-million dollar transactions in which media conglomerates, specifically Torstar and Maclean Hunter, expanded their holdings took place during and after the Kent Commission inquiry.

Unfortunately, the Kent Commission has undermined its own credibility because of its startling recommendation calling for governmental intervention—even if only through a complex form of Ombudsman system—in the editorial affairs of newspapers.

News presentation is a continuing process, with the overall picture of ongoing events shaped by mosaic components. News selection, Bagdikian has shown, is a multi-step filtering process with many factors—some technical, others objective and yet others subjective—playing a part in the decision-making process of the gatekeepers.

The control and supervisory process recommended by the Kent Commission could become a constraining influence. The idea of committees at both the local and national levels second-guessing journalistic decisions in the hindsight of later developments is likely to lead to a pallid product in which avoidance of controversy could become a major consideration in the information presentation process. This situation carries dangers of psychological self-censorship.

CHAPTER VIII

BROADCASTING: POLITICS, ECONOMICS AND CANADIAN IDENTITY

The first pay-television licences were granted in Canada in 1982, exactly 60 years after the start of commercial radio in 1922, 50 years after the start of public service broadcasting in 1932, 30 years after the beginning of Canadian television and Cable-television in 1952 and 10 years after the incorporation in 1972 of space satellites into the broadcasting structure. Each of the earlier developments—commercial radio, public broadcasting, television, Cable-TV and communications satellites—had a profound influence in shaping the Canadian broadcasting system.

The introduction of Pay-TV is seen as a watershed development that carries with it the promise of providing a financial base for the Canadianization of the contents of Canada's broadcasting system or the threat to enhance even further the dominant position of American TV programmes on Canadian television. The Canadian Radio-television and Telecommunications Commission, which held public hearings on Pay-TV licence applications in the fall of 1981, sought to ensure that Pay-TV should become part of the solution to the 60-year search for a dynamic Canadian presence in the broadcast offerings available to Canadians. The Broadcasting Act demands no less. It declares: The broadcasting system should "safeguard, enrich and strengthen the cultural, political, social and economic fabric of Canada."[1]

This chapter examines broadcasting in Canadian society and focuses on the great political, constitutional, economic and cultural controversies that are interwoven in the shaping of radio and television. The chapter begins with an overview of the broadcast industry. Later, there will be an examination of the characteristics of radio and television and an analysis of the role of the broadcast media in nation building.

---

1. *Broadcasting Act*, R.S.C. 1970, c. B-11, s. 3(6).

BROADCASTING IN CANADA: AN OVERVIEW

Canadians are served by one of the most developed broadcasting systems in the world. There are more broadcasting stations (originating and repeater) per capita than in any other country: one station per 8,000 people. Virtually the entire population, including persons living in remote outposts of our enormously big land, have access to both radio and television.

In 1982, there were 3,100 licensed broadcast operations in Canada. They include 1,191 television stations, 562 Cable-TV systems, 740 AM radio stations and 568 FM radio stations (Table VIII.I). There appears to be no slowdown in the dynamic growth pattern of the industry. In 1970, there were 1,296 licensed broadcast operations. Ten years later, there were 2,869—a 120 per cent increase.

Of the current 3,100 broadcast operations, 736 are originating stations while most of the others are involved in rebroadcasting. Together, they constitute one of the most diverse electronic media systems anywhere. Perhaps the most important point that can be made is that the broadcast system combines the "public interest" and "market" models: it accommodates publicly owned non-profit stations and profit-oriented private stations.

, **PUBLIC BROADCASTING**

Public broadcasting has been the dominant and sometimes exclusive approach to radio and television operations in many European countries and in other parts of the world. The stations are publicly owned, operated in the public interest and financed largely by tax monies or from the proceeds of licensing fees that owners of radio and TV sets may be required to pay.

In Canada, there is no pure public sector. First, the nationally owned Canadian Broadcasting Corporation (Radio Canada) derives part of its income (18 per cent) from television advertising. Second, there are joint interest operations between the CBC and privately owned affiliate stations that enable the national network to provide programming in places where there are no CBC stations. The smaller private affiliates benefit from the arrangement in that they have access to domestic programming that they could not afford to produce. Third, there are public sectors of broadcasting in several provinces—Quebec, Ontario, Saskatchewan, Alberta and British Columbia—that are operated to meet "educational interest," although in Quebec and Ontario "education" is so broadly defined that it includes movies and other popular programming, and thus to some extent becomes a "constitutional fiction."

The Public Sector of broadcasting incorporates the following services:

Canadian Broadcasting Corporation—1982 budget: $796 million

    CBC AM radio, English
    CBC FM radio, English
    Radio Canada AM radio, French
    Radio Canada FM radio, French

TABLE VIII.I Licensed Broadcasting Undertakings, By Type 1970-1981

TYPE	1970	1971	1972	1973	1974	1975	1976	1977	1978	1979	1980	1981[1]
Radio—AM	540	584	596	637	657	693	700	714	722	730	737	740
Radio—FM	84	86	86	92	101	121	174	278	323	416	470	568
Television	365	395	469	534	588	661	742	834	933	1045	1100	1191
Cable-Television	307	342	360	365	387	419	444	475	526	550	562	562
TOTAL[2]	1296	1407	1511	1628	1733	1894	2060	2301	2504	2741	2869	3062

[1]As at March 31 of each year
[2]Excluding Networks and Short-wave

Source: CRTC Annual Reports

Originating Stations Profile, 1981
Radio—AM	390
Radio—FM	197
Television	117
Networks	32
Total	736

CBC Television Network, English
Radio Canada Television Network, French
Radio Canada International—the CBC external service broadcasts in 11 languages
Northern Service—the CBC operated radio service broadcasting to the native peoples (Inuit, Denis, Métis) and non-native settlers living north of the 60th parallel in the Northwest Territories and Yukon.
Armed Forces Network—a special service for Canadian military personnel stationed abroad as part of Canada's North Atlantic Alliance (NATO) commitments or international peacekeeping operations.

Provincial Educational TV—1982 budget: $100 million

Radio Québec	$50 million
Ontario Educational TV	$30 million
Saskmedia (Saskatchewan)	$ 2 million
ACCESS (Alberta Communications Corporation)	$13 million
Knowledge Network of the West (British Columbia)	$ 2 million
Other provinces	$ 3 million

PRIVATE BROADCASTING

In the private sector, the stations are privately owned and operated for profit which they derive from the selling of advertising. Commercial broadcasting thus provides programming that is aimed largely at delivering audiences for the advertiser. In this way, the economic base of commercial broadcasting is similar to that of the print media. (Canadian newspapers and periodical publishers are very much involved in broadcast operations—radio, TV and Cable-TV—a practice that goes back to the earliest days of radio and is called cross-media ownership.)

There are, at the same time, some important differences in the economics of newspapers and commercial broadcast stations. All that Canadians need to start a newspaper is financial means; in radio and television, licences are necessary. Furthermore, there are limits to the amount of advertising that broadcasters can accommodate, since the broadcast day cannot be expanded beyond 24 hours. Newspapers, however, can be enlarged by adding pages and therefore have greater flexibility in increasing advertising content. Also, newspapers supplement their advertising revenue with incomes from subscriptions and street sales. Broadcasting generally does not have such additional sources of revenues, with the exception of Cable-TV, which presently has no advertising revenues and relies almost totally on subscribers. The introduction of Pay-TV in Canada will create yet another approach for the financing of broadcast operations in that viewers will pay for specific programming (or channel) which will not carry advertising.

The public and private sectors operate in a highly commercial environment, competing for audiences and to some extent even advertising revenues. In effect, the private and public sectors are concerned about numbers (the size of audience) and rating considerations are a major factor in the programme scheduling.

In 1982, this was clearly illustrated when the CBC introduced its 10-11 p.m. newshour incorporating *The National* (news) and *The Journal*. The fact that the newshour was drawing an average audience of two million in its first months of operation was seen as the principal yardstick of the project's early success.

The concern with ratings suggests that programme offerings are aimed at appealing to the largest possible audience, resulting in what is commonly called "lowest denominator" programming. This tends to limit the diversity of programming and supposedly neglects the "higher" interests of sophisticated audiences. In reality, the television viewing patterns of Canadians show a remarkable similarity of interests across all sectors of society in entertainment programming.

CHOICE OF PROGRAMMES

In both radio and television, Canadians have a wide choice of programme offerings. The CBC maintains a thriving and vital national radio service—the only one in North America—with a full range of programming on English and French networks disseminated by 146 originating AM and FM stations and 629 repeater stations. The highly developed private radio sector, with 441 originating stations across the county, has a local orientation.

In television, the figures speak for themselves: 99 per cent of the population has access to television services, 98 per cent has a choice of two channels, 91 per cent has three, and over 50 per cent has eight or more.[2] In 1982, steps were taken to increase television services to northern and remote communities where half a million people receive only one or two channels. A satellite delivery system is adding four TV channels—three English stations and one French channel—incorporating programmes from a variety of sources.[3] CANCOM (Canadian Satellite Communications) has been licensed as the wholesale provider of the Supplemental TV services which are distributed in the remote regions from satellite ground stations by cable (at $4 a month) and low power relays. Other initiatives involving satellite delivery packages are being undertaken by the major French (TVA) and English (CTV) networks in the private sector.[4]

In addition to receiving the offerings of their own broadcasting stations, most Canadians readily receive TV programmes from American stations, either through direct reception from border stations or, more commonly, via their

---

2. John Meisel, Notes for an address to Canadian Association of Broadcasters, Quebec City, April 6, 1981.
3. CRTC, *Annual Report* 1980-81. pp. 9-10.
4. *Ibid.*

Cable-TV hook-up. Canada is the most wired country in the world: eight out of ten homes have access to cable service, and more than four-and-a-half million households—57 per cent of all households—subscribe to Cable-TV (Chart VIII.1).

CHART VIII.1.   Cable-TV Penetration in Canada (January 1, 1981)

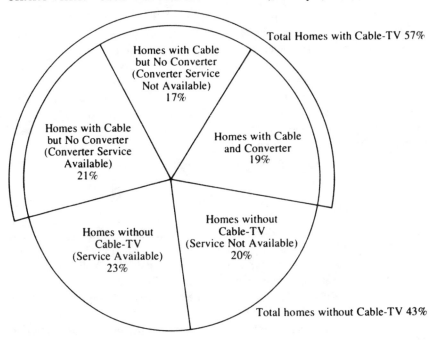

Source: CBC Annual Report 1980/81

Through regular TV broadcasting stations, cable and satellite transmissions, Canadians have greater programming choice than any other people in the world. Most of Canada's cable subscribers, for example, are provided with more U.S. programming than are most Americans themselves.[5] Access to 36 channels is becoming common for households linked to cable (and converter) services; present technology makes it possible to extend the capacity to 100 channels.

POPULARITY OF RADIO AND TV: SATURATION

The almost universal access to radio and television and the wide choice of programme offerings have contributed to the popularity of broadcasting. Canada has achieved "practical saturation." There are many more radios than people in Canada. Nearly all households have television sets; the home without indoor

---

5. Alphonse Ouimet, "The Television Revolution and the National Interest," in *The Computerized Society: Implications for Canada*, The Walter L. Gordon Lecture Series, 1979-80, Vol. 4, (Toronto: The Canadian Studies Foundation, 1980), p. 62.

plumbing is more common than the home without television. About 40 per cent of households have more than one TV set—in fact, there is one TV set for every two persons in the population. Over the past 10 years, there has been a 32 per cent increase in the number of households and a 56 per cent increase in the number of TV sets. (Table VIII.2)

TABLE VIII.2 Television and Cable in Canadian Households, 1971 &1981 (in thousands)

	1971		1981	
No. of Households	5,963	100%	7,907	100%
Households with TV	5,755	97%	7,693	97%
Households with more than one TV	1,403	24%	3,012	39%
Households with colour TV	1,080	18%	6,497	82%
Households with cable	1,370	23%	4,506	57%
Total No. of TV sets	*7,646*		*11,855*	

Source: CBC, Annual Report 1980/81

Television viewing and radio listening are by far the most important components of leisure-time activity. In one week, the average Canadian watches 24 hours of television and listens to 19 hours of radio. More time is devoted to the broadcast media than to the job.

BROADCASTING INDUSTRY: ECONOMICS

Broadcasting in Canada is a big industry involving in 1982 an estimated $2.5 billion in the combined revenues of the non-profit (public) and private sectors (Chart VIII.2). Advertising revenues for commercially sponsored radio and TV programmes account for $1.3 billion or 52 per cent of all broadcast revenues. Parliament in Ottawa provided $650 million for the Canadian Broadcasting Corporation, which also had $146 million in commercial revenues. The provincial broadcasting authorities operated on a combined budget of just under $100 million. Cable-TV operators had revenues of $440 million. The private sector of broadcasting (including Cable-TV) accounted for 64 per cent of the revenues, the public sector, 36 per cent.

The money flow in broadcasting, while significant at $2.5 billion, does not place it in the forefront of Canadian industries. Broadcasting is well behind the natural resources industries (for example, oil and gas, minerals) the automobile industry, the telephone industry and the print and publishing industry, among others. But the economics of broadcasting, in the primary activities of programme creation and transmission, do not reflect its social and political impact. Furthermore, the economic evaluation of the industry—measured in revenues, spending and capital investments—fails to appreciate the manufacturing and service operations tied to the existence of broadcasting. The public's investment in the purchase of radio and television sets is about 20 times more than the equipment investments of broadcast stations. Television marks the first time in a mass

CHART VIII.2. Broadcasting Revenues in Canada, 1982 (Estimated)

Total Revenues: $2.5 Billion—Radio, TV and Cable

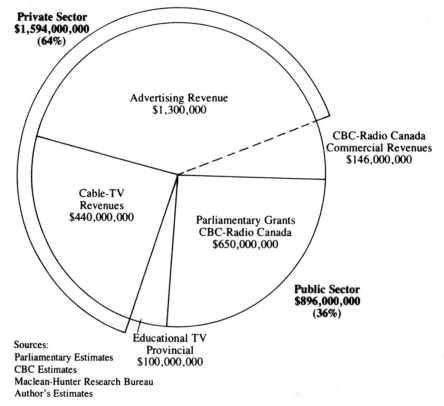

Sources:
Parliamentary Estimates
CBC Estimates
Maclean-Hunter Research Bureau
Author's Estimates

communications industry where the public paid most of the direct cost of equipment.[6] Spendings on the repair of radio and television sets are about equal to or in excess of the advertising revenues of Canada's broadcasters. Also, broadcasting gives rise to a whole series of support services, ranging from market research to advertising, film-making, engineering, industry publications, etc. In 1980, 28,000 Canadians were employed in radio and television broadcasting and another 6,000 in Cable-TV. These figures do not realistically reflect the economic impact of the industry.

Commercial broadcasting is highly profitable, with the rate of return on investment among the best in the Canadian industrial sector. Operating profits for television, radio and Cable in 1980—the latest year for which complete figures were available—amounted to $340 million on revenues of $1.3 billion, or 26 per cent.[7] The pre-tax profits for the same year (after taking into account deprecia-

---

6. Bagdikian, *The Information Machines, op. cit.*, p. 227.
7. CRTC, *Facts Digest*, 1982, pre-publication report.

tion, interest and other adjustments) were $189 million or 30 per cent of net fixed assets, an incredibly good performance.[8]

THE RECURRING CONTROVERSIES

Canadian broadcasting is beset with controversy. The public discussions in 1982 on introducing Pay-TV focused on many of the same basic issues that created controversies and surfaced repeatedly when Canada debated policies for radio, television and Cable-TV. Conflicts over constitutional, economic and cultural aspects of broadcasting are as old as the industry itself. Specifically, the major recurring controversies include the struggle between the federal and provincial levels of government for jurisdictional rights, public ownership versus profit-oriented private ownership and Canadian versus U.S. content in programming.

The great controversies have become "constant factors" that give rise to a continuing process of bargaining. Sometimes, this results in contradictions between broadcast policies and practices in Canada. Professor Frank Peers observed in 1969 in the *Politics of Canadian Broadcasting* that "official statements have not always meant in practice what they seemed to say; those who lost a battle were not convinced they had lost the war, and ways were found to alter the intent of Parliament's decisions."[9]

An overview of the development of broadcasting provides useful background for an examination of today's problem areas.

THE DEVELOPMENT OF BROADCASTING

The link between magnetism—one of the fundamental forces of nature—and electricity was basic to the development of electronic communications in the nineteenth and twentieth centuries. The telegraph and telephone were stepping stones to electronic communications without wires.[10]

Radio and television have a common history. Their base is in electricity: sound and light are converted into electromagnetic waves. The theoretical foundations for broadcasting were put forward in the theory of electromagnetism unveiled by the British scientist, James Clerk Maxwell, in 1864, or about the time of Canadian Confederation. The existence of electromagnetic waves, which travel at the speed of light and have other characteristics similar to light waves, was confirmed in the experiments of Heinrich Hertz of Manheim, Germany, in the late 1880s. This major breakthrough stimulated a "radio race" in the 1890s among scientists in Germany, Russia, Britain, the United States and Italy.

In 1896, Guglielmo Marconi, unable to find financial support in his native Italy, went to England at the age of 22 to promote his wireless invention as a means of communicating with ships at sea. Britain was the leading maritime

8. *Ibid.*
9. Peers, *Politics of Canadian Broadcasting, op. cit.*, p. 3.
10. Melvin L. De Fleur and Sandra Ball-Rokeach, *Theories of Mass Communication,* (New York: David McKay Co., Third Edition), 1975, p. 73.

nation at the time and Lloyds of London, the international shipping insurer, was a ready customer for Marconi's wireless devices. The British Admiralty provided Marconi with £20,000 a year for wireless equipment used by the Navy. The Italian Navy also became a customer. These sources of income provided funding for Marconi to continue his radio experiments.

Marconi, who received the Nobel Prize for Physics in 1907, had limited scientific training; his great strengths lay in finding practical applications for the electronic breakthroughs of his time. He was an outstanding organizer and an excellent businessman. Marconi also knew how to attract attention: he used vessels equipped with wireless transmitting equipment to provide coverage of such famed yacht racing events on both sides of the Atlantic as the America's Cup and the Irish Regatta. He set up a wireless communications link between Queen Victoria's summer palace and the royal yacht on which the heir to the throne, Prince Edward, was recuperating from an illness. Most important, Marconi's wireless telegraphy equipment on ships was proving highly effective, especially in accident situations.

One of Marconi's great objectives at the turn of the century was to provide a wireless link across the Atlantic. Toward this end, he set up a radio station with 60-metre high masts on the English coast at Poldhu in Cornwall. In 1901, Marconi went to St. John's, Newfoundland, where he established a receiving station on what is now called Signal Hill. Using kites to lift an aerial wire to great heights, Marconi received clear Morse code transmissions from Poldhu on December 12, 1901—a milestone date in the development of radio.

THE CANADIAN INVOLVEMENT

Partly because of geographic location in a trans-Atlantic communications link and partly because of vested interests, Canada became involved in a major way in the international enterprise that produced radio. The history of broadcasting in Canada is a record of significant achievements and at the same time a story of missed opportunities. The Liberal government of Sir Wilfrid Laurier made $80,000 available for Marconi's wireless station, built in 1902 at Glace Bay, Nova Scotia. But even this involvement in the Marconi experiments had its unhappy side. In backing Marconi, Canada turned its back on its own Reginald Aubrey Fessenden, who is sometimes described in the history books as the "American Marconi."

Fessenden was born in 1866 in Bolton in Quebec's Eastern Townships and was educated at Bishop's University in Lennoxville, Quebec. He was the first North American to make a major contribution to the development of radio. The Fessenden approach emphasized voice radio, a far more complex undertaking than Marconi's Morse code transmissions. In 1900, using the heterodyne system he had developed, Fessenden successfully carried out the first-ever voice transmissions—for the U.S. Weather Bureau—from his laboratory at Cobb Island on the Potomac River to the receiving station at Arlington, Virginia. He had found a way of superimposing a voice: sending it piggy-back on a radio wave. The first voice ever heard on radio was that of a Canadian.[11]

Fessenden spent most of his working life in the United States, where he was employed by such noted personalities in the electrical field as Thomas Edison and George Westinghouse. He taught electrical engineering at Purdue University and the University of Pittsburgh, but McGill University turned him down when he applied to fill a vacancy.

In 1906, Fessenden gave up teaching to devote himself fully to his inventions. He was involved at the time in trans-Atlantic voice broadcasting experiments, among other projects, and sought backing in Canada, where his supporters included Sir Robert Borden. The Fessenden Wireless Company of Canada was formed in 1906 by an act of Parliament, but the Canadian government gave Marconi the exclusive right to build wireless stations and Fessenden was for all practical purposes squeezed from the Canadian scene.

On Christmas Eve in 1906, Fessenden was back in the United States and carried out the first major broadcasting venture in the modern sense when he transmitted an entertainment programme—voice, music and recordings—from Brant Rock, Massachusetts to ships of the United Fruit Company that were carrying bananas between the United States and Puerto Rico.[12] Fessenden obtained more than 500 patents; his many inventions included the fathometer, which measures depth of water by means of reflected sound waves. Canada never invested in Fessenden's talents, and he never received the recognition he deserved.

Other principal actors in the development of radio included Thomas Edison in the United States and John Ambrose Flemming in England. Their research led to the invention of the vacuum tube, especially important for improved voice and music transmissions, by Lee de Forest. In 1908, de Forest brought his wireless transmitter to Paris, where his broadcast of recorded music from the Eiffel Tower could be picked up on radio receivers as far away as London. The voice and music broadcasts of Fessenden and de Forest were not taken seriously, for the emphasis was on radio for transmission of messages for ships at sea, weather information and business transactions.

Just how important radio could be for ships at sea was dramatically illustrated in April 1912 when the "unsinkable" S.S. Titanic struck an iceberg in the Atlantic on her maiden voyage and promptly went down. David Sarnoff, transmitting business messages between New York and Philadelphia, picked up the distress signal from the Titanic and helped to coordinate the rescue of passengers by sending out messages to other ships in the Atlantic. Sarnoff and wireless operators at Cape Race, Newfoundland kept the world informed about the shipping disaster. The incident was a catalyst for broader applications of radio, especially

11. For background on Fessenden's role in the development of radio, see Warner Troyer, *The Sound and the Fury*, (Rexdale, Ont.: John Wiley & Sons, 1980); also Sandy Stewart, *A Pictorial History of Radio in Canada*, (Toronto: Gage Publishing, 1975).
12. *Ibid.*

at sea. In World War I (1914-1918), wireless communications were used by both sides in naval engagements and other military and diplomatic activities. The technological improvements in wireless during the war set the stage for new ventures in broadcasting as a medium for information and entertainment.

EXPERIMENTAL RADIO: THE CANADIAN INITIATIVE

The manufacturers of wireless receivers, seeking a market for their products, initiated broadcasting to the public. Marconi's Station WAX in Montreal began broadcasting on an ͬxperimental basis in 1918 and on a regular schedule in 1919. The Montreal Marconi station, now known as CFCF, was the world's first radio station involved in regular broadcasting.

On May 21, 1920 the Montreal station inaugurated long-distance broadcasting when it transmitted a special programme to Ottawa (a distance of about 200 kilometres) to a meeting of the Royal Society of Canada at the Château Laurier Hotel.[13] On November 11th of that year, the first American station, KDKA in Pittsburgh, owned by the Westinghouse Corporation, began transmitting the results of the 1920 American presidential election that had taken place that day. At about the same time, similar experimental radio stations began broadcasting in Britain, Holland and other European countries.

RADIO IN THE 1920s: THE UNREGULATED PERIOD

Commercial radio was introduced in Canada with the licensing in April 1922 of stations owned by the rival Winnipeg newspapers, *The Tribune* and the *Manitoba Free Press*. Other newspapers that obtained licences in the early days were the French-language Montreal daily, *La Presse*, the *Toronto Daily Star* and the *Daily Province* in Vancouver. Newspapers saw radio stations as a natural extension of their communications business ventures: broadcasting could promote goodwill through local community identification and at the same time protect dailies from potential competition for audiences and advertising revenues.

For newspapers, radio was a secondary occupation. The same was true for most of the other radio station owners. Electronic equipment manufacturers operated stations to attract listeners who would buy receivers. Department stores operated stations to promote their names and also to sell radios. Church organizations set up stations to promote their religious beliefs. Universities saw radio as a possible extension of the classroom, and one that could play an important educational role. Owning a station was regarded as an investment for the future. It was a relatively cheap investment. Obtaining a radio licence was simple: a fee of $50 for the commercial broadcaster, a $5 fee for amateur radio clubs. Those who owned a radio receiver had to pay a one dollar yearly licence fee. Radio stations sprang up all over the country.

Canadians obviously liked radio. The first year they bought 10,000 sets, the

---

13. E. Austin Weir, *The Struggle for National Broadcasting in Canada*, (Toronto: McClelland and Stewart, 1965), p. 1.

next year an additional 20,000. By 1925, 100,000 Canadians had radios in their homes; five years later, in 1930, there were half a million radio sets. In 1937, the figure climbed to one million.[14] Radio was becoming a household item. These figures are on the low side because they are based on the number of licences issued to owners of receivers, and some did not pay the licence fee.

The Canadian interest in radio, as reflected in the licensing pattern for receivers, was widespread and existed in all parts of the country, both in cities and rural areas. The location of stations, however, was based on economic considerations tied to the size of potential audiences. Consequently, the emphasis was on broadcasting to the urban populations, although 50 per cent of Canadians lived in rural areas. In 1927, when Canada had 75 commercial broadcasting stations, more than 60 of them were located in the big cities. Toronto, for example, had 10 stations, Vancouver seven, Montreal five. Nineteen of the 23 stations in the Prairies were located in Calgary, Edmonton, Regina, Saskatoon and Winnipeg. In the Maritimes, there was a similar pattern of station location in the principal cities. In 1931, Canada had 80 commercial radio stations with a combined power output of 34,000 watts. Approximately half of this power was concentrated in Toronto and Montreal.[15]

The vested economic interests of the owners meant extensive coverage for large cities, but poor or no service for small communities. As Al Shea noted in *Broadcasting the Canadian Way*, "Canadians living in smaller communities and rural areas remote from the main centres of the population were beyond the reach of the magic waves"[16] . . . at least Canada's magic waves. American stations could be readily picked up by most Canadians, stimulating the sale of radios. Even in the big cities, all was not well. Competing stations were causing interference with one another's transmissions and many stations were on the air only intermittently. Furthermore, American stations with their stronger signals were often drowning out the Canadian broadcast signals. At night, there was also interference from powerful Mexican stations transmitting on frequencies that had been reserved for Canada.

The problems of radio for French-speaking Canadians were even more serious. Partly because the commercial sector in Quebec province was dominated by the English-speaking population, French-language radio was underdeveloped. CKAC, owned by *La Presse* in Montreal, was the only French-language broadcasting station of significant power. Quebec's large rural population had limited access to French radio. Statistics for 1929 show that there were only 50,000 radios in use in Quebec, compared to 150,000 in Ontario.[17]

The offerings of Canadian stations, French and English, were unexciting. Broadcasting stations were operating on low power and on the cheap. Major stations in Montreal and Toronto linked up by wire to the U.S. networks, and supplemented their American programming with little Canadian content. The

---

14. Royal Commission on Broadcasting, 1957, *Report* (Fowler Commission) Appendix II.
15. *Ibid.*
16. Albert Shea, *Broadcasting the Canadian Way*, (Montreal: Harvest House, 1963), p. 102.
17. Peers, *Politics of Canadian Broadcasting, op. cit.*, p. 21.

principal French-language station in Montreal also became a U.S. network affiliate.[18]

To a considerable extent, Canadians were either receiving U.S. broadcasts directly or getting U.S. material, in the form of records, via Canadian stations. The Canadian presence on our airwaves was small; Canadian content was less than 20 per cent of programme time. Canada simply plugged into American radio.

The implications of the "U.S. connection" were enormous and not always fully appreciated. The domination of American fare on the Canadian airwaves was not a passing problem that could be resolved in time by simply increasing Canadian programming. On the contrary, time worked against Canadian interests because the audience was developing communication habits, specifically entertainment and information tastes that would continue to grow. American humour, American entertainment personalities and the value system that they projected penetrated Canada and were readily appreciated. Basic communication habits and tastes tend to have their roots in early experiences with a medium. When television came along, the newer broadcast medium built on radio; early television was radio that you could see as well as hear. It was only natural for Canadians to appreciate TV offerings from the United States.

NATIONAL THRUST: CANADIAN NATIONAL RAILWAYS RADIO

The first national thrust to broadcasting, and in effect an element of public ownership, came as early as 1923 when Canadian National Railways introduced radio on the trains. The CNR was formed from the bankrupt railway systems that had run into financial difficulties in the Depression after World War I.[19]

According to Weir, Sir Henry Thornton, the first CNR president, perceived the communications industry from a broad perspective: ". . . carriers of goods and people by rail cars, transmitters of messages by telephone and telegraph and carriers of ideas and ideals by way of radio."[20] The first railway broadcasts began in June 1923 in Montreal. In December, the CNR arranged the first network broadcast in Canada by simultaneously transmitting the same program in Montreal and Ottawa over stations that had been linked by telephone wires. CNR built radio stations in Ottawa, Moncton, New Brunswick and Vancouver. Through the leasing of stations in Montreal, Toronto, Winnipeg, Saskatoon, Regina, Edmonton and Calgary, the CNR was able to entertain its passengers on transcontinental journeys. On July 1, 1927, to help celebrate Canada's sixtieth birthday, the CNR radio system carried a Diamond Jubilee programme that originated in Ottawa, could be heard across Canada and, through special arrangements in the United States and Europe, drew an audience of about five million.

The CNR broadcasts were setting an example as to what Canadian radio could achieve: there were live classical programmes (the Toronto Symphony, the Hart

18. *Ibid.*, p. 58 (fn).
19. Weir, *The Struggle for National Broadcasting in Canada, op. cit.*, p. 4.
20. *Ibid.*

House Quartet), school programmes and radio drama dealing with Canadian history.

By 1930, the CNR network included 80 rail cars equipped for radio, and there were 14 CNR (owned and leased) transmitting stations providing coast-to-coast broadcasting that could be picked up not only on the trains but also in homes across the country.[21] In addition to pioneering network broadcasting in French and English, CNR radio also introduced the concept of public ownership. The railway's Crown company status meant limited political interference. The earliest initiatives in nationally owned broadcasting were thus at an arm's length from politicians, providing a model for the insulation of broadcasting from political interference.

The CNR network served as the nucleus for the later development of public sector broadcasting.

THE PROBLEMS: A SUMMARY

The inspiring story of CNR radio must be seen in the context of the broader development of commercial radio.

The neglect of rural broadcasting, frequency interference, the American domination of Canadian radio and the underdevelopment of French-language radio did not exhaust the list of major problems. Controversies surfaced over religious programming. There were allegations of censorship and government favouritism in granting licences. There was controversy over the amount of advertising, the nature of advertising, the hours of advertising (it was argued that there should be no direct advertising on the air after men came home from work), and fears were expressed that the airwaves were becoming an "atmospheric billboard."

There was no meaningful policy direction in Canadian broadcasting for the entire decade of the 1920s, the formative years of broadcasting. The regulatory provisions were vague, largely ineffective and often disregarded. Technological and economic considerations and individual initiatives were far more important than governmental policy in shaping the broadcast system in the 1920s. It was a decade of trial and error and one that was filled with controversy.

In the United States, radio's phenomenal growth pattern was out of control and in 1927 the Radio Act passed by Congress established the Federal Radio Commission, giving it strong regulatory powers. Britain opted for publicly owned broadcasting and set up the British Broadcasting Corporation in 1927.

THE INQUIRIES: 1928-1982

Searching for a meaningful policy, Canada appointed the first Royal Commission on Broadcasting in 1928, headed by Sir John Aird. The Commission reported in 1929 that it had found divergent viewpoints in its extensive hearings across Canada on how broadcasting should be operated but there was consensus

---

21. Shea, *Broadcasting the Canadian Way, op. cit.*

on one fundamental point: *Canadian radio listeners wanted Canadian broadcasting.*[22]

The Aird Commission report, only nine pages long, put forward fundamental principles that continue to shape Canadian broadcasting policy today. The recommendations were aimed largely at the creation of a publicly owned and operated broadcasting system "behind which is the national power and prestige of the whole public of the Dominion of Canada." In the transition stage, however, private stations would provide a provisional service. The recommendations called for the building of seven high-powered stations—one in the Maritimes and one each in Quebec, Ontario, Manitoba, Saskatchewan, Alberta and British Columbia—to provide good reception over the entire settled areas of the country.[23]

The report put forward the expectation that Canadian broadcasting should provide a support structure for Canadian nation building and national unity: "In a country of the vast geographical dimensions of Canada, broadcasting will undoubtedly become a force in fostering national spirit and interpreting national consciousness."[24] But almost in the same breath, the Aird Commission warned about the foreign (American) influences in programme content that threatened to undermine Canadian identity:

At present, the majority of programmes heard are from sources outside Canada. It has been emphasized to us that the continued reception of these has a tendency to mold the minds of young people in the home to ideals and opinions that are not Canadian.[25]

Ottawa waited three years before it acted. The Great Depression began shortly after the publication of the Report and this was no time to launch expensive broadcasting ventures. There was a change of government following the general election in 1930 and a great deal of sensitivity about free enterprise. Furthermore, the rights of provinces in the broadcasting sector still had to be resolved.

The Aird Commission marked the beginning of a continuing process of Canadian soul-searching on broadcasting. Broadcasting policy has been examined, re-examined, reviewed and reshaped on a regular basis. There have been more than 40 inquiries in 50 years by Royal Commissions (Aird-1928, Massey-1949, Fowler-1955, Glassco-1963), Special Committees (Fowler-1965, Boyle-1977, Clyne-1979, Applebaum-Hébert-1981) and Parliamentary Committees.[26]

Some of the inquiries have dealt with all aspects of broadcasting, others have focused on broadcasting in the broader context of cultural policy and yet others

22. Royal Commission on Radio Broadcasting, 1929 *Report*, (Aird Commission), p. 6.
23. *Ibid.*, p. 8.
24. *Ibid.*, p. 6.
25. *Ibid.*
26. The Royal Commissions are: The Royal Commission on Radio Broadcasting (Aird); the Royal Commission on National Development in the Arts, Letters and Sciences (Massey Commission); Royal Commission on Broadcasting (Fowler) and Royal Commission on Government Organization (Glassco). The Special Committees include Advisory Committee on Broadcasting (Fowler); Committee of Inquiry into the National Broadcasting Service (Boyle); Consultative Committee on the Implications for Canadian Sovereignty (Clyne); Federal Cultural Policy Review Committee (Applebaum-Hébert).

have examined specific issues, such as the organizational structure of the CBC and the divisive aspects of French and English broadcasting in Canada. As Professor Peers has noted: "Inquiry succeeds inquiry; commissions report, and committees review the work of the commissions; finally governments act. Yet the debate goes on."[27] Parliament, for its part, has passed four Broadcasting Acts (1932, 1936, 1958 and 1968) in a continuing effort to fine-tune the regulatory process to changing economic and technological conditions. Consequently, there exists in Canada more than in any other country a greater awareness of the power and influence of communications and information resources in furthering unity, cultural identity and economic development.[28]

What is significant about many inquiries and the four Broadcasting Acts that evolved is a consistent philosophy of national consciousness and purpose that is attached to broadcasting.

There has been a continuing echoing of support for public sector broadcasting. The Royal Commission on Development in the Arts, Letters and Sciences (Massey-Levèsque Report) said in 1951: "The system recommended by the Aird Report has developed into the greatest single agency for national unity, understanding and enlightenment." The Fowler Committee reported in 1965 that the "CBC . . . is the most important single instrument available for the development of a distinctive Canadian culture." In 1977, the Boyle Committee, which focused its attention on weaknesses of the national broadcasting service declared, "If we did not have the CBC, we should have to invent it . . . the Canadian public wants the CBC and has a need for it."[29]

There have however, been cross-pressures and inconsistencies in translating the philosophy of national consciousness into practice. David Ellis in his study *Evolution of the Canadian Broadcasting System* notes that successive governments have failed to act upon specific recommendations in a remarkably consistent manner.[30] Professor Peers, in his eloquent analysis of Canadian broadcast policy (a two-volume study) concludes, "There have been increasing contradictions between the objectives declared by Parliament and the broadcasting pattern that has emerged in practice . . . Over the years we have evolved a system increasingly concerned with public gain."[31] The realities of Canadian broadcasting are quite different from the expectations. The directions taken by the Canadian broadcasting system, said CBC President A.W. Johnson, are a mockery of the Broadcasting Act.

CANADIAN FEDERALISM: JURISDICTION IN BROADCASTING

The national interest in broadcasting has long had the support of the courts. The

27. Peers, *Politics of Canadian Broadcasting, op. cit.*, p. 4.
28. Oswald H. Gangley, "Communications and Information Resources in Canada," *Telecommunications Policy*, December 1979, pp. 267-289.
29. Committee of Inquiry into the National Broadcasting Service (Boyle), 1977, *Report*, p. 9.
30. David Ellis, *Evolution of the Canadian Broadcasting System*, (Ottawa: Supply and Services, 1979), p. 79.
31. Frank Peers, *The Public Eye: Television and the Politics of Canadian Broadcasting, 1952-1968* (Toronto: University of Toronto Press, 1979), p. 438.

British North America Act 1867, our main constitutional document until 1982, was drafted a half-century before broadcasting became a reality, but the courts had no reservations about placing broadcasting within the jurisdiction of the federal level of government.

The *Radio Case*[32] of 1932 set a pattern of affirming federal jurisdiction and has been extended over the years to include television, satellites and Cable-TV. The Judicial Committee of the Privy Council (the highest court of appeal at the time) in its ruling in 1932 found three specific reasons as to why broadcasting should be in the federal sphere. Most significantly, the Judicial Committee recognized that radio was so important for all of Canada that it came under the peace, order and good government clause of Section 91 of the BNA Act. Furthermore, radio was seen as an extension of the telegraph [Section 92 (10) (a)], which connects one province to another and therefore was under federal jurisdiction. A third reason stems from the federal obligation relating to international treaties (Section 132). Canada was a party to the International Radio Telegraph Convention of 1927 and although this was not a British Empire treaty as specified in the British North America Act, Ottawa's international obligations with regard to broadcasting are logically derived from Section 132.

In a whole series of cases going back to the *Radio Case*, the national interest—that is, the power to make laws for the peace, order and good government of Canada—has been a key factor in determining federal jurisdiction in broadcasting, even on the question of control and regulation of the intellectual content of radio (and by extension television) broadcasting.[33]

The provinces, however, have strong and legitimate broadcast interests, especially as they relate to the educational role of communications. (Section 93 of the BNA Act gives provinces exclusive jurisdiction over education.) Giving in to the pressure from provinces, the federal Cabinet directed the CRTC in the early 1970s to issue licences (radio and TV) to "independent" educational broadcasting corporations at the provincial level. Provincial public sector broadcasting is most developed in Quebec (Radio Québec), Ontario (TV Ontario) and Alberta (ACCESS).

New technologies for communications delivery systems have created new openings for an expanded provincial involvement. The constitutional question has shifted largely, but not entirely, from the legal to the political arena, with the provinces continuing to press their case at federal-provincial conferences for some jurisdiction in the so-called "grey areas" of closed circuit television, including Cable-TV and Pay-TV. Quebec province, in particular, has been demanding jurisdictional rights in broadcasting in the interests of the cultural sovereignty of Quebecers. The case for the provinces goes beyond the interests of regional culture, regional economic development and regional community

32. Re Regulation and Control of Radio Communication (1932) A.C. 304.
33. Re C.F.R.B. and the Attorney-General of Canada (1973), 3 O.R. 819; (1974), 38 D.L.R. (3rd) 335.

building.[34] The computerized society and the wired city are bringing about the age of what Alphonse Ouimet has called *"telethis* and *telethat"*—electronic newspaper, telemedicine, tele-education, telepurchases, tele-surveillance, television viewing on demand, telelotteries and most importantly, tele-information (via Telidon, the highly sophisticated videotex system developed by the Department of Communications) which will have the potential to link Canadians with information banks globally.[35] The stakes in broadcast jurisdiction are growing rapidly and the provinces want part of the action.

In 1982, the provinces have been demanding the right to select which companies will distribute Pay-TV networks to be licensed by the CRTC. The British Columbia government, for example, served notice to the CRTC that it intends to regulate the non-broadcast segments of the pay-television industry.[36] Two provinces, Manitoba and Saskatchewan, regulate closed-circuit television. Obviously, there are many battles yet to be fought in the courts and the political arena on the complex jurisdiction issue in broadcasting. Martha and Frederick Fletcher, in a sensitive article "Communication and Confederation" argue that Ottawa has greater powers in communications than it needs and the provinces should have more authority to meet provincial aspirations (for example, delivery of social services through "wired city" technology).[37]

GOVERNMENT INVOLVEMENT: THE NATIONAL INTEREST

In Canada, as in other countries, the government regulates and supervises broadcasting. There are two reasons. First, the broadcast frequencies are considered public property and there is a need for the orderly rationing of the airwaves, a scarce resource. However, new technology, including the use of fibre optics, satellite transmissions and cable have enormously expanded the capacity to disseminate broadcast programs. The importance of the orderly use of broadcast facilities should not be underestimated, as the Canadian experiences of the 1920s, including the spillover of radio signals from the United States and Mexico, clearly shows. Broadcasting requires some national and international regulation.

The licensing requirement provides a convenient opening for regulatory practices in the "national interest," the second reason for public policy in the broadcast sector. Radio and television reach into virtually every household in the nation, providing information, ideas, opinions and entertainment. The electronic media are perceived as having an enormous influence in shaping values about all sectors of the society: economic, political and cultural. Broadcasting can be used

---

34. Martha Fletcher and Frederick J. Fletcher, "Communications and Confederation: Jurisdiction and Beyond," in R. B. Byers & Robert W. Reford (eds.), *Canada Challenged: The Viability of Confederation*, (Toronto: Canadian Institute of International Affairs, 1979), pp. 157-187.
35. Ouimet, "The Television Revolution and the National Interest," *op. cit.*, p. 57.
36. *Globe and Mail*, January 29, 1982.
37. Fletcher and Fletcher, "Communications and Confederation," *op. cit.*, p. 186.

as "an instrument of social control" and, as the American scholar Sidney Head notes, "No country can afford to leave so powerful and persuasive an avenue of public communication completely unregulated without shaping it to some degree in accord with public policy and national interest."[38]

In Canada, broadcast policies take on special significance because of the salient role of communications generally, and the electronic media specifically, in the development of nationhood. As the Federal Cultural Policy Review Committee (Applebaum-Hébert) reminded us in 1982, broadcasting is the only cultural industry whose activities are regulated under a comprehensive federal statute: the Broadcasting Act of 1968.[39]

As early as 1900, the Ottawa government asserted its jurisdiction in wireless operations by placing radio under the control of the Department of Public Works. In 1905, Parliament passed Canada's first radio legislation, the Wireless Telegraphy Act, which set up licensing requirements for radio transmitters and receivers. (This legislation became Section IV of the Telegraph Act of 1906.) In 1909, control over wireless was transferred from Public Works to the Department of Marine and Fisheries, reflecting the importance of radio as an aid to navigation. In 1913, Parliament enacted the Radio Telegraph Act that specifically included voice transmissions and continued the licensing requirements for transmitters and receivers set out in the 1905 legislation. In 1914, the year World War I broke out, the Department of Naval Services took over jurisdiction and operated more than 200 stations in Canada and in offshore waters. Naval Services also inspected and licensed privately owned stations and was the government department that licensed the Marconi experimental broadcast station in Montreal in 1918. In 1922, control over broadcasting reverted to the Minister of Marine and Fisheries who licensed the first commercial broadcast stations.

There was effective political control over navigational, military and commercial operations of point-to-point wireless transmissions, perceived as the important element of radio communication. The national interest was protected to the point that the government could take over any transmitting station or order stations to send messages. The 1913 legislation was suitable for "confidential messages" transmission but not for the mass medium that was to evolve in the 1920s.

THE REGULATION OF BROADCASTING

Broadcasting in Canada today is regulated by the Canadian Radio-television and Telecommunications Commission, an agency with broad powers to license and

38. Sydney W. Head, *Broadcasting in America*, (Boston: Houghton Mifflin, 1978, Third Edition), pp. 4-5.
39. Canada. Federal Cultural Policy Review Committee (Louis Applebaum & Jacques Hébert, co-chairmen), *Summary of Briefs and Hearings*, (Ottawa: Supply and Services, 1982). See also: Robert E. Babe and Philip Slayton, *Competitive Procedures for Broadcasting-Renewal and Transfers*, Study prepared for the Department of Communications, Ottawa, September, 1980, pp. 4-5.

supervise radio, television, Cable-TV, Pay-TV and telecommunications. The CRTC is the sixth regulatory authority established in the 60-year history of broadcasting. In chronological order, the regulatory agencies are:

1. 1922-1932. *The Minister of Marine and Fisheries* granted licences to stations. He operated in a policy vacuum using discretionary power that created political controversies. This was the decade of largely unregulated radio. In 1929, the Aird Royal Commission recommended public broadcasting. In 1930, Graham Spry and Alan B. Plaunt established the Canadian Radio League and helped rally public support for public ownership of broadcasting. The Court ruling in 1932 supporting federal jurisdiction in broadcasting cleared the way for major policy initiatives.

• 2. 1932-1936. *The Canadian Radio Broadcasting Commission.* Established by the first Canadian Broadcasting Act (1932), the Commission had two main functions: to regulate and control broadcasting and to carry on the business of broadcasting. This marked the start of public sector broadcasting. The Commission took over the Canadian National Railways radio facilities and expanded the network. Although the Commission had authority to literally take over broadcasting in Canada—it could set up new stations, lease or purchase privately owned stations, originate and transmit programmes—its accomplishments were limited. Inadequately financed, the CRBC also encountered administrative and political problems. Public radio made little headway, while the private sector continued to expand.

3. 1936-1958. *The Canadian Broadcasting Corporation.* Established by the second Broadcasting Act (1936), the CBC, a Crown Corporation, took over from the CRBC and moved quickly to build high-powered regional transmitters and parallel French and English networks. In 1936, the CBC could reach less than 50 per cent of the population; by 1939, the reach had been extended to 90 per cent. (In 1939, when King George VI and Queen Elizabeth were in Canada for a Royal Tour, the CBC was truly tested with what was perhaps the world's biggest broadcasting venture until that time. There was daily coverage in both French and English of the 11,000-kilometre journey through Canada. Four decades later, the Royal Tour is still looked back upon as the great coming-out feat of a truly national broadcasting system.)

The broadcast content was primarily Canadian and the innovative CBC programming included school and farm programs, later to be adopted in many other countries.

In addition to operating the national service, the CBC regulated the private sector, which continued to grow. The commercial stations saw the CBC as both regulator and competitor. The CBC recommended to the government the licensing of stations. This practice continued until 1958.

4. 1958-1968. *The Board of Broadcast Governors.* The third Broadcasting Act (1958) created a separate body that regulated both public and private broadcasting and recommended licensing. The Act was, however, unclear

on such issues as the BBG's power over the CBC, which reported directly to Parliament and had its own board of directors. There were no clear lines of authority between Cabinet, Parliament, CBC and the BBG. The Act was vague on other critical points but remained in effect for 10 years.

, 5. 1968-1976. *The Canadian Radio Television Commission.* The fourth Broadcasting Act (1968) created the CRTC, an independent public authority which regulates and supervises all aspects of the broadcasting system both in the public and private sectors. The Commission has the power to issue, renew, amend, suspend, or revoke licences and set any conditions of licence that it feels are necessary. The 1968 Broadcasting Act, among other things, defines broadcasting policy and remains in effect today.

6. 1976-present. *The Canadian Radio-television and Telecommunications Commission.* In 1976, the CRTC took over responsibilities for telecommunications previously regulated by the Canadian Transport Commission. The CRTC's enhanced powers over both broadcasting and telecommunications, two fields of enormous importance in Canadian society, make it one of the most visible regulatory bodies in Ottawa.

CANADIAN BROADCASTING POLICY AND COMMITMENTS

In the 60-year history of broadcasting, a number of national commitments and expectations have evolved. Most of these commitments are spelled out in the Broadcasting Act of 1968, some have their roots in the Constitution and others flow from broadcast practices. They include:

- The airwaves (radio frequencies) belong to the public.
- Broadcasting undertakings constitute a single system that comprises both public and private sectors.
- There is a commitment to provide radio and television service to all of the people—that is, equality of service. Initially this called for broadcasting in the densely populated areas but now includes the entire country.
- All Canadians are entitled to broadcasting service in both French and English. This broadcasting challenge has been further expanded to meet the Canadian commitment to multiculturalism, with accompanying linguistic requirements, and the commitment to meet the special needs of Canada's original peoples: the Indians and Inuit.
- Broadcasting should be effectively owned and controlled by Canadians so as to safeguard, enrich and strengthen the cultural, political, social and economic fabric of Canada (a national sovereignty commitment).
- There is a freedom of speech commitment. The tradition of freedom of the press in Canada resulted in expectations that there be freedom of information on the air. The Bill of Rights in the Canadian Constitution (1982) modernizes the free press concept by guaranteeing also freedom of the "other media of communication" (that is, electronic media).
- The programming provided by the broadcast system is to be varied, compre-

hensive and should provide balanced opportunity for differing views on matters of public concern.

- There are expectations of high standards with broadcasters using predominantly Canadian creative and other resources. The programme content should be predominantly Canadian.
- There are special expectations for the publicly owned national service CBC (Radio-Canada). They include:
  (i) Balanced service, meeting the needs of all sectors of society.
  (ii) Contribution to cross-cultural and interregional communications flow.
  (iii) Contribution to the development of national unity and provision for a continuing expression of Canadian identity.
- In the case of conflict between the public and private sector, paramount consideration will be given to the national broadcasting service.

CHARACTERISTICS OF RADIO TODAY

The long love affair Canadians have had with radio did not end with the introduction of television in 1952. Radio moved into the background and has thrived, away from the limelight, over the past 30 years. Figures for 1982 show that nearly 90 per cent of the adult population listens to radio every day for an average of over three hours. Radio thus continues to have an enormous influence on Canadian society. The characteristics of radio include:

- It is a universal medium with total saturation in Canada: there are many more radios than people, virtually all households have more than one radio and virtually the entire population has access to radio.
- It is a predominantly Canadian medium. Radio programming consists mostly of two elements, talk and recorded music, and both are cheap. Nearly all of the talk is Canadian but until 1970, nearly all the music (about 95 per cent) was foreign. CRTC regulations requiring that at least 30 per cent of the music on AM radio should qualify as Canadian have brought about a dramatic increase in Canadian content. CBC radio has about 60 per cent Canadian content; in the private sector, it is also well above the minimum. In FM radio, the Canadian content requirements vary with the kind of music in which a station specializes: country-and-western stations must meet the 30 per cent level, classical music stations, 10 per cent.
- It is a fragmented medium. In 1982, there are 1,308 radio stations—740 AM and 568 FM—competing for audiences. Nearly half of them are originating stations, and the rest are rebroadcast operations. The advertising revenue for radio is about $500 million and more than 500 stations in the private sector are competing for these funds. There is, then, fragmentation of audiences and revenues.
- Radio is largely a local medium. Seventy-five per cent of the advertising revenues are local sales. The programming has a local orientation. The major exceptions of course, are CBC (Radio-Canada) stations that provide network service with a local flavour in both English and French.

- Radio caters to personal taste. Programmes are categorized to appeal to specific audience tastes largely in music, but also in news and chit-chat. The image of the radio in the living room with the family sitting around has long disappeared. Radio does not cater to group entertainment. In the household, every member of the family may be tuned in to a different station. In 1942, Canada had one radio for three persons; today, there are about 1.5 radios per person.
- Radio is mobile. Nearly every automobile in Canada (93 per cent) has a radio. Many radios are portable and others like clock radios, serve additional functions. Only 10 per cent of the radios sold in Canada today are ordinary home radios.
- Radio listening is often a secondary activity. We listen to radio when we drive, picnic, in the home while engaged in other activities and even at the workplace. The heaviest listening periods are 6:30 a.m.-9:30 a.m., when there is a strong interest in wake-up music, news, weather and traffic conditions. Noon and the 4:00-6:00 p.m. (driving home) period are also heavy listening times. Radio thus does not compete in the heavy TV-viewing hours. Each medium has found its own place in the day cycle.

CHARACTERISTICS OF TV

In 1932, when Canada was formulating radio broadcast policy for the first time, Sir John Aird told a Parliamentary Committee: "It is coming, gentlemen, . . . we should be prepared to keep the question of television before us." It would be another 20 years before the first Canadian TV stations went on the air (in Montreal and Toronto). But Canadians were not strangers to television. All along the U.S. border, perhaps as many as half a million Canadians were watching American TV. There were 150,000 TV sets in Canadian homes before Canada had its own TV stations.

When TV came to Canada in its own right, the growth rate was phenomenal (Chart VIII.3). In no other country has there been a similarly rapid television penetration rate. In 1953, 10 per cent of Canadian households had TV; three years later, there were TV sets in 75 per cent of the households.

The CBC, the regulatory authority at the time, operated the first Canadian TV stations. There were, however, strong pressures from private entrepreneurs, especially owners of radio stations, who rightly foresaw that TV would be extremely profitable and wanted part of the action. By 1953, the first private sector stations went on the air; by 1955, the CBC "had lost its dominant position in the broadcasting system."[40]

The characteristics of TV in Canada today include:
- It is a universal medium. There are about 12 million TV sets. Nearly all households have TV: more than 40 per cent of the households have more than one TV set and 82 per cent of the households have colour TV.

---

40. Ellis, *Evolution of the Canadian Broadcasting System, op. cit.* p. 36.

CHART VIII.3. Television Growth in Canada (in percentages)—
Households with Television 1953-1981

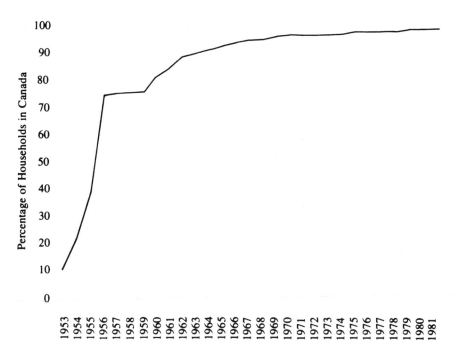

Source: CRTC, Industry Statistics and Analysis Division

- It is the dominant mass medium for entertainment, information, persuasion, education, advertising and cultural activity.
- It is the costliest and most profitable of all media. In 1982, more than $825 million in advertising money was channelled into TV (three-quarters of which was for national advertising). Grants for the public sector, national and provincial, amounted to about $650 million. Total TV revenues were about $1.5 billion. The profits on return on assets for the private sector of TV matches the outstanding profit performance of the newspaper industry.
- TV programming is a mosaic in that an evening's offerings include news and public affairs, hospital and police dramas, movies, detective shows, travelogues, comedies and the supernatural (for example, Incredible Hulk and Superwoman). There is thus considerable "mental gear shifting" as we move from one environmental immersion to another.
- TV is regarded as the most persuasive of the mass media. The Boyle Committee declared: "Television, which surpasses all other media in vividness and power of impact, provides the means for concerned Canadians to get the kind of information they need about their country."[41]

---

41. Inquiry into the National Broadcasting Service, *op. cit.*, p. 15.

- TV, by using satellites, has been able to conquer space and distance, considered among the most pressing mass communication problems. Over the past 10 years, television service has been extended to the entire country.
- Cable has enabled Canada to expand enormously the number of TV channels available to the public. Coaxial cable, fibre optics and satellites have overcome the "the scarce resources" aspects of public air waves.
- Pay-TV opens the way for charging directly for specific programmes or channels, with the consumer getting what he pays for. This approach to TV financing, not dependent on government subsidies, licence fees (which were discontinued in Canada in 1953) or advertising, will have a major impact on what the consumer will get on what is now called "free television."
- TV is by far the most popular leisure-time activity: the average Canadian spends more than three hours a day in front of a TV set, compared to the two hours a week that he devotes to reading books.
- Canadian TV content is dominated by American programming. It has been federal policy for more than 20 years to require a minimum amount of Canadian-produced programmes on TV stations. The present regulation requires all TV stations to have 60 per cent Canadian content between 6 a.m. and midnight, calculated on an annual basis. Between the hours of 6 p.m. and midnight, the CBC must have 60 per cent Canadian content, private stations, 50 per cent. As far as the privately owned stations are concerned, Canadian content is a burden on profitability; at best, Canadian programmes are reluctantly scheduled, preferably when few people are watching TV. The CRTC intent, of course, is quite different: not only must Canadian programmes exist, but they should be viewed.[42] Between 8 p.m. and 10:30 p.m., the peak viewing period, Canadian content has generally been declining (except on the CBC networks). In the 1978-79 period, CTV averaged under 6 per cent Canadian content in this prime time period. While CTV's Canadian content was lowest, most privately owned stations and networks averaged less than 25 per cent Canadian content in the 8 p.m.-10:30 p.m. time slot.

A report prepared for the CRTC draws an obvious conclusion.

". . . When most people are watching television, there are very few alternatives to U.S. programming fare. Overall, however, CBC has been most successful in maintaining a Canadian presence on the television screen. What Canada has at the present time is a system (if both off-air and cable carriage are considered) which is dominated by foreign programming in peak time and which is heavily oriented to foreign programmes throughout the day".[43]

---

42. *Canadian Broadcasting and Telecommunications: Past Experience and Future Options*, A report prepared for the CRTC, (Ottawa: Supply and Services, 1980), p. 25.
43. *Ibid.*

CABLE TV

Before there was Canadian TV, Cable-TV came to Canada as a carrier of American programmes. In 1952, E.R. Jarmin, a London, Ontario dry cleaner with electronics as a hobby, built a rhombic antenna to bring in TV signals from Cleveland, Ohio where the closest television transmitter was located.[44] He ran a successful test programme into 15 households. Today, London is probably the most wired city in the world, with more than 90 per cent of the homes having cable.

The incredible growth of TV sets in Canadian households (Chart VIII.3) brought in its wake a cable rush. Cable provided better signals (clearer pictures) and most importantly, additional stations from across the border. Colour TV, introduced in the United States before it came to Canada, further heightened interest in cable, which provided a better colour picture than off-air reception. Cable gave Canadian viewers the best of two worlds: not only did it bring a flood of additional programs beyond the offerings of Canadian stations, but it provided good reception for programmes originating in Canada and in the United States.

No country took to cable like Canada. In the 1970s, the spread of the copper wires of the cable companies was reminiscent of the breath-taking speed with which the Canadian Pacific Railway was built a century ago. In 1968, 700,000 households had cable, representing 13 per cent of the population. Five years later, well over 2,000,000 households—one-third of the population—subscribed to cable. In 1982, 60 per cent of households are linked to cable and fully 80 per cent of the nation's homes have access to cable (Chart VIII.4).

This is the national average. In Vancouver, 90 per cent of the households are linked to cable, and nearly 100 per cent of British Columbia households have access to cable. Remote locations often cannot have cable because of the prohibitive costs for wiring isolated communities where direct satellite transmissions provide a more practical approach for bringing additional programming.

The cable revolution removed some of the technological restraints in television transmission: more channels, a better picture and improved colour reception. But it also built irrigation ditches channeling American programming—sometimes more than Americans themselves can receive—into Canadian homes. Our enthusiasm for cable is just one indicator of how very popular American programming is in Canada.

BROADCASTING: THE CULTURAL HIGHWAY

Broadcasting was seen as the answer to many of the communications problems that stood in the way of Canadian nationhood. It would provide a cultural highway of national self-expression and serve as a unifying force. Our analysis shows that television is the dominant medium. "The long-term input of television on national identity," says Alphonse Ouimet, "is greater than that of all media combined."

---

44. *Cable Television in Canada.* Information Booklet. Canadian Radio-Television Commission. January, 1971, p. 4.

The notion of highway is important, for it suggests a conduit for a dynamic linkage in the harvesting of common experiences—the creation of a usable Canadian memory—from the diversity that is an integral part of the meaning of Canada. There is no suggestion of a stamp of imposed uniformity across Canada; rather, the emphasis is on sharing, on communicating experiences, attitudes and values. Identity, said John Grierson, "is something you create in action."[45]

CHART VIII.4.   Cable Growth in Canada—Households Subscribing and with Access to Cable 1968-1981

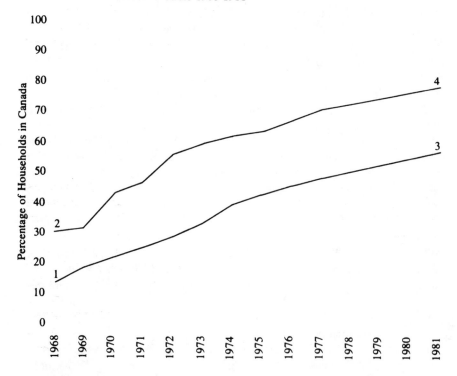

[1]710,000 Cable Households
[2]1,607,000 Households with Access to Cable
[3]4,506,000 Cable Households
[4]6,326,000 Households with Access to Cable

Sources: CRTC, Industry Statistics and Analysis Division
          CBC Research, Annual Report 1980/81

Broadcasting can facilitate identity formation, the cultural dimension of unity, but it cannot in itself create it.

The key to Canadian unity lies not in the "melting pot" but in the dynamics of cross-regional and cross-cultural interaction. The link between culture and com-

---

45. Grierson is quoted in *Report*. Committee of Inquiry into National Broadcasting, *op. cit.*, p. 5.

munications is inseparable; culture has been described as primarily a system of communication.[46] Culture, as Bernard Ostry has said, "is central to everything we do and think."[47]

NATION BUILDING AND BROADCASTING: THREE DIMENSIONS

There are three critical dimensions in the role of broadcasting in relation to Canadian unity and Canadian identity.

The first can be called *Canadian presence* and is measured by the amount (air time) of Canadian programming. It is usually referred to as the *Canadian content* of radio and television programming vis-à-vis the American programming available to the broadcast audience. This is the issue that has received the greatest attention, since the absence of *Canadian presence* is perceived as a national threat: a distinctive national identity cannot be nurtured by almost all-American programming.

The often-echoed assertion of the Aird Commission that Canadians want Canadian broadcasting is not supported in the TV viewing patterns. This is especially true and problematic in English TV, where the time spent watching Canadian programmes is lower than the proportion of Canadian programmes available.

Only one-third of all programmes on English TV (including the stations and cable mix) originates in Canada. These programmes do not attract their share of audiences although presumably they are tailored to meet specific Canadian interests. In fact, only one out of every four hours of TV viewing is devoted to Canadian programming, and this consists mostly of news, public affairs and sports. The other three hours are spent on American programming (Chart VIII.5). Half of Canada's TV time is spent watching drama and in this area, English TV has virtually surrendered the field to foreign offerings: 97 per cent of the drama we watch is foreign. In variety programming (including music and quiz shows), Canada's input is limited to 31 per cent and it attracts only 20 per cent of the audience share; 80 per cent of the substantial viewing time of variety shows goes to foreign programming.

In French-language TV, the language barrier provides some protection from inundation by foreign programming. The Canadian content on French TV is a respectable 64 per cent of the available programming and it attracts 62 per cent of the viewing time. As Chart VIII.6 shows, in nearly all categories of programming, including news, public affairs, sports, drama and variety shows, viewing time corresponds and sometimes exceeds the proportion of broadcast time. In the category of drama, which accounts for 39 per cent of the viewing time on French TV, only 12 per cent is Canadian content, but it attracts 20 per cent of the view-

46. E.T. Hall and Wm. Foote White, "Intercultural Communication: A Guide to Men in Action," in A.G. Smith (ed.) *Communications and Culture*, (New York: Holt, Rinehart and Winston, 1966), pp. 567-75.
47. Bernard Ostry, *Cultural Connections*, (Toronto: McClelland and Stewart, 1978).

CHART VIII.5. English-language TV Viewing Time, by Canadian and Foreign Programming, 1979-80

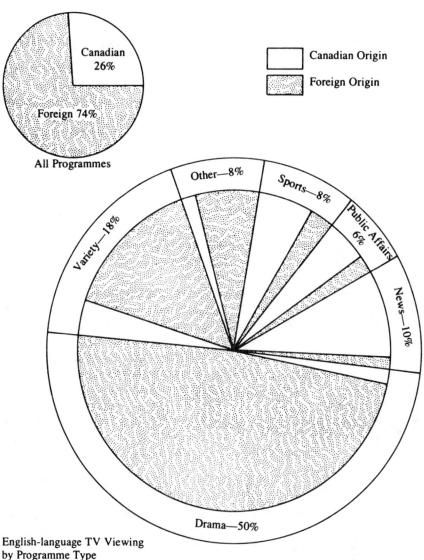

Canadian
26%

Foreign 74%

All Programmes

☐ Canadian Origin

▨ Foreign Origin

Other—8%
Sports—8%
Public Affairs 6%
News—10%
Variety—18%
Drama—50%

English-language TV Viewing
by Programme Type

	Canadian Origin	Foreign Origin
News	89%	11%
Public Affairs	71%	29%
Drama	3%	97%
Sports	71%	29%
Variety-Music-Quiz	20%	80%
Other	18%	82%

Source: CBC Research

CHART VIII.6. French-language TV Viewing Time, by Canadian and Foreign Programming, 1979-80

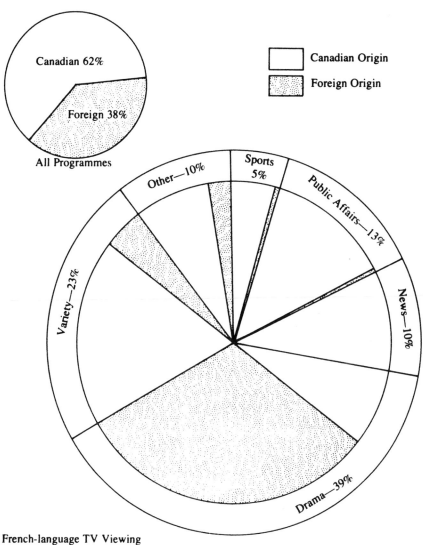

French-language TV Viewing
by Programme Type

	Canadian Origin	Foreign Origin
News	100%	
Public Affairs	98%	2%
Drama	20%	80%
Sports	96%	4%
Variety-Music-Quiz	82%	18%
Other	78%	22%

Source: CBC Research

ing time. In variety programming, 78 per cent is Canadian content and it attracts 82 per cent of the viewing time.

"Economic realities" are the principal reasons for the massive importation of American entertainment. It is far cheaper to buy the U.S. product than to produce "equivalent" Canadian programming. The Federal Cultural Policy Review Committee (Applebaum-Hébert) was given some stark figures by the CBC. It cost $1 million per episode to produce the *Lou Grant* series in Los Angeles. The CBC buys *Lou Grant* at $30,000 per show, or $800,000 for a series of 26. The CBC, for its part, has to spend $300,000 for each episode of a "substantial" Canadian series or a total cost of $8 million for 26 weeks.[48] The figures speak for themselves. The CBC can purchase *Lou Grant* for one-tenth the cost of producing its own series (and for three per cent of the original cost of the *Lou Grant* programme).

For the private broadcasters, the "dumped" American shows are irresistible. The CBC also finds the American imports important in its mix of Canadian/foreign programming. The Applebaum-Hébert Committee in its preliminary report noted that the marketplace provides a "double disincentive" that works against Canadian programming in favour of American.[49] Firstly, the "dumped" programmes are cheap and, secondly, there is the appeal of American programmes to advertisers. The private broadcasters make up to 500 per cent profits on the purchase price of American programmes, while they often lose money on the prime time programmes that they themselves produce. The Canadian Association of Broadcasters, a lobbying group for the private broadcasters, says, "Private broadcasting must be a successful business before it can effectively embrace public service requirements."[50] American programming has made private TV extremely profitable.

The CRTC recognizes that Canadian content regulations in their present form do not work, for there are no requirements or incentives for private broadcasters to produce quality programming that would attract Canadian viewers. On the contrary, much of what passes for Canadian content—outside of news, public affairs and sports programmes—encourages Canadians to seek something more substantial of foreign origin. Canada has failed, so far, in its efforts to mesh the profit-making motives of the private sector in broadcasting with the country's social and cultural objectives.[51] In the Canadian experience, it is unrealistic to speak, as the Broadcasting Act does, of a single system of broadcasting, comprised of the private and public sector and operating in the national interest specifically "to safeguard, enrich and strengthen the cultural, political and social fabric of Canada."

The weakness of *Canadian presence* on TV has deflected attention from two other fundamental problems. Regional communications interaction and cross-

48. Federal Cultural Policy Review Committee, *Preliminary Report, op. cit.*
49. *Ibid.*, p. 219.
50. *Ibid.*
51. *Canadian Broadcasting and Telecommunications, op. cit.*, p. 34.

cultural communications between the French and English broadcasting systems are essential elements in the harvesting of common experiences on a national scale. Both the private and public sectors have failed to make meaningful contributions.

The Boyle Committee reported in 1977 that practically all CBC English network TV series were produced in Toronto with Ottawa contributing some political programming.[52] Programming from other provinces ranged from very little to next to nothing in the Atlantic region and Prairies. British Columbia contributed some significant regular-season television in drama (for example, *The Beachcombers*). On the whole, the regional programming tends to be most frequently aired in the light-viewing summer months. The Boyle Committee concluded: "The regions of English Canada, from sea to sea, exist chiefly during the summer vacation."[53] On French CBC (Radio-Canada), the regional presentation of Canada beyond Quebec is extremely limited.

Television has played an almost insignificant role in explaining French and English societies to each other. The private sector networks (CTV in English, TVA in French) have virtually no programme exchange arrangements. In the CBC, the situation is hardly better, although some measures for French-English interaction have been taken since CBC President A.W. Johnson issued his "Touchstone for the CBC" document in 1977, when French-English problems in the national service created grave concern.[54] The structural arrangement within the CBC encourages the "two solitudes" of Canada, reinforcing differences in outlooks by such creative elements as journalists and entertainment producers rather than bridging them. French and English television in Canada have far more in common with American TV than with each other.

52. Committee of Inquiry into the National Broadcasting Service, *op. cit.*, pp. 56-57.
53. *Ibid.*, p. 57.
54. A.W. Johnson, "Touchstone for the CBC," Statement by CBC President, June 1977.

CHAPTER IX

SUPPORT STRUCTURES IN THE POLITICAL NEWS FLOW: CANADIAN PRESS AND THE PARLIAMENTARY PRESS GALLERY

This chapter focuses on The Canadian Press news agency and the Parliamentary Press Gallery. These two institutions with low public profiles are powerful forces in the Canadian news flow. The Canadian Press can be perceived as a super newsroom that services daily newspapers and broadcast stations with news about Canada and the world. The Parliamentary Press Gallery is a highly specialized organization that provides the infrastructure for the coverage of national political news. (There are similar press gallery organizations in provincial capitals.) The Canadian Press and the Press Gallery are basic structures in the machinery of political journalism. How they are organized and how they operate has a profound influence on Canadian media content.

I. NEWS AGENCIES: AFFORDABLE NEWS SUPPLY

The mass media brings us a picture of the nation and the world. No newspaper or broadcast station has the financial resources to cover the world on its own and consequently there are organizations that function as great marketplaces for news. They specialize in news collection and processing, and distribute news files at affordable costs. News and information are collected not for the exclusive use of one newspaper or broadcast network, but are provided to many subscribers who thus share in the costs of national and international news processing. There is a variety of marketing approaches for news material that includes pooling, cost-sharing, bartering on an exchange basis in cooperative ventures and the commercial sale of news files. The organizations involved in the wholesale marketing and distribution of news files are called news agencies, wire services, press agencies and telegraphic agencies.

THE CANADIAN PRESS: CP

"Ottawa (CP)," "Quebec City (CP)" and "New York (CP)" are examples of datelines of newspaper stories. CP stands for The Canadian Press news agency. If all the material supplied by The Canadian Press—news stories, feature articles, news analysis, stock market quotations, pictures, etc.—were removed from the pages of Canadian daily newspapers, there would be many blank spaces. If CP material and stories inspired by CP items were removed from radio and TV newscasts, there would be much awkward silence. CP provides enormous quantities of political, social, economic and entertainment news—much more than even the largest newspapers can handle—but the news agency is hardly noticed by the public. Few readers know the meaning of the (CP) logotype in newspaper datelines and the dailies choose to keep it that way; they do not want to emphasize the fact that an outside organization is providing so much of the content. Dailies prefer to give the impression that they are preparing a highly personalized and distinctive product. The broadcast media, for their part, hardly refer to The Canadian Press, CP thus remains anonymous to a large segment of the population.

Professor Carman Cumming describes CP as one of the most overlooked institutions in Canadian life.[1] CP has a pervasive national role. Silently and efficiently, it reaches out to almost every Canadian on a daily basis through more than 900 media institutions: 110 daily newspapers, about 500 private radio and TV stations, 115 Cable-TV systems and the 200 radio and TV stations of the CBC Radio-Canada networks.

CP: NATIONAL AGENCY WITH INTERNATIONAL LINKS

The Canadian Press is a national news agency. Most of its editorial energy and budget are spent in collecting, processing and disseminating domestic news for the Canadian mass media. At the same time, CP, much like national news agencies in numerous other countries, is linked with international press services. In this way CP provides a roadway for world news into Canada and for Canadian news to the world.

CP, of course, functions to meet specific Canadian news and information needs and is adapted to the unique Canadian communications environment. But news agencies generally have much in common. News is an international commodity and external factors have been important in the emergence and the shaping of news agency operations in Canada. It is useful to examine briefly the history of news agencies.

THE HISTORY OF NEWS AGENCIES

News agencies are an integral part of the mass media today and have especially

---

1. Carman Cumming, "The Canadian Press: A Force for Consensus?," in G. Stuart Adam (ed.), *Journalism, Communication and the Law*, (Scarborough, Ont.: Prentice Hall of Canada, 1976), p. 86.

close ties with newspapers. The origin of news bureaus as collectors and distributors of information, however, predates the media link: the early bureaus in Europe sprang up to meet the needs of shipping, commerce and international diplomacy. For example, the international insurance organization, Lloyds, collected and disseminated information on world shipping—news about arrivals, departures and disasters—in the early 1700s and had correspondents at major world ports.[2] In the early 1800s, the Rothschild banking family had its private news bureau and was the first in England to know about Napoleon's defeat at Waterloo.[3]

A study by the United Nations Education, Scientific and Cultural Organization (UNESCO) traces the origins of the modern news bureau to 1825.[4] In that year, Charles Havas set up a news bureau in Paris. Correspondents in various European capitals and centres of commerce were sending him news of interest to diplomats, traders and financiers which was translated and edited for the private subscribers. European newspapers at the time were more interested with "principles and polemics" than with current events and declined to buy the Havas file.[5] This situation changed in France around 1836 with the emergence of the affordable newspaper of mass appeal. To meet the demand for general news, newspapers turned to Havas.

In Britain, the emergence of the "cheap press" was held back by the tax stamp. Circulation climbed rapidly after newspapers became more affordable with the reduction in the tax on newsprint in 1836, and took off following the repeal of the tax in 1855.[6] A former Havas employee, Julius Reuter, opened a London news bureau in 1851, concentrating on financial information for stockbrokers and other commercial clients. By 1858, Reuter was supplying news to the British dailies. In Germany, Bernard Wolff, also formerly with Havas, started a Berlin news bureau in 1848.

The development of news agencies reflected the rapid change of communications technology in the nineteenth century. Havas emphasized speed and enhanced his reputation by creating an information network across much of Europe. He used the postal services, special couriers, carrier pigeons and the semaphore signal system. The big breakthrough was the electric telegraph, which came into wide use around 1848. The cable connection between London and Paris was in place in 1851, the year Reuter opened his London bureau. The UNESCO study shows that the decade between 1850 and 1860 saw the organization and development of the great European news agencies.[7] It was only a matter of time before there were trans-Atlantic and global links for news agencies.

2. Richard R. Cole, "News Agencies," in Fedler, *An Introduction to the Mass Media, op. cit.*, p. 246.
3. *Ibid.* This information was extremely useful for buying stocks that rose sharply with the spread of the news about the British military victory.
4. UNESCO, *News Agencies: Their Structure and Operation*, (New York: Greenwood Press, 1953), p. 9.
5. *Ibid.*, p. 9.
6. *Ibid.*
7. *Ibid.*

In the United States, the demand for news from Europe was the catalyst for establishing the first news agency, the Harbour News Association, in 1848 in New York. Newspaper rivalry, especially after the introduction of the penny press in 1833, led to an emphasis on "first with the news." New York newspapers were sending representatives in row boats to meet incoming ships in the harbour to collect newspapers and information dispatches from Europe, instead of waiting for the ships to dock and unload. Later, the New York dailies sent fast-sailing schooners (newsboats) far out into the Atlantic to meet incoming ships.[8] (Some newspapers made arrangements for news transmission by carrier pigeons, which were released when the ships were within flying distance.) This practice proved costly and seven New York dailies formed the Harbour News Association through which they shared the costs of newsboats.

New York was the major port of entry for foreign news and the telegraph was used to transmit it to newspapers in other regions. To share the cost, regional news agencies sprang up in the 1850s, including the N.Y Associated Press, the Western Associated Press, Southern Associated Press and New England Associated Press. These agencies also became involved in the exchange of news and news collection and later amalgamated into the Associated Press. The American approach was cooperative cost-sharing, compared to the private enterprise news agencies in Europe.

Towards the end of the nineteenth century, there were four major news agencies in the world: the Associated Press in the United States, Reuters in Britain, Havas in France and Wolff in Germany. They formed a global cartel by dividing the world into areas of exclusive news collection and distribution, and by exchanging news with each other. The Associated Press had the United States and Canada; Reuters collected and supplied news in the British Empire (excluding Canada) and the Far East; Wolff served Central, Northern and Eastern Europe (including Russia); Havas had the rights for Western and Southern Europe and countries in Central and South America.[9]

The cartel's global arrangement came under some pressure in the first decade of the twentieth century when two U.S. newspaper chains formed commercial international press agencies. Scripps established United Press (UP) in 1907 and William Randolph Hearst formed International News Service (INS) in 1909. In World War I, conflicting national interests disrupted cartel operations. Wolff disappeared with the rise of the Nazi party in the 1930s. Havas was a victim of World War II when it came under the indirect control of Germany during the occupation of France.

Today, five news agencies, all in competition with each other, dominate the world's news flow and are sometimes referred to as global agencies. They are:

Associated Press (AP)—non-profit cooperative based in the U.S.

United Press International (UPI)—commercial service based in the U.S.

---

8. Newspapers, *Collier's Encyclopedia*, 1952, Vol. 14.
9. UNESCO, *News Agencies, op. cit.*, p. 12.

Reuters—cooperative jointly owned by press associations in Britain, Australia and New Zealand; headquarters in London.

Agence France-Presse (AFP)—administered as a cooperative involving French daily newspapers and the French government's broadcasting organization.

TASS[10]—the official news agency of the Soviet Union.

As the 1980 UNESCO study *Many Voices, One World* points out, these agencies dominate the world news flow because of the size and technological strength of their news collection and distribution systems.[11] Each of these agencies is enormous by any standards of measurement. They each have networks of correspondents in more than 100 countries and supply news to thousands of clients including national news agencies, subscribing newspapers, radio and television organizations in over 100 countries. All have regular daily services in at least seven major world languages.[12] (AP alone has 10,000 subscribers, UPI about 6,500.)

Associated Press, which is establishing a Canadian bureau in 1982, has had especially close ties with Canada for over 100 years. This has given rise to an oft-heard criticism that Canadians see the world through U.S. eyes. A U.S. Supreme Court ruling in 1945 forbade AP to engage in a cartel with CP to prevent the two news agencies from furnishing news to each other exclusively.[13]

All of the global agencies either directly or indirectly have access to Canadian news. CP receives news from Associated Press, Reuters and Agence France-Press, partly for pay and partly in compensation for providing these agencies with Canadian news. This arrangement leads to a massive inflow of international news and a small outflow of Canadian news.

CANADA: TELEGRAPHIC NEWS

The national news agency came late to Canada. It was not until 1917 that CP was established partly at government convenience to meet national communication interests during World War I. At first glance this is surprising because Canada was one of the first countries to use the telegraph and the wires were carrying news as soon as the poles went up in 1846. The problem was that newspapers, which were less developed than those in the United States and Europe, simply were customers for news—the telegraph companies were the *collectors* and the *carriers*. The unsound practice developed—and it continued for 60 years into the first decade of the twentieth century—where news gathering was largely in the hands of telegraph operators, not journalists.[14]

10. Telegrafnoie Agentsuo Sovetskovo Soyuza (TASS).
11. UNESCO, *Many Voices One World*, Report of the International Commission for the Study of Communications Problems, (London: Kogan Page, 1980), p. 59.
12. *Ibid.*
13. Cole, "News Agencies," *op. cit.*, p. 250.
14. M.E. Nichols, *(CP) The Story of the Canadian Press*, (Toronto: The Ryerson Press, 1948), p. 5.

The Great North Western Telegraph Company, owned by the Grand Trunk Railway, was the dominant news supplier for about three decades. The building of the Canadian Pacific Railway in the 1880s brought Canadian Pacific Telegraph into the news business.

Two major railway companies had a monopoly in the supply of press news because they controlled the telegraph, the only means of speedy communication. The rapid growth of the "cheap" daily newspaper heightened the demand for news packages. The telegraph companies profited from the arrangement: the press could be serviced at slack times; and news stories were sandwiched between commercial messages in the daytime. Most press copy went out overnight when there was little demand for other telegraphic services.[15]

The national reach of Canadian Pacific—in 1885 it linked the country from east to west and was the largest railway in the world—led to its becoming Canada's most important supplier of telegraphic news. This dominance was enhanced in 1894 when Canadian Pacific gained exclusive rights to the Associated Press file, which it picked up at border points for distribution to Canadian newspapers.[16]

The Associated Press news file digest was prepared in the United States with American audiences in mind and this contributed to the evolution of Canadian tastes for American news. Some of the more important Montreal and Toronto newspapers supplemented their "railway packages" by subscribing to special news files from Chicago and New York dailies.

The AP file contained little news about Britain and the Empire countries, areas of special interest to Canadians. Montreal, Ottawa and Toronto newspapers tried to remedy this situation in 1903; they formed the Canadian Associated Press and engaged a full-time correspondent in London. This "mini news agency" inaugurated the first commercial cable between Canada and Britain. There were political as well as journalistic reasons for the British news link and Ottawa shared in the cost by contributing $8,000 a year.[17]

The news files provided by the telegraph companies appeared to meet the quantitative needs of most newspapers, but there were problems of quality: (1) Canadian news received little emphasis compared to foreign news, (2) there was an oversupply of U.S. news and (3) there was a low supply of overseas news which came to Canada through American channels and took on a colouration related to U.S. interests. To deal with the shortage of Canadian news, a few of the larger papers hired special correspondents in provincial capitals, but dailies in smaller cities lacked the financial resources for supplementing the news offerings of the telegraph companies. For news from Britain, there were the Canadian Associated Press dispatches for the successful papers in Ottawa, Montreal and Toronto. The ingredients described above provided a support structure both for regional communications gaps and for qualitative differences between news-

15. *Ibid.* p. 11.
16. *Ibid.* p. 13.
17. UNESCO, *News Agencies, op. cit.*, p. 80.

papers available to readers in large and small cities. What was common to all newspapers was a plentiful supply of news from the United States.

COOPERATIVE NEWS GATHERING

There was little cooperative news gathering in Canada until 1907, when the three Winnipeg dailies formed the Western Associated Press (WAP) in a revolt against the Canadian Pacific monopoly. Canadian Pacific had gone too far. Without consultations, it doubled rates and reduced service for the Winnipeg papers. The AP file would now be routed via Minneapolis, the Canadian news summary package would be discontinued and Winnipeg dailies would have to bring in Canadian news from the East at their own expense. The new terms were rejected and unexpectedly brought together the Winnipeg dailies, which were of very different political allegiances.[18]

The Western Associated Press linked up with United Press and later also with International News Service to replace the AP file for international news. Other Western papers were signed up and a cooperative news collection and distribution system evolved. The railway company retaliated by charging higher telegraphic rates for the WAP file. An appeal to the federal Railway Commission resulted in a 1910 ruling in favour of WAP: equal press rates for all press material.

Canadian Pacific's monopoly-hold, which stemmed from its control of the technology, dissipated, and it gave up its rights to the AP report. A national holding company, Canadian Press Limited, was established in December 1910 specifically to take over the AP rights. Nearly every daily was a member and thus had access to the news file from the United States.

Meanwhile, the cooperative news-sharing practices developed by Western Associated Press—which eventually included nearly all dailies in British Columbia, the Prairies and Northwestern Ontario—spread to other regions. In 1910, the Central Provinces agency brought together newspapers in Ontario and Quebec and the Maritimes dailies were linked through the Eastern Press Association.[19]

There was, however, no national link for the three separate regional press associations, since the cost for large-volume telegraphic transmission across the vast distances separating the news agencies was prohibitive. In World War I, the need to promote national unity in times of crisis was a major concern and the government of Sir Robert Borden offered an annual grant of $50,000 to help pay for a nation spanning leased wire. Almost immediately, the regional news agencies in western, central and eastern Canada came together to form what is now called The Canadian Press. The grant was discontinued after seven years.[20]

For 65 years, The Canadian Press has been a basic support structure for the

---

18. Nichols, *(CP) The Story of the Canadian Press, op. cit.*, p. 20.
19. *Ibid.*, p. 3.
20. Keith Kincaid, *The Canadian Press*. A CP publication produced in cooperation with the London Free Press, 1978, p. 3. The annual meeting of CP in 1925 voted that the news agency should never again accept a grant or subsidy from any source whatever.

mass media in Canada. Created as a non-profit cost-sharing cooperative by the daily newspapers, it has also become a major news supplier for radio and television. The Senate Study on the Mass Media noted that "Canadian Press pervades the news scene so completely that it has been endowed with a kind of semi-official status as an arm of the public service, like the Post Office and Air Canada."[21] The Royal Commission on Newspapers (1981) described CP as "Canada's voice in print, and increasingly radio and TV as well."[22]

In 1982, CP is operating on a budget of $27 million, with nearly 40 per cent coming from the broadcast media. The private sector in broadcasting (radio, TV and cable systems) in French and English receive their news from a CP subsidiary called Broadcast News (BN), while the publicly owned CBC is supplied through Press News, a subsidiary that looks after special services.

The 110 member newspapers pay a total of $10 million in basic assessment fees that are based largely on circulation and the number of newspapers in a city. The assessments in 1982 ranged from $600,000 for the *Toronto Star* to about $15,000 for the *News* in Thompson, Manitoba. Newspapers can pay additional fees for other CP services that they may want as a group or individually. (CP also supplies special services to a number of government offices, Canadian diplomatic missions, educational institutions, etc. Canapress Wire is a special service focusing on economic news for the business community.)

Canada has "other" news agencies and news bureaus serving the media. For the print media, they include:

United Press Canada (80 per cent owned by the *Toronto Sun* and 20 per cent by United Press International) is a commercial supplier of news and pictures, operating on a budget of $3 million. The Canadian content of the news file is small compared to the massive offerings of news copy from CP.

Southam News Service, with a budget of $2.5 million, provides a distinctive file for the 14 papers in the Southam chain, with a heavy emphasis on news analysis and backgrounder. Its staff of 23 operates out of six Canadian bureaus and five abroad.

The *Globe and Mail* news bureau system. In 1981, the *Globe and Mail* spent $1.7 million to maintain correspondents in Washington, London, Peking, Mexico City and in eight Canadian cities. The paper plans to open two more bureaus—one in Canada and one abroad—in 1982. The *Globe and Mail* file is essentially for its own news and is not available to other dailies in the Thomson chain.

The Thomson News Service, with a budget of less than $500,000, provides a supplemental file, compiled in Canada only, for the 37 small papers in the Thomson chain.

---

21. Special Senate Committee on Mass Media. *Report. op. cit.*, p. 229.
22. Royal Commission on Newspapers. *Report. op. cit.*, p. 119. For a detailed study of CP and other Canadian press services, see Carman Cumming, Mario Cardinal and Peter Johansen, *Canadian News Services*, Vol. 6, Research Studies for the Royal Commission on Newspapers. (Ottawa: Supply and Services, 1981).

Prestigious foreign news agencies—The *New York Times*, the *Los Angeles Times-Washington Post*, the *Times* of London, *Le Monde* of Paris, the *Christian Science Monitor*, *Chicago Tribune*, the *Economist* (Britain)—are among the foreign news services that supply news and/or feature material to a number of Canadian dailies, either directly or through two major Canadian syndicated feature services. In all, there are several dozen agencies and syndicated services, some of which offer feature material only by mail.

Southam, Thomson, the *Globe and Mail* (and the CBC in broadcasting) operate news bureaus for private use; CP and United Press Canada are for general consumption. The services of CP, or at least its main rival, UPC, are indispensable for Canadian daily newspapers aiming to provide well-balanced national and international coverage.

CP: A BIG AGENCY

CP is a big news agency for three reasons: it is a news clearing house, it provides its own reporting, and it receives international news from three global agencies—AP, Reuters and AFP. The global agencies provide indirect links to numerous other national wire services.

News Clearing House: The Giant Newsroom

CP's network of news collection extends into the newsroom of 110 member dailies. Almost every reporter working for these papers is a potential contributor to the CP file. For example, in Thunder Bay, Ontario, a reporter covering a shipping disaster on Lake Superior is collecting information not only for the *Chronicle-Journal* which employs him but also for the *Toronto Star*, the Halifax *Chronicle-Herald*, the *Victoria Times-Colonist* and other newspapers, as well as CP's broadcast clients. In this way, news from 90 newspaper cities across Canada flows into the CP system. The agency describes itself as "a giant newsroom where all the elements of Canada's individual newspapers come together on a national scale for mutual benefit."[23]

The news agency sorts the stories, usually rewrites and edits them, and distributes stories under the (CP) logotype. Stories that originate in Thunder Bay, Moose Jaw, Windsor or Chicoutimi thus appear in newspapers in St. John's, Halifax, Ottawa, Winnipeg, and Vancouver, among other cities. In the few cities where there is more than one daily, news supplied by one paper is not passed on to the competition.

CP: News Reporting in Canada

In addition to acting as a news exchange broker, CP is also involved in original reporting. In fact, 60 per cent of the Canadian news content on the CP wire is

---

23. Kincaid, *The Canadian Press, op. cit.*, p. 4.

supplied by CP staff; 10 years earlier, it was only 40 per cent. The increased emphasis on reporting is partly a response to increased demands for pooled cost-sharing journalism in Canada's non-competitive newspaper system and partly an effort to bolster weak editorial coverage in some regions.

CP's own reporting work is especially important in the coverage of national affairs in Ottawa where 24 reporters, among the 31-member CP editorial staff, cover Parliament, the Parliamentary committees and the departments of government. No Canadian newspaper has sufficient Ottawa staff to provide more than surface coverage of the Ottawa political scene and the affairs of Parliament (especially Committee proceedings), and CP thus is the major source of Canadian political news. (CP provides comparatively modest but nevertheless important coverage of provincial legislatures.)[24]

There are eight CP bureaus across Canada: Halifax, Quebec City, Montreal, Ottawa, Toronto, Winnipeg, Edmonton and Vancouver. Staff correspondents are stationed at six other cities: St. John's, Newfoundland; Saint John, New Brunswick; Fredericton, New Brunswick; Regina, Saskatchewan; Calgary, Alberta; Victoria, B.C.; and Yellowknife, N.W.T. (a new operation in 1982).

International News

The international news transmitted by CP is at once a strong and weak point of the agency. The volume is impressive. The sources are varied: three global agencies, each with its own world-spanning network, make their news available to CP, which gobbles it up in great quantities. Keith Kincaid, CP's General Manager, says, "Newspapers of no other country carry an international news report so broad, so complete, so closely tuned to their needs as that by CP."[25]

The problem is that CP does very little to project a Canadian perspective in world news; its own foreign coverage is minimal. In 1970, the Senate Study on the Mass Media urged a more vigorous international news-gathering role: there should be more Canadian reporters abroad providing reports that reflect "the kind of bias that Canadians tend to share, rather than the bias that Americans, or Frenchmen or Englishmen tend to share."[26] In the 12 years since the Senate Study, CP has actually become even more dependent on the global agencies. It closed down a one-man bureau in Paris, reduced its staff in New York and London and withdrew its correspondents who served for short periods in Moscow and Brussels. Today, CP has six correspondents abroad: two in London and four in the United States (Washington and New York). CP has opted in recent years to send reporters abroad to cover specific stories or countries, especially in times of dramatic news developments. Severely criticized by the Kent Commission for its

---

24. For a discussion of provincial press galleries, see F. Fletcher, "The Crucial and the Trivial: News Coverage of Provincial Politics," in Donald C. MacDonald (ed.) *The Government and Politics of Ontario*, (Toronto: Van Nostrand Reinhold, 1980).
25. Kincaid, *The Canadian Press, op. cit.*, p. 1.
26. Special Senate Committee on Mass Media, *Report. op. cit.*, pp. 233-34.

foreign coverage, CP increased its "international spendings" in 1982 to $500,000, still less than two per cent of its total budget.[27]

News Distribution

CP has its national decision-making desk for English news in Toronto and for French news in Montreal. However, the news agency divides the country into regions, and the bureaus in the largest cities play a key role in deciding whether a story is of national or regional interest. The regional decision-making centres are Halifax for the Atlantic region; Montreal for Quebec; Winnipeg for Manitoba and partly Northwestern Ontario; Edmonton for Alberta, Saskatchewan and the Northwest Territories, and Vancouver for British Columbia and the Yukon. The Toronto centre, in addition to its national centralizing function, also has a desk looking after the Ontario regional needs.

Central to the news distribution is CP's 90,000-kilometre system of leased wires. Stretched end to end, the CP wires could be wrapped around the world twice and there would still be a lot of wire left over. The trunk circuit, leased from Canadian Pacific Telecommunications, runs from St. John's, Newfoundland to Vancouver Island and the Yukon. This trunk circuit is linked to a whole network of connecting wires that reach into more than 90 communities. One connecting circuit out of Toronto links 30 Ontario dailies.

The leased wire system as a cooperative venture is one of the major reasons that CP is affordable for Canadian dailies. On a toll basis, the price would be prohibitive.[28] The traffic on the CP wire staggers the imagination: about 250,000 words a day on the main circuit, which amounts to about 300 columns of news, about 10 times as much as a newspaper can conveniently utilize. Thirty newspapers pay surcharges to receive the full 300-column Datafile—all the copy that CP has, including six regional circuits—on computer-to-computer transmission at the rate of 1,200 words a minute. Forty dailies have lesser computer facilities and receive a condensed file—70 to 80 columns—at speeds of about 100 words a minute. (French dailies get their news supply on a fast-speed wire of 300 w.p.m.) All 70 dailies with computer-receiving facilities can edit the wire copy on video display terminals without interfering with automatic typesetting. The remaining 40 dailies receive their wire news—about 55 columns—in column-width lines, permitting automatic typesetting, but making editing difficult.

CP AS AN AGENDA SETTER

The Canadian Press, like Reuters, Associated Press and other principal press associations, divides its flow of news into p.m. and a.m. reports for afternoon

---

27. I am indebted to CP General Manager Keith Kincaid for information about CP's 1982 operations. (The $500,000 international spendings budget is about double the CP spendings for this purpose in 1979.)
28. For further details on CP news wires in Canada and maps of the CP news wire circuits, see Kincaid, *The Canadian Press, op. cit.*, pp. 8-13.

dailies and morning papers. Perhaps the most eagerly awaited dispatch from CP by Canadian newspaper editors is the "budget" or checklist, a rundown of the major national and international stories that CP will be transmitting. Stories of importance that break in the course of the day's transmissions are usually slugged "urgent" or "bulletin"—and on rare occasions, "flash"—so that they will receive special handling and come to the quick attention of the editors who are planning the contents of the papers. Frequently, when CP is working on a story, but has not yet prepared sufficient copy for distribution, it will send a message slugged "attention editors," advising them as to what they can expect. These messages sometimes come in the form of "add budget," which means they should be considered part of the budget list. "Important" stories understandably receive preferred treatment in transmission. Studies have shown that time of delivery of a story on a news agency wire is a critical factor in the decision-making process of whether it will be used.

CP gives further direction as to what might be regarded as "important news" by sending advisories on its wires indicating the stories that are receiving front-page play in eight of the country's major newspapers. Similar advisories list the stories featured on the national TV newscasts of the CBC (at 10 p.m.) and CTV (at 11 p.m.) networks.

Newspaper editors, it is generally argued, have become so dependent on the judgement of what CP regards as important, that the wire service has, for all practical purposes, become the principal suggestion board, or reference point, for setting the agenda for most Canadian dailies. This is especially true for the 80 papers that rely on CP for nearly all of the news that originates beyond their immediate region of publication. There is, however, no empirical evidence for this. In fact, CP does not seek this agenda-setting role. The new fast-speed computerized delivery systems give newspaper editors far greater leeway in making their "own" decisions.

The news agency can be likened to the main water pipe leading to the reservoir in a community with every household linked to this pipe. The use of water in the individual homes, however, depends on a variety of factors that include the size of the family, the social habits of the individuals, the kind of plumbing, etc. Similarly, Canadian media outlets—newspapers and broadcasting stations— select what they want from the universe of CP offerings and can pass it on "as is" to their audiences, or they may edit, rewrite, cut, add or adapt. While CP is a major influence in setting a national news agenda, there is some evidence that other factors, such as language, regionalism, localism and metropolitanism, are even more powerful influences.

"The Something-for-Everybody File"

Canadian Press faces the staggering task of producing news files that meet distinctive regional communications interests reflecting the country's diversity. This is one of the reasons CP places so much emphasis on quantity, or what some critics call "news by the pound." The daily masterfile (Datafile) of 250,000 words is equivalent to two books. All newspapers, including those receiving the condensed files, have far more copy than they can use and presumably find enough material to satisfy their special needs in the "something-for-everybody file."

Quantity of copy is one major characteristic of CP. The all-purpose facts story—the neutralization of news—is another.

Neutral and Unbiased News

The all-purpose facts story is a pragmatic response to meet the common interests rather than the individual outlooks of newspapers. Keith Kincaid, the General Manager of CP, declares that the agency has "no interest except to fulfill its purpose—unbiased fearless recording of fact," providing an accurate, impartial picture of Canada and the world.[29]

Unbiased recording of facts means among other things that CP must be non-partisan politically and ideologically. It strives for neutrality in federal-provincial relations, French-English interaction, constitutional change and the aspirations of Quebec society as interpreted by separatist and federalist factions. An emphasis on facts, as James Reston has pointed out, may be useful for stories dealing with accidents, violence or sports, but can be "a limiting and distorting technique" in dealing with important and complicated events.[30] In Canada, facts by themselves oversimplify what is one of the most complex governmental systems in the world. Facts have to be placed in the context of history, region, biculturalism, federalism (political and societal) and national interest. Otherwise, they distort the "Canadian reality."

The Canadian reality can be projected by the media only through a complex flow of information, of which the outward thrust of federal news to the provinces is only one of several dimensions. For our purposes, language and region require further examination.

FRENCH SERVICE

French-language newspapers were among the charter members of the Canadian Press. But for 34 years, from 1917 until the formation of the French Service in 1951, the French dailies received their news in English and had to translate it. (There was a brief experiment in 1922-23 with CP delivering news files in French to five evening papers.) Starting in 1929, French-language dailies were given a translation grant: they received a rebate of one-third of the general CP assessment. The discount price could hardly make up for the inconvenience, translation expense and time delay, not to mention the cultural and linguistic disadvantages that flowed from this arrangement. Prime Minister Louis St. Laurent, speaking at the official inauguration of the French Service, described it as a major event in Canada's development as a nation.

29. *Ibid.*, p. 1.
30. James Reston, *The Artillery of the Press*, (New York: Harper & Row, 1966), pp. 13-22.

French CP, headquartered in Montreal, has some of the characteristics of a subsidiary and regional operation but is at the same time a largely autonomous service. At its start in 1951, there were six editor/translators. While the number of French dailies has declined in the past three decades, the CP French Service has expanded significantly from what started out largely as a translation operation to incorporate a vital news collection system. The greater emphasis on original reporting in CP's English-language side has been paralleled by a similar thrust on reporting in the French Service.

In 1982, the French Service had 31 reporters, editors and translators: 20 in Montreal, seven in Quebec City, three in Ottawa, one in Toronto. English-speaking Canada is covered by the French Service almost exclusively through translation and adaptation of copy prepared by English-language reporters.

CP supplies far more material in English than in French. The coverage of Parliament and Ottawa is broader in English than in French. English CP correspondents file copy from all over Canada, including Quebec province, while the original offerings in French are mainly from Montreal, Quebec City and Ottawa. Some of the criticisms of the French Service made in 1970 by Claude Ryan, then publisher of *Le Devoir*, are still valid. Mr. Ryan said French CP coverage tended to be thin (or synthetic) compared to the fresher or more complete coverage of the English wire.[31]

The Royal Commission on Newspapers described French CP as "unwell" and called for a greater infusion of money and authority.[32] But as Mr. Ryan noted in 1970, there are harsh realities of economics that account for the lesser quality of CP's French Service. It is already felt that CP's French Service is subsidized to an abnormal extent in relation to the contribution of the French-language members alone. Canada's 11 French-language dailies pay total basic assessment of $1.7 million, compared to $8.3 million contributed by the far more numerous English-language dailies.

What is significant about the French Service is not so much its shortcomings as compared to English CP, which are very real, but its rapid rate of improvement. Since 1980, for example, the delivery speed of the French wire has been increased to 300 words from 66 words a minute. The reporting and editorial staff increased by 43 per cent over the past decade. Furthermore, some effort is being made to disseminate over the English wire material collected by French reporters. Situationals and features are translated from French to English, providing what CP calls "an original and authoritative perception of the Quebec fact."[33] But these efforts are insufficient to bridge the gap between the French and English service.

In terms of technology, the CP French Service ranks among the most advanced in the world. The 11 French dailies—nine in Quebec, one in Ontario and one in New Brunswick—are provided with news day and night. CP has been equipped

---

31. Special Senate Committee on Mass Media. *Report. op. cit.*, p. 232.
32. Royal Commission on Newspapers. *Report. op. cit.*, p. 122.
33. Canadian Press, *Submission to the Kent Commission*, April 16, 1981, p. 9.

with video display terminals (VDT) for bilingual operation since 1974, and the copy is delivered for automatic typesetting.

The improved technology and resources of both the French and English services have made them more autonomous in relation to each other. Current practices tend to encourage cultural and regional isolationism rather than a cultural distinctiveness which could be strengthened by the dynamics of communications exchanges.

For domestic news, the two great meeting points for French and English CP staff are in Ottawa and Quebec City. Hawley Black, in his study of CP, notes that French-language reporters in the federal capital are formally part of Ottawa's CP bureau, but in practice they deal almost exclusively with the French Service head office in Montreal. Thus, there is virtually no liaison between the French and English CP news operations.[34] In Quebec City, says Black, English-speaking CP staff operate almost like foreign correspondents.

In international news, CP's structure tends to encourage different perceptions of the global scene along linguistic lines. The French-language news from the international agencies flows to Montreal where the CP selections are made, while the English-language selections on international news are made in Toronto. The problem is not that the selection of the French- and English-language services may be different; rather, the two services have limited knowledge of each other's interests and perceptions of newsworthiness. This arrangement hampers "communication awareness" across linguistic and cultural lines.

CP has not moved effectively to bolster bilingualism in the news service operation.[35] The linguistic separation reinforces different perceptions of news values in domestic and international news. There is limited encouragement for a sharing of common ground across cultural barriers.

On the whole, the English service dominates the CP structure. There are nine times as many English-language newspapers as there are French, and collectively English dailies feed far more information into the CP news flow than the French papers. Furthermore, the corporate structure at head office in Toronto is dominated by English-speaking directors. A considerable amount of the French-language file continues to be based on translation.

INTERREGIONAL COMMUNICATION

CP is a reflection of the Canadian newspaper system: strong newspapers supply good copy while weak newspapers have relatively few offerings of interest to the national service. The picture of reality projected by the news media (and CP) is not only based on what is happening but is shaped by the resources utilized by the newspapers in the coverage they extend to their respective cities and regions of operation.

34. Hawley L. Black, "The Role of the Canadian Press News Agency in Gatekeeping Canada's News," unpublished Ph.D. thesis, McGill University, 1979, p. 208.
35. *Ibid.*, p. 209.

Intensity of news coverage in provinces varies significantly. Ontario has 45 dailies, Quebec, 11—an enormous difference even if population sizes are taken into consideration. There is an uneven distribution of newspapers in Canada (see Table VI.1) that affects the comprehensiveness of national newspaper coverage. The result is a spotty news flow and in some cases regional news deprivation. News value of events does not necessarily coincide with population density. The most undercovered news area in Canada is the vast northland, the frontier region of resources development.

The predominance of small newspapers in Canada means that, except for a few large cities, the resources of newspapers for journalistic coverage are limited. The disappearance of competition, most recently in Ottawa and Winnipeg, means that only one newspaper is covering the local scene rather than two, suggesting a significant quantitative decline. Furthermore, the local coverage is deprived of the dynamics of competition and the news flow to CP, and thus the national news flow, is presumably weakened in quality also.

In summary, CP is a remarkably efficient organization that plays an absolutely vital role in providing a national communications link and a roadway for the entry of international news into Canada. It has a pervasive reach in the media and is a great training ground for Canadian journalists. Its strong points and its shortcomings are a reflection of the strengths and weaknesses of the Canadian newspaper system. In the 1980s, the broadcast media, now supplying 40 per cent of CP revenues, will play an increasingly important role in shaping the organization that has generally been regarded as a preserve of the printed press.

II. THE PARLIAMENTARY PRESS GALLERY

The Press Gallery is at the centre of the flow of national political news, and its importance in parliamentary government is universally recognized. In 1944, Prime Minister Mackenzie King observed that the correspondents of the Press Gallery as a body formed an "adjunct" of Parliament itself.[36] Twenty-five years later, the Task Force on Government Information (1969) in its Report *To Know and Be Known* described the Gallery as "perhaps the most powerful Gatekeeper of Federal Government Information. . . . unquestionably, the most important instrument of political communication in Canada."[37] More recently, the Royal Commission on Newspapers referred to the Gallery as "the inner temple" of political journalism, but expressed concern that its performance and prestige had declined in recent years.[38]

PARLIAMENT AND THE GALLERY: RELATIONSHIP

The relationship between Parliament and the Gallery, steeped in precedent and tradition, is loosely defined. The decision that the press should be allowed to

36. Robin Adair, "Parliament and the Press," *The Canadian Liberal*, Vol. 4, No. 1, Spring 1951, p. 37.
37. Task Force on Government Information. *Report.* (Ottawa: Queen's Printer, 1969), Vol. II, p. 116.
38. Royal Commission on Newspapers. *Report, op. cit.*, p. 141.

cover Parliament was resolved in Britain nearly a century before Confederation. (Opponents had argued that parliamentarians would be inhibited from speaking their true mind in the presence of journalists.) The press has always been welcome in Canada's federal Parliament. There is, all the same, no absolute privilege to print what is said in Parliament, although newspapers can reproduce what is printed in Hansard,[39] the official record of proceedings.

In practice, however, there are few restraints on press coverage of Parliament and the mass media are institutionalized in the parliamentary process. As the Speaker of the House of Commons, James Jerome, observed in 1977:

> The Press Gallery function is more than a commercial news reporting service. It is an integral part of our (Parliament's) work; a service which Parliament must safeguard for the Canadian public who are entitled as of right to the fullest information on activities here.[40]

HISTORY OF GALLERY: EARLY PERIOD

There had been press coverage of legislatures in British North America for half a century before Confederation. It therefore came as no surprise that when the first Parliament met in 1867, space and services were provided for journalists.[41] In fact, the press reports of the first decade of Parliament are the best "unofficial" records of parliamentary proceedings. (Hansard, the verbatim account of the proceedings of Parliament, was not introduced until about 1878.)

The journalists in the early Parliaments recorded conscientiously speeches that were of special interest to the newspapers they represented. This was the era of the partisan press and journalists covering Parliament had close ties with the politicians they supported.

Paul Bilkey, writing about his experiences when he went to the Press Gallery in 1903, said it "was divided on party lines almost, if not wholly, as distinctly as was the House of Commons."[42] Arthur Ford, who was sent by the Winnipeg *Telegram* to the Gallery in 1907, observed that most of the papers were "either owned or directed by political parties or politicians, or controlled by publishers or editors who took their politics seriously."[43] Journalists and parliamentarians gave each other advice and developed an open relationship; there was no pretense about their ties.

The fact that Gallery reporting reflected the party line had its advantages and disadvantages. Government ministers handed out news, much like patronage,[44] to supporting papers. Taken into the government's confidence, the loyal reporter

39. Friedland, *National Security: The Legal Dimensions, op. cit.,* p. 64. There are procedures to empty the House of the public, the media and Hansard reporters if Parliament opts for a secret meeting in a war crisis or similarly grave situation.
40. The Speaker, Mr. Jerome, made his comments on the role of the Gallery in a letter in December 1976 to the General Manager of Canadian Press, Mr. Dauphine, during a controversy relating to a strike by CP members in Ottawa. Part of the letter is quoted in Doug Small, "Politicizing the Press Gallery," *Carleton Journalism Review*, Vol. I, No. 2, Winter 1977, p. 5.
41. W.H. Kesterton, *A History of Journalism in Canada, op. cit.,* p. 162.
42. Paul Bilkey, *Persons, Papers and Things,* (Toronto: Ryerson Press, 1940), p. 49.
43. Arthur R. Ford, *As The World Wags On,* (Toronto: Ryerson Press, 1950), pp. 43-44.
44. *Ibid.*

became much like a back-bencher. He could grumble under his breath and offer advice in private but ''he was gagged by the responsibilities of partisan journalistic connection.''[45] He virtually forfeited the right to be a watchdog on government activity or even indulge in realistic news analysis. The ''Opposition press,'' on the other hand, thrived on leaks, rumours and ''underground sources,''[46] and while not always accurate, was often ''nearly right,'' which seemed to be good enough.[47]

Telegraph transmission was costly. Detailed accounts of parliamentary proceedings were sent by mail while the most urgent matters—specifically, the speeches of party leaders supported by the newspaper—were transmitted by wire. ''A Conservative paper,'' says Ford, ''covered the speeches of its leaders and more or less ignored the speeches of the Liberals and vice versa.''[48] There was nothing fair or unbiased in the reporting. Press Gallery members were not only observers but also participants in raw politics. There are several cases where Gallery reporters were elected to the House of Commons, appointed to the Cabinet and Senate, made official advisors or given senior posts in the Ministries.[49]

The Gallery was a small and exclusive club. Only the wealthiest papers, or those with especially strong vested political interests, sent representatives to Ottawa. Sometimes a correspondent would represent several Canadian dailies and one or two papers abroad. The membership included the publishers of papers, editors (often important political figures in their own right) and their most favoured reporters. It is no coincidence that some of the famous names of the early Galleries are also famous names in Canadian political history.

The Kent Commission speaks with great nostalgia about the ''good old days'' of the Gallery: of influence, of prestige, of ''legendary figures . . . who were more like ambassadors for their newspapers than mere correspondents.''[50] A number of famous Gallery members in their memoirs also reminisce romantically about memorable Ottawa correspondents. Olivar Asselin, for example, the founder and editor of *Le Nationaliste*, spent a month in jail for assaulting Quebec Premier Sir Lomer Gouin. Another colourful Gallery correspondent, Ernest Cinq-Mars of *La Presse*, on one occasion, after having a few drinks, sent a message to his paper that both Sir Wilfrid Laurier and Sir Robert Borden had committed suicide, the former by jumping off the Interprovincial Bridge and the latter by taking poison in a Hull hotel.[51] The telegraph clerk went over to the House to verify the story and found both Laurier and Borden alive and well. The Cinq-Mars message was never transmitted.

---

45. Bilkey, *Persons, Papers and Things, op. cit.*, p. 49.
46. ''Underground sources'' presumably included speculation, tips from Opposition politicians, talkative government officials, etc. See Ford, *As The World Wags On, op. cit.*, p. 43.
47. Bilkey, *Persons, Papers and Things, op. cit.*, p. 49.
48. Ford, *As The World Wags On, op. cit.*, p. 43.
49. Even today, there is some movement between the Gallery and the Government. The present Gallery includes at least two former Members of Parliament, one a former Cabinet Minister, and numerous former Gallery members are employed in government departments.
50. Royal Commission on Newspapers. *Report, op. cit.*, p. 141.
51. Ford, *As The World Wags On, op. cit.*, p. 68. The stories on Asselin and Cinq-Mars are outlined in detail by Ford, pp. 65-70.

These lighter stories do not detract from the rather remarkable journalistic work of Asselin, Cinq-Mars, George Pelletier, Arthur Ford, Paul Bilkey, Wilfrid Eggleston, Israel Tarte, Joseph Howe, Charles Bishop, Henri Bourassa and John W. Dafoe, among others.

GALLERY CHANGES

The "Gallery" developed into an exclusive institution, a club that was extremely jealous of its loosely defined privileges. Housed in a Parliament that was itself reluctant to reform, the Gallery was highly resistant to change.

But change did come to the Gallery in dramatic form. This change was inevitable because the Gallery has only one foot in Parliament. The other is in the media, and as the media changed, the Gallery was hit by a successive series of shock waves, especially in 1917, 1959 and 1977.

The 1917 Change: CP in the Gallery

The partisan interaction between parliamentarians and journalists continued into World War I. There were about 25 members in the Gallery, all men, representing a score of newspapers. The wartime (W.W.I.) need for national support from papers of all political outlooks was a factor in creating CP in 1917, Canada's first national medium. The news agency's Ottawa bureau and the CP correspondent in the Gallery had to serve newspapers of different political outlooks, and the approach was "unbiased" factual news. The process of "neutralization" of federal political news had begun. At the time Canada had 138 daily newspapers and nearly all of them started receiving impartial news supplied by CP staff in Ottawa.

Arthur Ford observed in his autobiography that Canadians, for the first time, were receiving a fair picture of Ottawa events. In Ford's opinion, "the credit for the development of independent political thinking in Canada and the breaking down of party lines—for better or for worse—must largely go to the Canadian Press."[52] (As noted in Chapter VI, economic forces were creating parallel trends to "neutral news" for everyone's taste.)

The old-time members of the Gallery at first were shocked by the CP approach; they felt their own jobs could become obsolete. Instead, the routine and thorough coverage of parliamentary proceedings by CP correspondents provided the other Gallery members with new opportunities. They now had more time to cater to specific regional interests, to explain Ottawa developments and to interpret the news.

Over the years, as government in Ottawa expanded enormously, the load on CP's shoulders in the capital increased. In 1917, CP began with one correspondent in the Gallery. By 1922 there were five, and this number climbed to 13 by 1959. In 1982, the CP bureau in Ottawa numbers 31 men and women editors and reporters providing coverage of Parliament (House of Commons, Senate and

---

52. *Ibid.*, p. 44. See also: Nichols, *The Story of Canadian Press, op. cit.*, pp. 194-201.

selected Parliamentary Committees), the Supreme Court and the departments of government and governmental agencies, among other sources of political news.

The Press Gallery: Membership

The Canadian *Parliamentary Guide* in 1925 for the first time provided a formal description of the Press Gallery: "A voluntary, self-governing body subject to the authority of the Speaker in matters affecting House of Commons discipline and management."[53] Two years later, however, the word "membership" replaced "management," a change that is important because it involves jurisdiction on membership. Speakers have made it a point to keep a hands-off policy on the Gallery. In practice, Speakers have delegated the responsibility of accreditation, permanent and temporary, to the Press Gallery itself, unless there is "some indication of injustice or impairment in the right of the public to be informed about Parliament."[54]

The membership question has always been important for the Gallery, which traditionally fostered something of an élite status for itself. There was no Gallery constitution until 1935, at which time the membership became concerned that the "club" was becoming too big. The Gallery expanded during the Commonwealth Economic Conference held in Ottawa in 1932. Furthermore, the Great Depression saw journalists looking around for work and some ended up in Ottawa in the hope of picking up free-lance assignments from papers not represented in the Gallery. The Gallery members, who saw themselves at the top of the ladder in journalism, moved quickly to create a "closed shop": membership was restricted to *bona fide* representatives of recognized daily newspapers and news agencies who earned most of their income from the daily printed press. The 1935 constitution shut the door to freelancers and journalists working for magazines or radio.

In 1942, the first magazine journalist from *Maclean's* was grudgingly admitted as an Associate Member. In the decade of the 1940s, representatives from the *Financial Post, Saturday Night, Time, Life, Weekend Magazine* and the *Glasgow Herald*, among others, became Associate Members.[55]

By 1949, the Gallery membership numbered 64, including nine Associate Members. The CP representation was eight, and six members represented foreign newspapers and news agencies. Despite the enormous growth of Canadian government during and after World War II, membership in the Gallery was small, and far too few persons were covering what had become a major capital.

The 1959 Change: Broadcasters in the Gallery

The Gallery policy to keep out broadcast journalists, enforced for nearly 25

---

53. Canada. *Canadian Parliamentary Guide*, (Ottawa: King's Printer, 1925).
54. The Speaker, Mr. Jerome, is quoted in Small, "Politicizing the Press Gallery," *op. cit.*, p. 5.
55. Associate Membership was strictly controlled: (1) two-thirds voting at a General Meeting had to approve, (2) the journalists had to be the full-time staff of periodicals, national or international, which focused on national affairs and were published at least twice a month.

years, was self-serving. Newspapermen covering Parliament regularly appeared as panelists and commentators on radio and TV public affairs programmes.[56] These moonlighting activities, which were an important source of income, created great controversy in the 1950s. It was suggested that Gallery members were hesitant to criticize government policy on the nationally owned CBC (Radio-Canada) networks. The CBC, for its part, sought to establish a broadcast gallery in Parliament if it could not send its own correspondents to the Press Gallery.

In 1959, broadcasters were allowed into the Press Gallery. They were not permitted, however, to bring their tape recorders and TV cameras into the Gallery; like the print journalists, they could take notes.

To accommodate the special film needs of television, a room in the basement of the Parliamentary Building was made available. Here, MPs could face the TV cameras and microphones after the all-important (for the media) Question Period to re-enact some of the House highlights. The broadcasters would elaborate on the Question Period of the House and ask their own follow-up questions, bringing a new and unreal perspective to the Question Period. This led to a situation, says Professor Westell, where newspaper editors were demanding that their reporters provide coverage of the "Question Period follow-up" instead of the actual Question Period.[57] The broadcasters began to erode the supremacy status of the print journalists, which had prevailed unchallenged in the Press Gallery for 92 years. The prestige of the Commons was partly undermined. What was going on in front of the TV cameras in the basement seemed to be more important than the proceedings on the House floor.[58]

The 1979 Change: the Electronic Hansard

A new chapter in the history of the Canadian Parliament began on October 17, 1977, as radio and television moved into the House of Commons on a permanent basis. The live broadcast coverage of the House introduced a new dimension in the interaction of mass media and Parliament.

For about a century, every word spoken in Parliament became part of the printed record of proceedings, commonly called Hansard, that has been and continues to be of enormous value to the press, researchers and anyone in Canada with an interest in parliamentary affairs.

The radio and television record of the House of Commons (begun on an historic occasion in the Senate Chamber with the Queen opening a new session of Parliament) is referred to as the Electronic Hansard. Radio and TV now have access to a record of proceedings of the House of Commons that is suited to their special needs.

---

56. Task Force on Government Information. *Report. op. cit.*, p. 117.
57. Anthony Westell, "Reporting the Nation's Business," in Adam (ed.), *Journalism, Communications and the Law, op. cit.*, p. 64.
58. Hawley Black, "Live Commons' Broadcasting—How It's Rated By Canada's MPs," *Cable Communications*, Vol. 47, No. 11, November 1981.

Parliament was slow in opening its doors to the electronic media. Off and on for about a decade, parliamentarians debated the merits of bringing radio and television into the Commons.[59] Some of the same arguments heard in the British Parliament two centuries earlier for keeping out newspaper journalists from the House were brought forward by those who had reservations about the Electronic Hansard: the normal proceedings of Parliament could be adversely affected. There was apprehension that the generally leisurely ways of the legislators would come under some pressure if parliamentarians tried to meet the deadlines of broadcasts. The concerns that Parliament would try to serve TV, instead of the other way around, were unfounded.

Neither cameras nor production personnel are visible on the floor of the House. The House itself, under the authority of the Speaker, owns and operates the broadcast system which is neutral toward politics, without commentary and observations. The telecasts tend to be boring because the camera is always focused on the person making a speech and no mood shots of the House are provided. The broadcast stations decide what they want to use. Excerpts from the Question Period are now frequently integrated into the national network newscasts.

The parliamentary broadcasts are transmitted live via satellite to numerous Cable-TV systems across the country. These feature the Electronic Hansard on one of the previously unused channels. More than half of Canada's households have access to the live proceedings or same-day reruns from the House and the audience appears to be bigger than had been envisaged. Furthermore, the Electronic Hansard has become the source for a number of regular radio and TV programmes of House highlights. The House telecasts have been so successful that consideration is now being given to extending the Electronic Hansard service to selected Parliamentary Committee meetings.

The Electronic Hansard has opened a new link between Parliament and the public that enables political leaders to bypass the filtering influences of the print and broadcast journalists. It has helped to focus attention on the real Question Period instead of the substitute session in the basement TV studio. A greater public awareness of, and interest in, Parliament enhances the importance of the Press Gallery.

THE PARLIAMENTARY PRESS GALLERY TODAY

Critics of Parliamentary Press Gallery performance, including the Task Force on Government Information (1969), have often based their analyses on the membership list, or nose count.

The conventional wisdom is that government activity has expanded far more

---

59. Television was supposed to have come to the Commons in 1973. One reason for the four-year delay was that Canada had a minority government in 1973, a situation that may create an element of instability and certainly tends to enhance the influence of third parties holding the balance of legislative power. A minority Parliament is usually perceived as a pre-election period. The presence of previously untried telecasts, it was feared, could have undermined legislative programmes, while the House membership concentrated on political advantages to be gained by individual television performances.

quickly than the growth rate of the Gallery, and the Ottawa press corps has been swimming against the tide. Professor Anthony Westell of Carleton University, in a sensitive analysis "Reporting the Nation's Business," argues convincingly that the media "are not doing as well as they could and should" in providing information about federal politics and the institutions of government.[60] But the Gallery has expanded considerably in the past 10 years and has become more professionalized.

In 1982, the Gallery had a membership of about 240 journalists, consisting of editors, reporters, syndicated columnists, broadcasters and foreign correspondents. About 150 Gallery members, or 60 per cent, represent the print media: newspapers, magazines, and press agencies. The other 100 members serve the electronic press. Only 18 Canadian dailies have their own representatives in the Gallery, compared to 22 dailies 60 years earlier. But these naked figures do not reflect the full influence of the Gallery in the national news flow.

The structure of the Gallery has changed. In 1975, for example, there was one freelancer in the Gallery; in 1981, there were 15. The number of wire and news services now stands at 30, a three-fold increase since 1960.

Television networks, radio news services, specialized news services and freelancers (including specialists in economics, foreign policy, science and law) have professionalized the Gallery, resulting in an improvement in media coverage of the federal capital. The Gallery today bears little resemblance to the 133-member body that existed a dozen years earlier at the time of the Senate Committee Study on the Mass Media. As Professor Fletcher has observed, more specialized and analytical copy is flowing out of Ottawa and on the whole, coverage of federal affairs has both increased and improved.[61]

One important change is that far more correspondents are working on pooled and cost-sharing assignments for press services, and they are supplying both the print and broadcast media. Others, especially freelancers, have developed their own clientele, often by offering special coverage not previously available. A number of newspaper columnists, housed in the Gallery, have large national audiences through syndication, thus overcoming some of the problems of newspaper fragmentation.

The Gallery turnover has been high, ranging between 25 and 40 per cent a year. Consequently more journalists are gaining experience in covering the federal capital, although it is sometimes argued that the newcomers do not have the background and personal contacts that can be so important in reporting on politics. At the same time, the high turnover has made the Gallery a more open place. More women reporters than ever before are covering the Ottawa scene. They are, on average, younger and better-educated than their male colleagues.

On balance, the Gallery has become more dynamic and more professionalized. The leisurely days of Gallery members staying in Ottawa for the parliamentary session and leaving the city during the parliamentary recess are gone forever.

---

60. Westell, "Reporting the Nation's Business," *op. cit.*, pp. 54-69.
61. F. Fletcher, *The Newspaper and Public Affairs*, Research Study, Vol. 7, Royal Commission on Newspapers. (Ottawa: Supply and Services, 1981), p. 53.

CHAPTER X

THE MASS MEDIA AND CANADIAN FEDERALISM: THE IMPACT OF LANGUAGE AND CULTURE

The dissemination of federal government news is important in a country like Canada where, it is often noted, there are relatively few natural forces to bind the nation together. The maps of the world, and especially of Canadian affairs, drawn for us by the media are important clues in evaluating the pressures for integration and disintegration.

It was observed earlier (Chapters II and VI) that while federalism requires good internal communications, the characteristics of Canadian federalism, and particularly the importance of provincial legislative powers in relation to our most immediate interests, tend to bring about regional communications interests of an extreme form and an accompanying regional containment of news.

In this chapter, the focus of attention is on the mass media, both print and broadcast, as support structures for Canadian federalism and nation building. Particular attention is given to the influence of language. There will be an analysis of the differences between the French and English media in their perception of Canadian federalism and Canadian unity.

The sociologist Frederick Elkin, in his essay on the role of Canadian communications in the development of a Canadian identity, expressed the view that the content of the English and French media, "although basically following similar lines, often reflect different cultures."[1] The Canadian Senate Study on the Mass Media (1970) observed that in journalism, "the traditions, the audience preferences, the mythologies, the economics of publishing and broadcasting—all are shaped by the French Fact, to the extent that the province's [Quebec] media cannot be viewed simply as part of the Canadian whole."[2] In 1981, the Royal Com-

---

1. Frederick Elkin, "Communications Media and Identity Formation in Canada." In *Communications in Canadian Society*, edited by Benjamin D. Singer (Toronto: The Copp Clark Publishing Co., 1972), p. 222.
2. Special Senate Committee on the Mass Media. *Report.* (Ottawa: Queen's Printer, 1970), Vol. I, p. 95.

mission on Newspapers noted that Quebec journalists were deeply engaged in the socio-political transformation of Quebec. "The practice of French-language journalism differs in a number of respects from the norms of English-speaking Canada."[3]

DUAL FEDERALISM

Language and cultural considerations in the Canadian communications flow cannot be divorced from federalism. This is because the Canadian federal system combines two distinctive dimensions: "two federal systems, of very different types, compelled to co-exist within the same constitutional structure."[4]

One basic component is organized around the traditional perception of federalism, an American invention, providing for a division of powers between the central government (that is, Ottawa) and the regional governments, or provinces, as they are called in Canada. Both levels of government derive their substantial powers from the constitution and are each, "within a sphere, co-ordinate and independent."[5] The British North America Act prescribed a federal system that departed in important ways from the "classical" definition; it has been described as quasi-federalism.[6] But Canada has, over the years, moved in the federal direction, and not towards the unitary governmental system that so many Fathers of Confederation envisaged. As Donald Smiley puts it: "Canada is in the most elemental way a federal country, and it seems that it is becoming increasingly so."[7] The federalism that binds the 10 provinces in the national framework finds its dynamism not only in the constitution and governmental institutions but also in the very nature of Canadian society, where such basic considerations as natural resources, economic development and identity allegiances have a territorial base.[8]

The second and distinctive component of Canadian federalism is that we are also a union of two "founding peoples"—the French and the English—each fostering its autonomous cultural and linguistic traditions. French-English duality was perhaps the most important, but certainly not the only, reason for establishing Canada as a federation instead of a unitary state.[9]

The "founding peoples" aspect of our federal structure is not specifically prescribed constitutionally either in the British North America Act of 1867 or the Canada Act of 1982. It stems from cultural and political factors that predate Confederation and found a fertile soil in the economic, political and social systems as

3. Royal Commission on Newspapers, *Report, op. cit.*, p. 171.
4. J.R. Mallory, *The Structure of Canadian Government* (Toronto: Macmillan of Canada, 1971), p. 393. See also J.R. Mallory, "The Five Faces of Federalism," in P.A. Crepeau & C.B. Macpherson (eds.), *The Future of Canadian Federalism* (Toronto: University of Toronto Press, 1965).
5. K.C. Wheare, *Federal Government* (London: Oxford University Press, 1953), p. 11.
6. Mallory, "The Five Faces of Federalism," *op. cit.*
7. D.V. Smiley, *Canada in Question: Federalism in the Eighties* (Toronto: McGraw-Hill Ryerson Ltd., 3rd edition, 1980), p. 1.
8. *Ibid.*, p. 2.
9. *Ibid.*, p. 214.

Canada moved from a largely rural-based society to a highly industrialized nation. The Royal Commission on Bilingualism and Biculturalism came forward with recommendations which held up the viability of the two linguistic and cultural groupings as an essential goal and basic principle of Canadian existence. This French-English founding peoples notion has been developed into a whole series of concepts and formulas for Quebec's position in Confederation including "special status" and the "bi-nation state." The aspirations of the Parti Québecois government for the separation of Quebec from Canada is an extremist perception of how the principle that Quebec "is not a province like the others" should be translated into reality.

In our examination of the interaction of the mass media and federalism, we will focus first on daily newspapers and later on the broadcast media.

I. FRENCH AND ENGLISH NEWSPAPERS: SIMILARITIES AND DIFFERENCES

Studies carried out in the mid-1960s for the Royal Commission on Bilingualism and Biculturalism noted significant differences in the attitudes of French- and English-language journalists toward their work.[10] English-language journalists saw their principal function as straight news reporting while French-language journalists were much more inclined to perceive their journalistic function to include interpreting the news. The findings suggest a sense of involvement in the news on the part of the French language journalist.

This sense of involvement of French-language reporters and their newspapers is especially pronounced in the coverage of politics, particularly when it relates to Quebec nationalism and Canadian federalism.

In 1966, when the politicization of separatism was still in its infancy, Quebec newspapers provided a strong support structure for the newly formed separatist Rassemblement pour l'Indépendence Nationale party in the provincial general elections. (In the vote on June 5th, the Liberal Party of Premier Jean Lesage, a principal figure in Quebec's Quiet Revolution, was toppled from power by the Union Nationale headed by Daniel Johnson.) Professor Guy Bourassa's analysis of Quebec newspaper coverage of the election campaign showed that the Liberals received a bad press. In contrast, the separatist RIN received the most favourable coverage: "it was never shown in a bad light."[11] The RIN received the best headlines, the most favourable treatment in background and analysis stories and in picture coverage of its leader, Pierre Bourgault. In fact, in every avenue of analysis the RIN received the best press compared to the other parties.[12] The

10. F. Chartrand-McKenzie, "Les Journalistes Anglo et Franco-Canadiens: Leurs Opinions et leurs Comportements vis-à-vis de la Coexistance des deux Cultures." See also H. Black, "French and English Canadian Political Journalists: A Comparative Study." Both are research reports of the Royal Commission on Bilingualism and Biculturalism.
11. See Guy Bourassa and Francine Despatie, "La Presse Québecoise et les Elections du 5 Juin," *Cité Libre* 17 (Nov.-Dec. Supp. 1966): 5-32.
12. *Ibid.*

most important aspect of the 1966 election campaign coverage in the press, largely overlooked at the time, was the support for separatism. Ten years later, the Parti Québecois was elected to power.

The Quebec newspaper support for the RIN was only one dimension of the French print media's outlook toward federalism in the late 1960s. A content analysis study of French and English newspaper coverage of the Federal-Provincial Constitutional Conference in February 1969 (the first such meeting after Pierre Trudeau had become prime minister) showed significant differences in the press coverage provided by French and English papers.[13] The French papers projected a two-nation parity concept of federalism, with Quebec leaders representing French Canada and Mr. Trudeau speaking for English Canada. In contrast, English papers perceived a federalism of provinces and not "nations." Quebec journalists displayed a more sophisticated understanding of the nuances of federalism and outlined well-defined Quebec demands on such matters as international relations, family allowances, medicare, education and telecommunications, issues largely neglected in the English press. A general conclusion of this study was that French- and English-language dailies covering the same political event stressed different subject matters, were different in style, reflected different interests both editorially and in news coverage, and had different orientations on federalism. French and English newspapers provided different "mappings of reality" of Canada's federal framework for their respective audiences, thus providing a political communications dimension for what Hugh McLennan has called "two solitudes" in the broader social context.

OCTOBER 1970: THE FRONT DE LIBERATION DU QUEBEC (FLQ) CRISIS

Press coverage of the Canadian Emergency in October 1970, commonly referred to as the FLQ crisis, provided an excellent vehicle for finding out more about the "Canadian reality" as presented by French and English newspapers and evaluating the implications of the differences in the interaction of press and politics.[14]

A crisis situation tends to reveal basic characteristics of the political and social systems, including such matters as stability, flexibility and responsiveness of the institutions.[15] It is in a situation of this nature that the political system is confronted with the unusual and its response is likely to bring to the surface characteristics that remain latent in what are regarded as more normal times. In other words, a crisis situation precipitates a moment of truth for the political system. It

13. A. Siegel, "Public Opinion, the Mass Media and Plebiscites in Canada," House of Commons, Committee on Justice and Legal Affairs, *Proceedings*, Appendix "JLA-7," February 22, 1979.
14. A. Siegel, *Canadian Newspaper Coverage of the FLQ Crisis: A Study on the Impact of the Press on Politics*, unpublished Ph.D. Thesis, McGill University, 1974.
15. Crisis was defined as a situation involving the following aspects: (1) a threat to the goals of the political system, (2) outside initiation, (3) surprise, (4) escalation of risks, and (5) time pressure in the sense that the situation is acute, not chronic. See James Robinson, "Crisis," *International Encyclopedia of the Social Sciences*. See also Daniel Latouche, "Mass Media and Communica-

is also a moment of truth for the mass media. Communications studies have shown that in time of crisis, coverage tends to become more alike, and many differences are submerged with the filtering out of unimportant political details. The focus is on the common interest and the differences that do show up are seen as being of a fundamental nature.[16]

In the FLQ crisis—and this is characteristic of most crises—the media were drawn into an active role in the events themselves. The events of October 1970, as Professor Daniel Latouche has noted, could be seen as a battle for the temporary control of the communications system in Quebec.[17] The media occupied a central position in the communications flow between principal actors in the crisis, serving as channels of communications between the FLQ and the authorities, the FLQ and the public, and the authorities and the public. The public was thus drawn into the crisis in an intimate manner. Furthermore, newspapers also were advocates of solutions in what was really a "new" situation when "mass communications is widely believed to be quite efficient in creating opinions."[18] Consequently, the political power of the press, stemming from the politicians' perceptions of the influence of the press, increased.

The Crisis

The crisis involved a series of events which began on October 5, 1970 with the kidnapping of the British Trade Commissioner in Montreal, James Richard Cross, by the Front de Libération du Québec. In the next two weeks or so, there were to be such other notable traumatic events as the kidnapping and murder of the Quebec Minister of Labour, Mr. Pierre Laporte, the proclamation of the War Measures Act by the federal government in Ottawa, and the deployment of armed troops for the maintenance of internal security. The FLQ crisis was intimately linked to the French-English confrontation in Canada. In a sense, one can view the crisis as an attempt to resolve the constitutional question by violence and to break up the Canadian union.

Involved in this crisis were the issues of Quebec's place in the Canadian federation and whether there was to be a federation at all. The way the government perceived the developments in October 1970, the very life of the political system was under attack. The invocation of the War Measures Act, in effect declaring a state of emergency, marked the first time that the government took this step in time of peace. Matters very much related to the crisis were civil rights in time of emergency, the role of Parliament during a grave crisis, and the power and role

tion in a Canadian Political Crisis," in Singer, (ed.) *Communications in Canadian Society, op. cit.*, pp. 296-297.
16. J.T. Klapper, *The Effects of Mass Communications* (Glencoe, Ill.: The Free Press, 1960), pp. 53-61.
17. Daniel Latouche, "Mass Communications in a Canadian Political Crisis," in Singer (ed.), *Communications in Canadian Society, op. cit.*, p. 302. See also: Arthur Siegel, "The Use of the War Measures Act in October 1970: A Communications Analysis." Paper presented at the inaugural meeting of the Canadian Association of Survey Research, Quebec City, May 30-31, 1976.
18. Klapper, *The Effects of Mass Communications, op. cit.*, p. 60.

of the federal government in the emergency. Another very important consideration, apart from the fact that the jurisdiction of the federal government is sensibly enlarged by an emergency situation,[19] is the role of the provincial government, which has exclusive constitutional jurisdiction for the "administration of justice" in the field of "law and order."

A multi-dimensional content analysis of a representative weighted sample of 22 dailies was used to examine the versions of realities presented to French and English readers. Five main avenues of analysis were used to slice into the content: (1) intensity and scope of coverage, (2) the subject matters receiving attention—that is, the themes, (3) personalities receiving prominent attention, (4) a geographic profile examining the geographic sources of stories and (5) a detailed examination of opinions expressed in the editorial columns.

It was found that the French and English dailies in their coverage of the *acute* stage of the crisis, beginning with the kidnapping of the British Trade Commissioner and ending with the funeral of Quebec Minister Laporte 17 days later, attached similar overall importance to the October developments, as revealed by similarities in the intensity of coverage. In every other main sphere of analysis (themes emphasis, personality emphasis, geographic profile, editorial position), there were significant differences.

Two news themes, *negotiations* and *manhunt*, were especially important in setting the patterns for front-page news coverage (see Table X.1). For the French papers, the highest-ranking theme was *negotiations*, which could be interpreted as stressing a compromise approach to resolving the crisis. For the English dailies, *manhunt* was the most prominent theme. These stories dealt mostly with police activities to apprehend the kidnappers and free the hostages, a very different manner of resolving the crisis than through *negotiations*. The fact that the English and French groups of papers stressed these two differing aspects of the crisis means that most of the differences that appear for the other themes of front-page emphasis can be accounted for. The most important matter for *negotiations* to come about was, of course, the position of the authorities: the *federal government* and the *Quebec government*. These two themes ranked immediately after *negotiations* in the French group of papers, but were not nearly as prominent in the English dailies. The notion of time, so important in the definition of crisis, provided a sense of urgency to bring about negotiations, for otherwise the hostages would be killed. This was yet another theme receiving greater prominence on the front pages of French dailies.

19. The War Measures Act (Rev. Stat. Canada 1952, c. 288) is a grant of power so sweeping that it conveys to the Governor-in-Council most of the war-time emergency powers made available to the Dominion Parliament under the "peace, order, and good government" clause of Section 91 of the British North America Act. As Professor Mallory has pointed out in "The Five Faces of Federalism," there is nothing either in the Confederation debates or the B.N.A. Act which addresses itself to the distribution of powers in an emergency. It was the courts that have made this opening in the federal system regarding the federal distribution of powers a peace-time luxury which must be forgone in war-time. Emergency federalism, in effect, makes Canada "a unitary state for the duration." See J.R. Mallory, "The Five Faces of Federalism," in P.A. Crepeau and C.B. Macpherson (eds.), *The Future of Canadian Federalism, op. cit.*, pp. 7-9. See also Smiley, *Canada in Question, op. cit.*, pp. 49-52.

For the English papers, the most prominent theme, as noted above, was *manhunt*. Very much related to the *manhunt* theme were *security* and the *War Measures Act*. *Security* involved stories dealing mainly with the role of the army for the maintenance of public security. The *War Measures Act* gave emergency powers to the authorities to expand the *manhunt* and in a sense helped to uphold the principle of law and order. All these themes received greater emphasis in the English dailies.

TABLE X.1. Themes of Front-Page Emphasis, by Coverage in French and English Papers (in mean number of stories appearing daily on Page One)

THEME	FRENCH MEAN	ENGLISH MEAN	PERCENTAGE DIFFERENCE BETWEEN MEANS (LOWER MEAN = 100%)	SIGNIFICANCE LEVEL IN t TEST
Negotiations	.5185	.4292	French + 21%	.20*
Federal Government	.4568	.2968	French + 54%	.02
Quebec Government	.4444	.1598	French + 178%	.000
Manhunt	.4198	.5388	English + 28%	.20**
Kidnapping	.4074	.4110	Equal	—
Time	.3086	.2237	French + 38%	.15
Security	.2963	.3165	English + 7%	—
Religious-Funeral	.2469	.1416	French + 74%	.05
Parliament	.1728	.3151	English + 82%	.03
Murder	.1481	.1689	English + 14%	—
War Measures Act	.1111	.2603	English + 134%	.01

*Significance level in F test: .01
**Significance level in F test: .02
N (F) = 81
N (E) = 219

Yet another theme that was highlighted in the English front pages, but not in the French, was *Parliament*. Parliament was asked to approve the War Measures Act policy, and concern about the resort to emergency powers would therefore be accompanied by interest in the reaction of the legislative branch of government. The tendency on the part of the English dailies to stress the legislative branch of government, while the French dailies emphasized the positions of the political executives (the federal and Quebec governments), was one of the strongest findings in the statistical analysis.

As the focus of attention shifted from the front pages to the contents of the whole newspaper (see Table X.2), it was found that French dailies were especially interested in international reactions to the FLQ developments. French papers stressed the *civil rights* theme and gave considerable prominence to the *protest movements* (labour groups, civil rights groups, students, etc.). The picture which emerged from the French newspapers suggested far more popular opposition to the authorities than one would have envisaged from reading the English dailies.

TABLE X.2. Emphasis of Coverage of Selected Categories, by Language of Newspapers (in mean number of stories)

THEME	FRENCH MEAN	ENGLISH MEAN	PERCENTAGE DIFFERENCE BETWEEN MEANS (LOWER MEAN = 100%)	SIGNIFICANCE LEVEL IN t TEST
Canadian Reaction— Personalities	1.6914	.6164	French + 174%	.00
Background	1.1852	.8630	French + 37%	.08*
International Reaction— Press	1.0370	.2785	French + 272%	.00
Media	.8025	.5160	French + 56%	.05
Protest	.7778	.5297	French + 47%	.07**
International Reaction— Personalities	.5432	.2694	French + 102%	.05*
Civil Rights	.1481	.0594	French + 149%	.02*

*Significance level in F test: .00
**Significance level in F test: .04
N (F) = 81
N (E) = 219

There was an emphasis on background stories in French dailies which explained the ramifications of the FLQ crisis and related matters. These background stories were often "think" pieces and intellectual journalism prepared by outside experts such as political scientists and sociologists. This finding showed greater media involvement on the part of French papers compared with English dailies through interpretive journalism. Also, the French dailies had more stories classified in the *media* theme.

In the personality analysis, it was found that the French papers gave far greater emphasis to personalities involved in the crisis while English papers tended to focus on institutions.

The geographic analysis, focusing on the sources of stories, showed that the French dailies concentrated for the most part on Quebec province and Ottawa, while the English dailies had a far wider Canadian perspective. There was also a difference between the number of stories appearing from foreign cities, with the French dailies having far more from virtually every foreign country except the United States.

The French/English differences outlined above show that there were two distinct patterns of news coverage, which meant that the FLQ crisis looked different to French and English readers. The different patterns of coverage reflected an organization of information which projected different perceptions in an overall context of what was taking place and which aspects were important in the resolution of the crisis.

Editorializing

The extent to which editorial positions were distinctly different in the French and English group of papers is shown in Table X.3. There were virtually no important issues pertaining to the crisis on which the French and English took similar positions, except the general concern expressed for the safety of the hostages. Of the 15 issues explored in detailed analysis, there were significant differences in 11.

English newspapers were more hostile to terrorism generally and the FLQ specifically, provided far stronger support for both the Ottawa and Quebec governments, enthusiastically endorsed the decision to invoke the War Measures Act and emphasized consistently their support and concern for Canadian unity.

French editorialists provided extremely strong support for negotiations, had a comparatively low support level for Canadian unity, generally did not relate separatism to terrorism and tended to differentiate between legitimate separatism (the kind advocated by the Parti Québecois) and the "bad" separatism that was associated with terrorism. Social and economic injustices, which were almost always associated with French Canadians in the editorials, were a frequently raised issue and a matter of considerable concern. French papers were far more concerned about what was happening to civil rights in Canada. The argument frequently made in the English dailies was that it was not the civil rights of Canadians that were so much in danger but the civil rights of the kidnapped victims.

The editorial analysis, then, revealed that the two groups of papers interpreted the crisis developments in different ways. The differences in outlook were broadly based and the perception of reality in the French and English papers was very different.

There was evidence of a strong association of editorial position with the patterns of news coverage. In the French dailies, the editorials stressed the need to resolve the crisis through a negotiated approach, in effect a compromise between the authorities and the FLQ. The English papers, in their editorials, stressed the law and order aspect which was, of course, associated with the emphasis on the police activity observed in the news themes. The findings in the editorial evaluation showed that news processing—that is, newspapers acting as a channel of communications—was in the FLQ case related not only to the developments taking place, but also to editorial opinions. There is, then, an intricate or very close relationship between editorializing and agenda setting, two major sources of political power of newspapers. In other words, the press as a symbolic institution providing interpretations of the society is a major factor in shaping the press as an operating organization, that is, a social institution.

Political Implications

The political socialization activities of mass communications are envisaged as a long-term process. Wright has pointed out that either deliberately or inadvertently, the individual at various times in his life probably obtains some of his

TABLE X.3. Editorial Evaluation on Specific Issues, by Language (frequency of indication of attitude and description of attitude in percentages)

Issue	FRENCH								ENGLISH								X² Test	Degrees of Freedom	Significance Level
	Rank	Frequency (%)	Strongly Favourable (%)	Favourable (%)	Neutral (%)	Opposed (%)	Strongly Opposed (%)	Mean Score*	Rank	Frequency (%)	Strongly Favourable (%)	Favourable (%)	Neutral (%)	Opposed (%)	Strongly Opposed (%)	Mean Score*			
Terrorism	1	85	0	0	11	23	66	4.54	1	95	0	0	0	2	98	4.98	28.14	2	.000
FLQ	2	73	0	0	10	23	67	4.56	2	85	0	0	0	5	95	4.95	18.36	3	.001
Quebec Government	3	66	30	22	22	22	4	2.48	6	53	56	29	12	4	0	1.63	12.07	4	.02
Federal Government	3	66	11	30	30	26	4	2.81	3	76	59	27	8	7	0	1.63	25.61	4	.000
Mr. Cross	5	51	48	43	10	0	0	1.62	4	55	67	26	6	2	0	1.43	3.06	3	NS
Mr. Laporte	6	44	61	33	6	0	0	1.44	7	41	65	27	5	2	0	1.44	.68	3	NS
Negotiations	6	44	62	23	15	0	0	1.54	10	35	17	26	23	14	20	2.94	11.14	4	.05
Civil Rights	8	37	40	13	27	13	7	2.33	9	36	11	17	33	28	11	3.11	5.88	4	NS
War Measures Act	9	32	46	23	8	15	8	2.15	8	39	80	13	8	0	0	1.28	11.19	4	.05
French Canadians	10	29	75	25	0	0	0	1.25	12	21	14	38	33	10	5	2.52	13.85	4	.01
Social and Economic Injustices	10	29	42	50	8	0	0	1.67	14	12	17	67	8	0	8	2.17	2.57	3	NS
Canadian Unity	12	24	30	30	20	20	0	2.30	5	54	95	5	0	0	0	1.02	32.82	4	.000
Separatism	13	17	0	0	86	11	0	3.14	11	30	0	0	16	27	57	4.40	15.60	3	.01
Army	14	10	50	50	0	0	0	1.50	13	14	93	0	7	0	0	1.14	7.97	2	.02
New Democratic Party	15	0	0	0	0	0	0	0	14	12	0	8	0	92	0	3.83			

N (F) = 81   N (E) = 219

* Mean score is theoretically not a valid figure. However, in practice it was found that the mean score was a fairly reliable indicator of overall editorial attitude. Guttman scaling: 1 = strong support, 5 = strong opposition.

social and political norms from the mass media.[20] Because the political culture of
a society is shaped partly by profound life experiences as well as historic incidents, the FLQ crisis is likely to become a reference point for present and future
generations for their perception of the political system.[21] A number of findings in
the FLQ study are regarded as reflective of values and norms that are part of the
transmission of political culture through the newspapers. The findings, summarized in Table X.4, are based on the analysis of news coverage as well as editorial contents.

**TABLE X.4. Some Major Findings Reflecting Different Values and Norms, and
Characteristics in the French and English Press.**

FRENCH	ENGLISH
Canadian unity not perceived as a major objective in the editorial evaluation of the crisis developments.	Canadian unity a major objective.
A strong concern with Quebec affairs and FLQ problems evaluated from a regional perspective.	A pan-Canadian perspective was taken in evaluation of FLQ developments.
Neither positive nor negative disposition towards French separatism.	Negative disposition towards separatism.
Emphasis on personalities in coverage of FLQ developments.	Emphasis on institutions.
Emphasis on executive branch of government.	Emphasis on Parliament.
Concern with international reaction to FLQ crisis.	Concern with Canadian reaction.
In foreign reaction coverage, greatest emphasis was given to European and Francophone countries.	Comparatively high interest in U.S. reaction.
Emphasis on historic and contemporary economic and social injustices experienced by French Canadians.	Strong interest in economic implications of crisis.
High media involvement in crisis as illustrated by frequent references to media and journalists, personalised coverage, signed editorials, first-person editorials, high input of intellectual journalism.	Relatively low media profile.
Homogeneity of coverage.	Variations of coverage associated with size of community, distance from crisis centre and distance from metropolitan areas.

20. Wright, *Mass Communication: A Sociological Profile, op. cit.*, pp. 90-112.
21. Lucian Pye, "Political Culture," in Sills (ed.), *International Encyclopedia of the Social Sciences, op. cit.*, p. 218.

The findings indicate that there are basic French-English press differences in viewing the political system, political institutions, Canadian and foreign reaction, economic implications and the role of the press.

The Political System

English-language papers, on the one hand, saw Canadian unity as a major objective in evaluating developments during the crisis period. This was further illustrated in the pan-Canadian perspective taken in their editorials and in their highly critical stand toward separatism. French papers, on the other hand, showed different priorities: there was little concern for Canadian unity and instead their major concern was with the impact of the crisis on Quebec. Editorials in the French papers generally evaluated developments from a Quebec perspective without giving much consideration to the national implications of the crisis. Their generally neutral disposition on the issue of separatism may be interpreted as keeping the options open in formulating attitudes towards the political system.

Political Institutions

Some of the strongest findings in the FLQ study relate to differences in disposition in the French and English papers towards political institutions. English papers gave strong emphasis to institutions of government while French papers stressed personalities. This personality emphasis may be a reflection of the political culture of French Canada. It may be argued that French Canadians have difficulties relating directly to the political institutions that are associated with the parliamentary system which they seem to perceive as alien to their traditions.

Pierre Trudeau, in his article "Some Obstacles to Democracy in Quebec," argued that in French Canada there was an "outward acceptance of the parliamentary game, but without inward allegiance to its underlying moral principles."[22] There is ample evidence that French Canadians have traditionally related to the personalities in power at the federal level of government, and it has been this emphasis on personality politics, with French Canadians sharing the helm, that has led to the strong support of the federal Liberal Party in Quebec province in national elections. The tradition, Mr. Trudeau observed, started with the choice of Laurier as the leader of the Liberals at the end of the nineteenth century. This development, combined with strong French-Canadian criticism of the way the Conservatives handled the Riel rebellion, brought French Canadians en masse into the fold of the Liberal Party.[23]

For English-speaking Canadians, the parliamentary institutions are often taken for granted, though not necessarily understood. These institutions are perceived

---

22. P.E. Trudeau, "Some Obstacles to Democracy in Quebec," *Canadian Journal of Economics and Political Science*, Vol. 24, No. 3 (August 1958), p. 299.
23. *Ibid.* Most historians would probably attribute the electoral behaviour of French Canadians as a form of bloc voting rather than an obsession with personalities. See H. Blair Neatby, *Laurier and a Liberal Quebec* (Toronto: McClelland and Stewart, 1973).

by English-speaking Canadians as part of their inherited traditions with which they feel comfortable. This sort of an outlook would lead to an emphasis on relating to institutions rather than the personalities in a leadership position in these institutions. The greater interest in the executive branch of government on the part of French dailies (compared with English papers, which stressed the developments in Parliament) is in line with such an argument.

Canadian and Foreign Reaction

French newspapers were especially concerned with international reaction to the crisis, with particular emphasis on the views of the press and personalities in European and Francophone nations. This finding may be related to a concern on the part of French Canadians about an international image. English papers, for their part, were primarily interested in Canadian reaction to the crisis: how the developments were being perceived in different parts of the country, including Quebec. In terms of international reaction, the English-language dailies concentrated on the United States, an area of low interest for the French dailies. There was a European thrust to French-language newspaper coverage compared to a North American emphasis in the English press. These findings, when seen in conjunction with the observation that French papers took a regional perspective of the crisis in evaluating developments in the Canadian setting, suggest that there is a strong element of parochialism—or Quebec-confined nationalism—while in the international setting there is a broad horizon to the outlook of French-language newspapers. This stance is in line with Quebec interests in international relations, which have produced some strains on Canadian federalism in the past decade.[24]

Economic Implications

The French dailies stressed the historic and contemporary economic and social injustices experienced by French Canadians. This indicates that the immediate economic implications of the crisis were of secondary importance when seen in a larger perspective. This overview took into consideration the emotional cost of being a minority sub-cultural group that sees itself in a disadvantaged economic position. The English papers, in contrast, stressed the immediate economic costs to the country (such as the value of the Canadian dollar and Canadian stocks), suggesting a strong relationship between economic and political factors in their appraisal of the crisis.

The Role of the Press

The findings indicate that the French and English press have different percep-

24. Canada, *Federalism and International Relations*, White Paper prepared by Department of External Affairs (Ottawa: Queen's Printer, 1968). For Quebec's aspirations in foreign relations, see: Québec, Ministère des Affaires Intergouvernementales. *Working Paper on Foreign Relations.* Québec, 1969.

tions of their importance in the political process. The French papers projected an image of self-importance in many ways, including frequent reference to media and journalists, personalised coverage which at times included the raising of rhetorical questions and editorials written in the first person. The enormous editorial comment in the French papers, all of it signed by recognized media intellectuals, and the massive editorial page backgrounding, much of it contributed by academic figures, are reflective of the ideological involvement of intellectuals in the French press system. This would suggest that values articulated in the French dailies are inserted by an intellectually oriented group that may be at a distance from the readership it is trying to lead. The fact that French dailies maintained a fixed editorial position, once they had indicated an attitude, would suggest that their editorial outlook was derived from a larger perspective, based on goals that went beyond the crisis. English newspapers, for their part, maintained a comparatively low profile as far as projecting their own image was concerned, with the coverage generally depersonalised.

Structural Characteristics

The homogeneity of coverage in the French-language newspapers was traced to the leadership of the Montreal dailies. It was found that Montreal plays a dominant role in the French press system, to such an extent as to create communications bonds which overshadow differences of ownership and regional dispersion of a limited nature. In this way, the Montreal French-language papers exert centripetal pull and the French-language service of The Canadian Press provides an organizational support structure for the Montreal dominance.

For the English-language press system, there was no single primate city that provided national newspaper leadership during the FLQ crisis. Variations in coverage were associated with numerous factors, including metropolitan status, size of city, distance from crisis area and local characteristics of the city. The findings are a reflection of the fragmented nature of the English press system. The local influences, while noticeable in the French dailies where they applied, were much stronger in the English dailies.

Canadian Press

The Canadian Press news agency failed to act as a nationalizing agent in the FLQ crisis. Even in cases where the papers were almost entirely dependent on CP, the gatekeeper role of the editors remained important despite the traditional argument that the wire services tend to take over the agenda-setting function. It is possible that the special circumstances of the news flow in the critical days of the FLQ crisis may have been the reason for the failure of a relatively uniform pattern of coverage to emerge on a national basis. But it is precisely in matters of great political significance that the dissemination of a national version of developments may be desirable if one takes into consideration the question of national integration. Eggleston and Kesterton, among others, in their studies of the Canadian press system have taken it for granted that CP is a nationalizing agent.[25] The findings here suggest that questions must be raised about the validity of this assumption.

Canadian Integration

Here we shall attempt to apply the various conclusions about the press system in order to evaluate their implications for national integration. The findings in Table X.4 demonstrate that the coverage of the FLQ crisis illustrated different sub-cultural interests which involved the basic question of French-English relations in Canada. There are polarizing implications to these findings. However, there were a number of modifying factors, with the structural characteristics of the press system in Canada being of particular importance. On the one hand, the homogeneity of coverage in the French press implies that this medium defined the crisis for its readers from a particular perspective and thus reinforced distinctive outlooks towards the political system, institutions and economic matters, among others. On the other hand, the fragmented nature of the English press system implies that the findings about values and norms summarized in Table X.4 (right-hand column) did not have a uniform impact throughout the English-language medium. Fragmentation and parochialism of the press, it is argued here, diffuse the polarizing tendencies of the French and English press systems and must therefore be regarded as a mediating factor. Furthermore, another phase of the study showed the existence of an editorial dialogue among the newspapers, most intense at the level of metropolitan dailies, and this also was a mediating factor. Another important finding was the tendency towards similarity of outlook in the dailies in Montreal and Toronto, Canada's largest cities and perceived as national metropolises, vis-à-vis the coverage in other large cities. The rule of thumb was that coverage became more different from the French (that is, more hard-lined), the further one moved from the crisis centre. But despite these and other mediating factors, the basic differences in the French-English outlook were observed, admittedly in a diluted form, even in cities where there are both French and English dailies.

On balance, then, the evidence shows that the press system in Canada, as illustrated by its performance in the FLQ crisis, had an unsettling effect on Canadian integration, or at least did not promote it. The empirical findings reveal that newspapers reinforced sub-cultural differences, rather than contributing to the unification of society by broadening the base of common norms, values and collective experiences shared by its members. It was found that the dissemination of the same basic information was socially divisive because it was organized in such a way as to emphasize particular interests coinciding with territorially based language divisions.

---

25. For an evaluation which argues that CP plays an important role in fostering a Canadian identity, see Elkin, "Communications Media and Identity Formation in Canada," *op. cit.*, pp. 226-227. See also W.H. Kesterton, *A History of Journalism in Canada, op. cit.* and Wilfrid Eggleston, "The Press of Canada," in *Royal Commission Studies*—A Selection of Essays prepared for the Royal Commission on National Development in the Arts, Letters and Sciences (Ottawa: King's Printer, 1951), pp. 41-53.

At the same time, it should be noted that by emphasizing sub-cultural interests, the French and English press systems helped to reinforce the bi-cultural characteristic of Canadian federalism. The homogeneity of the French press system can thus be regarded as a necessary supportive factor for a numerically disadvantaged sector of society.

II. FRENCH AND ENGLISH BROADCASTING: SIMILARITIES AND DIFFERENCES

On November 15, 1976, the Parti Québecois was elected to power, setting off shock waves across Canada and creating grave concern about the future of the Canadian federal union. A unity crisis had surfaced almost by surprise, and many Canadians "were shocked and angry that events had proceeded so far without their being fully aware of them."[26] And with the unity crisis came a crisis for the mass media. There were allegations by a number of noted personalities, including the Prime Minister and some Quebec members of his Cabinet, that Radio-Canada, the CBC French-language service, had a pro-separatist orientation and had contributed to the PQ election victory. At the request of the Prime Minister, there was an inquiry into the national broadcasting service by the CRTC, the regulatory and supervisory agency for Canadian broadcasting.

The Prime Minister attached great urgency ("given the profound significance of this situation"[27]) to the work of the Committee of Inquiry (the Boyle Committee) which presented its report in four months, on July 20, 1977.

The findings of the Boyle Committee provided a devastating indictment of the state of French-English interaction in the broadcast media: it was almost nonexistent. The findings of a series of content analysis studies of French and English newscasts and the results of a national survey of Canadian perceptions of the broadcast media led the Boyle Committee to the following conclusion:

As presented by the [broadcast] media, Canada is in a state of deep schizophrenia: if English and French Canadians were on different planets there could hardly be a greater contrast of views and information.[28]

The Boyle Committee said that all the broadcast media—the private and public sectors—were equally delinquent in this regard, but noted that only the CBC Radio-Canada had a mandate to work in the opposite direction.

The content analysis studies for the Boyle Committee examined major national television and radio newscasts of the French and English CBC during 10 days in May, 1977.[29] There was also a comparative examination of newscasts of the pri-

26. Committee of Inquiry into the National Broadcasting Service. *Report.* (Ottawa Canadian Radio-television and Telecommunications Commission, July 1977), p. 5.
27. Letter from Prime Minister Trudeau to CRTC Chairman Harry Boyle, March 4, 1977.
28. Committee of Inquiry into National Broadcasting Service. *Report. op. cit.*, p. 62.
29. A. Siegel, *A Content Analysis. The Canadian Broadcasting Corporation: Similarities and Differences of French and English News.* Background Research Paper. Committee of Inquiry into the National Broadcasting Service. (Ottawa: Canadian Radio-television and Telecommunications Commission, 1977).

vate and public sectors of TV broadcasting: CBC (English), CTV (English), Radio-Canada (French), TVA (French) and Global (English). The studies examined variations in the attention that news events receive, which aspects of the news are being stressed and the intensity and scope of coverage. Five avenues of exploration were used to slice into the content: time and space considerations, including order of appearance of news item; political classification, that is, the political or geographic entity discussed in the news item; an examination of the subject matter, that is, the themes; a personality analysis examining the names in the news and the frequency of mention; and a geographic profile analysis, which explored the sources of origin of news stories as well as the frequency of mention of cities, provinces and countries.

The major findings included:

• Differences between the French and English newscasts far outweighed similarities.

• A search for similarities in the pictures of the world and Canada projected in the French and English newscasts showed there was little common ground. Of the 1,785 stories examined, 259 appeared in both French and English. More than half of the stories in common dealt with international issues. A realistic estimate of common ground in the French and English newscasts was about 15 per cent.

• The comparison of patterns of coverage on French (Radio-Canada) and English (CBC) television newscasts showed there were differences in describing Canadian events, in viewing the international scene, in perceptions of what is newsworthy, in emphasis on personalities and in the geographic sources of news stories.

There were striking differences in the French and English treatment of Canadian news. The main thrust of French TV newscasts was Quebec; more than half of all the time spent on Canadian news was devoted to Quebec, as shown in Chart X.1. (One possible conclusion that can be drawn from Chart X.1 is that there may be an underlying concept of "parity" in the French news content, half devoted to French Canada and half to English-speaking Canada.) Furthermore, at least one-third of the Canadian-national stories had a marked Quebec point of view and some of the news classified as "other provinces" involved reaction to Quebec stories. Over the 10-day period in May, 1977, French TV made 130 specific references to Quebec for an average of 13 Quebec mentions per newscast.

• English TV newscasts provided much more intensive national news coverage out of Ottawa than the French news, and included reaction stories from other parts of the country to national developments. Quebec coverage on the English TV newscasts was low (17 per cent of air time devoted to Canadian news) considering the great interest in Quebec affairs in the wake of the Parti Québecois' electoral victory. Canada's four Atlantic provinces and the west coast province of British Columbia received little attention in either French or English news.

• There was a heavy emphasis on Quebec personalities in the French newscasts. Excluding Premier René Lévesque, Quebec ministers were mentioned

CHART X.1.   Political Classification of Canadian Stories—10 Days of TV Newscasts (based on time)

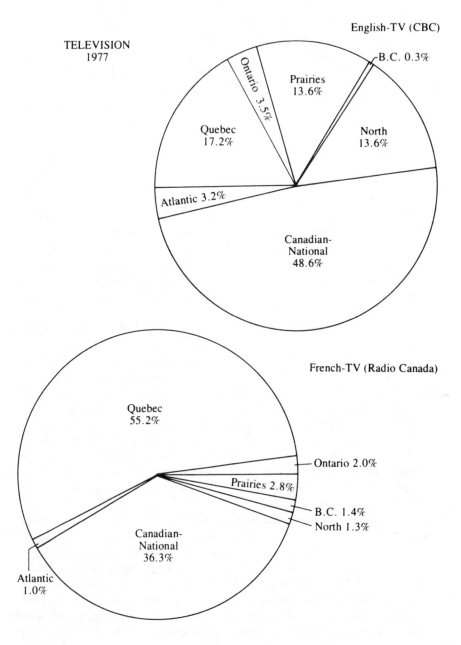

Source: CRTC, 1977

153 times in the 10-day period. Of these mentions, 145 were on French newscasts (82 television, 63 radio) and eight were on English newscasts (six television, two radio). The frequent mention of these names makes them readily identifiable personalities in Quebec, but in English-speaking Canada they are relatively unknown. In English newscasts, federal Cabinet Ministers received fewer mentions than Quebec ministers in French newscasts; provincial Cabinet Ministers receive hardly any attention.

- The theme analysis showed that different subject matters were emphasized in the French and English newscasts.
- In the coverage of international news, French and English newscasts were somewhat more uniform. However, some significant differences were observed: (1) English news devoted more than twice the time than French news to the United States (Chart X.2) and (2) French news gave greater emphasis to Western European news and personalities. The common ground in international news was about 25 per cent.
- In the French newscasts, 55 per cent of the stories dealt with politics, compared to 42 per cent in English. The French newscasts had three times as many stories dealing with constitutional issues than the English newscasts.
- The geographic analysis was especially revealing about the news flow in Canada. Four cities—Ottawa, Quebec City, Montreal and Toronto—were the sources of 73 per cent of the news disseminated by radio and television. Halifax, Winnipeg, Edmonton and Vancouver each supplied between one and two per cent of the news stories.
- In radio, French-English differences were even stronger than those observed in the television newscasts. Basically, the differences were along similar lines. In the four-month period of September through December of 1976, only three per cent of the stories in the major national evening newscast in French dealt with any part of Canada other than Quebec (excluding, of course, national news). In the English evening newscast, only nine per cent of the stories originated in Quebec at a time when a general election and the handing over of power from the Liberals to the Parti Québecois took place. International stories, including such major events as the death of Chairman Mao, the war in Lebanon, summit meetings, Rhodesian peace moves, earthquakes, and the U.S. presidential elections, accounted for more than half of all the stories in common.
- There is a fragmentation of perceptions about Canada that goes beyond the French-English newscasts of the CBC. A three-day analysis of the content of five television networks—CBC English, CTV, CBC French, TVA and Global—showed that only three of the 252 stories disseminated appeared on all five networks.
- Television, both French and English, is much more personality-conscious than radio; names are mentioned twice as often on TV. This may be important in political terms. For one thing, it makes TV an especially attractive medium for the personality-oriented politics associated with French Canada.

CHART X.2.   Political Classification of All Stories, Canadian and International—10 Days of TV Newscasts (based on time)

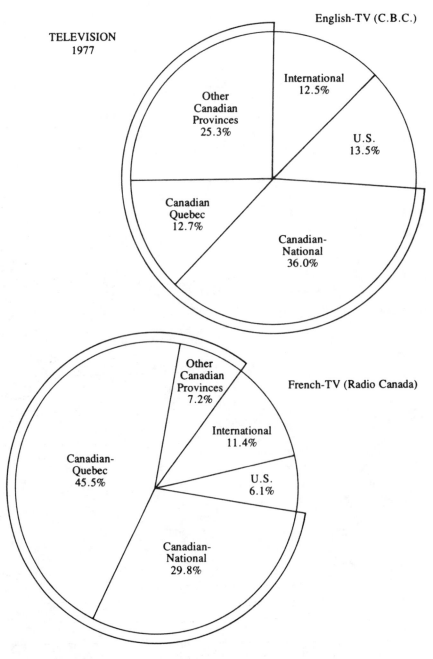

TELEVISION
1977

English-TV (C.B.C.)

Other Canadian Provinces 25.3%

International 12.5%

U.S. 13.5%

Canadian Quebec 12.7%

Canadian-National 36.0%

Other Canadian Provinces 7.2%

French-TV (Radio Canada)

International 11.4%

Canadian-Quebec 45.5%

U.S. 6.1%

Canadian-National 29.8%

Source: CRTC, 1977

The differences in the content of French and English newscasts, it would appear, are *imposed* by the structure and operational procedures of the broadcasting system and differences in journalistic norms; they do not reflect audience interests. The Boyle Commission's national opinion survey indicated "the Canadian public's interest, attitudes and sense of priorities about the news are much the same whether they speak English or French, or live near the Atlantic or Pacific."[30]

SUMMARY AND OBSERVATIONS

Many of the differences observed between French- and English-language broadcast news were similar, and even stronger, than the differences observed in French and English newspapers. The overwhelming emphasis in the French-language media (print and broadcast) is on Quebec province. A French-language media emphasis on personalities is evident in broadcast news as much as in the written press. In the English media, there is a much stronger emphasis on the institutions of government, especially Parliament. Differences in international news coverage in the French and English media run along similar lines in the newspapers as in broadcasting. Furthermore, the role of the broadcast journalist in French Canada appears to have an enhanced political component, with the journalist seeing himself as an important political actor, compared with the role of the journalist in the English broadcast media. This too is similar to the situation in the printed press. It is argued here that the electronic and print media complement each other in reinforcing the linguistic and cultural differences in Canadian society.

The Canadian identity dilemma, reflected in part by differences in the reality mappings provided by the French and English media, is intimately linked to the failure of our mass communications systems to meet the political and social responsibilities perceived over the years in the political debates, Royal Commission studies and broadcast policies. The shortcomings of the media are not so much the news messages and ideas they disseminate, but rather what they leave out. The President of the CBC in 1977, A.W. Johnson, said in a major policy statement *Touchstone for the CBC*, "The CBC has failed generally to adequately reflect English Canada to French Canada and vice versa."[31] Mr. Johnson committed the national broadcasting service to stimulating the flow of information between French and English societies and to promoting greater opportunities for the regions of Canada to express themselves to the rest of the country.

Of particular interest is the leadership role in French-Canadian society, in which journalists see themselves. The articulation of a clearly defined value system is evident in French-language journalism, a practice that goes back many years. It may, however, be argued that until about 20 years ago the impact of this was muted in political terms and the intellectual journalists may well have been

30. Committee of Inquiry into the National Broadcasting service. *Report, op. cit.*, p. 63.
31. A.W. Johnson, "Touchstone for the CBC." June 1977 statement, p. 39.

at a distance from the readership they were trying to lead. The media is only one among several social institutions that include the family, the educational system, the church, the peer group and the work environment which are believed to be especially important in shaping the value structure in society. However, the Quiet Revolution in Quebec combined with the youth revolution globally have resulted in diminishing the influence of the church and family in shaping attitudes and values, and as passers-on of political culture. Also, the educational system has undergone major reforms. The mass media and the new generation of teachers have emerged in comparatively more influential positions than before. It is no accident that former teachers and journalists have played extraordinary important roles in the Parti Québecois leadership.

In looking at the print and broadcast media together, it can be concluded that the "we-they" perception of Canadian federalism, with parity for French and English Canada, has long been built into the French-language communications system. There are basic French-English press differences in viewing the political system, political institutions, Quebec's international personality, economic and social history and the press as a political actor. Separatism has long been recognized as a viable proposition in the French press—printed and electronic—and there is evidence of a media support structure for a separatist political party as far back as 1966. The significance attached to an international personality for Quebec appears to be linked to a Quebec independence posture and is reminiscent of Ottawa using international relations as a stepping stone for achieving Canada's full sovereignty.

We see, then, the Quebec media system as an enormously important political factor. It has provided a support structure for the "founding nations" concept of Canadian federalism; it has taken on the role as watchdog of the political and cultural interests of Quebec vis-à-vis the rest of Canada. The influence of the media and media personalities in French society is an important dimension of the unity crisis precipitated by the Parti Québecois' referendum strategy to take Quebec out of the federal union.

III. THE MEDIA AND THE QUEBEC REFERENDUM

On May 20, 1980, 60 per cent of the voters in the Quebec referendum said "No" to the PQ government's demand for a mandate to negotiate sovereignty association.

***

The election of the Parti Québecois government in November, 1976, brought changes to the style of politics in Quebec and also in Canada generally. As part of its programme to take Quebec out of the federal union, the Parti Québecois government spent four years preparing for a referendum which it thought it could not lose. Public opinion surveys were used to ensure that the referendum question put to the people of Quebec would be a winning one. The timing of the referendum vote was carefully planned to ensure a successful outcome. Furthermore,

Quebec Cabinet Ministers indicated from the outset that if the "first" referendum did not produce the desired result, there might be a second referendum, or a third, until the voter support for sovereignty is achieved. It shaped up as a "win only" scenario for the PQ.

There are different kinds of referenda, including the self-determination plebiscite, referenda for constitutional change, legislative referenda, where voters rather than their elected representatives make the final decision on an important policy question, and local government decision referenda.[32]

The Quebec vote on sovereignty association was thus a specific kind of referendum—one involving the decision of the people on a question of sovereignty—and was, strictly speaking, a self-determination plebiscite. This type of plebiscite incorporates the principle of popular sovereignty. It was an offspring of the French Revolution, designed as an instrument to accomplish changes in sovereignty when the people of a territory so desired. An examination of the use of plebiscites since they were first introduced 191 years ago reveals some troubling characteristics:[33]

- Firstly, they are instruments of convenience when the outcome is obviously going to be in line with what the authorities want; that is, popular will coincides with governmental policy.
- Secondly, plebiscites are anything but a free expression of the will if the outcome is likely to be negative or doubtful. Persuasive methods including economic, political and sometimes military pressure have frequently been used.
- Thirdly, if the plebiscite outcome is doubtful and, for one reason or another, the voters cannot be intimidated, then generally the plebiscite is never held.
- Fourthly, the question that is posed in the plebiscite is critical and is often worded in such a way that a "yes" vote is assured.
- Fifthly, massive propaganda campaigns usually reflecting one viewpoint are part and parcel of recent plebiscites.
- Sixthly, plebiscites usually confirm a *fait accompli* and therefore are redundant.
- Seventhly, a frequent purpose of plebiscites is to attain international recognition for sovereignty change.

There have been some instances where plebiscites have performed a useful service in international relations, particularly during the wave of nationalism that swept Europe in the mid-nineteenth century. After World War I, a plebiscite in Schleswig helped Germany and Denmark establish their frontier. The separation of Norway from Sweden in 1905 can also be seen as a positive use of the plebiscite, though it was perhaps redundant in that the participating governments were entirely reconciled to the cession. The list of meaningful plebiscites is indeed short. On balance, plebiscites have been generally abused.

---

32. Colin Braham, Jim Burton, *The Referendum Reconsidered*. Fabian Tract 434. (London: Fabian Society, 1975), p. 17.
33. Siegel, "Public Opinion, the Mass Media and Plebiscites," *op. cit.*, p. 14.

Canadians are understandably confused about referenda and plebiscites. The last national referendum was in the war year of 1942, when the Ottawa government sought approval for a military conscription programme which was a reversal of promises it had made in the election campaign two years earlier. The outcome was divisive: Eight provinces voted "yes" for conscription, while Quebec voted overwhelmingly "no." The only other national referendum, also divisive in terms of religion and language, took place in 1898 on the question of alcohol: every province except Quebec voted for total abstinence, while Quebec voted overwhelmingly to be wet.

More recently, the people of Newfoundland voted in the "admission referenda" in 1948. There were two votes. The first provided three choices; the second, two. There was a clearly stated question and this referendum route was Newfoundland's approach for entry into the Canadian union.

(At the provincial level, Manitoba, Saskatchewan, Alberta and British Columbia have over the past 70 years adopted legislation providing for referenda or direct legislation. Alberta and British Columbia never held any referenda.[34] In Manitoba, the referendum law was declared unconstitutional in that it allowed for direct legislation that would bypass the legislature and the Lieutenant-Governor, thus interfering with the constitutional right of the Lieutenant-Governor to withhold Royal Assent. Saskatchewan has had five referenda, three dealing with the prohibition of alcohol, and one with time zones and one on the principle of direct legislation.)[35]

The introduction of referendum politics, as the experience in Canada and other countries shows, has an impact on the political process and in the interaction of media and politics. Among other things, it changes the political atmosphere: politics becomes more media-oriented, more personalised and polarized. The side effects include a lowering of the dignity and authority of Parliament. Most importantly, referendum politics related to national sovereignty is crisis politics. The very existence of the Canadian union in its present form was threatened by the Quebec referendum.

The Quebec referendum was not a democratic grass roots venture of people in search of sovereignty. It was an attempt by the PQ leadership to lead Quebec on the road of secession, although there is no *legal* right to secede from Canada. The late Hans Kelsen, whose teachings have influenced Pierre Trudeau, distinguished between two types of federalism: the federal state and the confederacy of states.[36] There is a right to secede in the confederacy of states but not in the fed-

---

34. Richard Theoret, "The Use of the Referendum in Canada," in Donald C. Rowat (ed.), *The Referendum and Separation Elsewhere: Implications for Quebec* (Ottawa: Carleton University Dept. of Political Science, 1978), pp. 20-23. See also H. Hahan, "Voting in Canadian Communities: A Taxonomy of Referendum Issues," *Canadian Journal of Political Science*, Vol. I, 1968.
35. *Ibid.*
36. Hans Kelsen, *General Theory of Law and the State*, (New York: Russell and Russell, 1961). For an example of Trudeau references to Kelsen, see P. Trudeau, "Federalism, Nationalism, and Reason," in P.A. Crepeau and C.B. Macpherson (eds.), *The Future of Canadian Federalism, op. cit.*, p. 28.

eral state. The Parti Québecois scenario for *Sovereignty Association* called for a fundamental change that would create a confederacy of two states where the right to secession exists. *Sovereignty Association* would have been a major step toward, if not the actual accomplishment of, Quebec's separation from the Canadian union.

Referenda have no legal status in Canadian constitutional practices, which provide for representative government. In fact, referenda are alien to the spirit of our parliamentary system. It is in Parliament that democracy is played out. Despite the obvious need for reforms to enable meaningful scrutiny of government activity, parliamentary procedures provide a suitable, if imperfect, approach for a Government to deal with the business of the country and at the same time subject the Government's actions to the criticisms of the Opposition. Many forces come into play in the House of Commons and Senate. Historic traditions, economic factors, the structure of society generally and the rights of the minority are incorporated in the shaping of the laws that govern the country. All these factors, and especially the interests and rights of the minority, take on added importance in Canada's federal society.

The politics of plebiscite are addressed directly to the people. The vote itself reflects the views of the majority at one particular moment on the highly emotional issue of sovereignty. The mass media are the great battleground for public opinion and, much more than in a general election, the media are the centre of public debate in a plebiscite.

A few days after the Parti Québecois came to power in 1976, Prime Minister Trudeau addressed the country on radio and television about the Quebec question. He said that a declaration of independence by Quebec would be unconstitutional without the concurrence of the federal government. The Prime Minister followed up his address to the nation with a nationally broadcast press conference the next day where much of the attention was focused on Quebec. He suggested that a national referendum involving all the people of Canada might be held if a sufficient majority of Quebecers indicated that they favoured independence. (The way Mr. Trudeau saw it, it's like a marriage. You don't just ask the husband or wife if he or she wants a divorce, you ask both of them.)

The Parti Québecois Premier, Mr. Lévesque, also using radio and television to speak to the Quebec people immediately after his Government was sworn in, reacted strongly. He used such terms as "ignorant" and "grotesque" in commenting on Mr. Trudeau's notion that there should perhaps be a Canadian-wide referendum. Mr. Lévesque said the people of Quebec have an unchallengeable right to decide their own future.

The televised statements of Prime Minister Trudeau and Premier Lévesque are unusual in Canadian politics. Traditionally, the floor of Parliament—the House of Commons in Ottawa for Mr. Trudeau and the National Assembly in Quebec City for Mr. Lévesque—would have been the appropriate setting for important policy statements by governmental leaders. What we were witnessing was the opening of the plebiscite campaign.

An examination of front-page headlines and stories in a sample of Canadian newspapers in the six months after the Quebec elections showed unprecedented emphasis on two personalities in Canadian politics: Premier Lévesque and Prime Minister Trudeau. There was a record number of press conferences, television appearances, public speeches and carefully staged media events. Mr. Lévesque's address to the Economic Club in New York in which he predicted Quebec independence and Mr. Trudeau's speech to the U.S. Congress proclaiming that Canada would stay united were part of the unity confrontation that was being played out in the media. When Quebec produced a study showing that federalism was a financial drain for Quebecers, it was a big media event. The federal government, for its part, produced its own study to show that Quebec was financially ahead because of federalism. The Quebec White Paper dealing with the language of education drew headlines across the country. The following day, Prime Minister Trudeau received his own headlines when he said Quebec's educational policy was a return to the "dark ages." These are but a few examples of the polarization of politics associated with plebiscite politics.

In the official referendum campaign, as in the FLQ crisis, the media helped to shape events. Parliament in Ottawa and the Quebec National Assembly were spectators as the principal actors in the "yes" and "no" camps sought to reach out to the people directly and via the media.

The Quebec referendum marked the first time ever that a plebiscite on secession aimed at establishing a new country was defeated. Under normal publicity practices in plebiscites in other countries, the Parti Québecois and the French media would have joined in a crusade.

The vote confirmed that Quebec is an integral part of the Canadian Union. Without Quebec, there is no real Canada; without Canada, there is no real Quebec.

The referendum was a moment of truth for journalists in Quebec. Marcel Pépin, the editorial page editor of *Le Soleil* (Quebec City), makes this comment:

> Politics is a family affair in Quebec. By overwatching the political war at home, Quebec journalists have lost touch with public opinion outside the province. Politics has divided the population into groups who are strangers to each other.[37]

As Mr. Pépin points out, the referendum debate was a very stressful and painful period to go through, because both sides had contradictory and irreconcilable stands. "The press learned how to walk slowly and carefully on eggs, without making an omelette."[38]

The media, both print and broadcast, presented as fair an account as was possible under the circumstances. Some papers experienced difficulties. For example, *Le Soleil* in Quebec City wanted its editorial page to reflect both the "yes" and "no" sides which divided Quebec society. None of the editorialists wanted

37. Marcel Pépin, "Prospects and Proposals," in *Politics and the Media, op. cit.*, p. 98.
38. *Ibid.*

to present the "no" side and as a result the paper took no editorial-page stand. At *Le Devoir*, the editor-in-chief favoured the "no" side, but all the other editorialists were in the "yes" camp.

The broadcast media, for their part, kept within the guidelines of the Broadcasting Act, requiring that the programming "should provide reasonable, balanced opportunity for the expression of differing views on matters of public concern." Journalistic standards were closely scrutinized during the campaign.

Considering the tradition of personal involvement of French-Canadian journalists in the political process and their commitment to political-social transformation of Quebec society, it is remarkable that the media coverage of the campaign presented an opportunity for free choice, unheard of in other national sovereignty plebiscites. Freedom of the press and the practices of fairness and accuracy have developed strong roots in Quebec.

CHAPTER XI

THE MEDIA AND POLITICS IN THE 1980s

The mass media are an integral part of the political process in democratic societies. Media and politics are so entwined that significant changes in one have profound implications for the other. In the 1980s, the Canadian mass media and the governmental system are in the process of readjusting their relationship. A number of factors, including constitutional change, government policy, the economics of the industry, the dominant role of television in media election campaign coverage and technological change give rise to cross-pressures in the interaction of media and politics.

These cross-pressures are creating contradictory trends in the media/government relationship. On the one hand, the foundation for freedom of the media is being strengthened in the new constitution and on the other hand, there is the threat of government intervention in the press, as recommended by the Kent Commission, in the interests of the "communications rights" of the society. In other words, the media as watchdog of government is faced with the dilemma of government as watchdog of the media.

CONSTITUTIONAL CHANGE

THE CANADA ACT, 1982

In 1982, Canada entrenched freedom of the press in its constitution. *The Charter of Rights and Freedoms* declares that the fundamental rights of everyone include: "Freedom of thought, belief, opinion and expression, including freedom of the press and other media of communications."[1]

Constitutional entrenchment means that there can be no tampering with the freedom of the media provision without formal constitutional change, a most unlikely development. It is, however, not an absolute guarantee, because the

---

1. *Canada Act*, 1982 S.2.

introductory section of the *Charter* states that the rights and freedoms are "subject only to such reasonable limits prescribed by laws as can be demonstrably justified in a free and democratic society."[2] There is yet a further dilution of the constitutional entrenchment in the so-called *override* provision (Section 33) which enables Parliament or a provincial legislature to pass legislation which may have precedence over certain sections of the Charter of Rights, including Section 2 which guarantees freedom of the media.

The constitutional entrenchment of press freedom is laudable, even in its imperfect form. It has, however, attracted little public comment because at first glance it does little more than give formal recognition to a tradition that evolved in Canada, despite occasional serious setbacks, over the past 150 years. As noted earlier, Canada is ranked near the top of the short list of countries that enjoy freedom of the press; many nations with ringing declarations in their constitution about press freedoms have little of it in practice.

Freedom of the press is fundamental to Canadian democracy. However, as one of its staunchest supporters, Canadian Human Rights Commissioner Gordon Fairweather, has observed, "The principle is neither expressed nor applied in absolute terms in this country."[3]

It is significant that Canada's two major inquiries into the press—the Kent Commission in 1981 and the Davey Senate Committee 11 years earlier—both quote in their opening paragraph Justice Hugo Black of the United States Supreme Court on freedom of the press.[4] Canadian courts have not spoken out as strongly on press freedom as the U.S. courts have. In Canada, the legal support structure for press freedom is not as developed, and is presumably more fragile, than in the United States. This does not necessarily mean that our press is less free. But freedom of the press, as we saw in Chapter V, evolved late in Canada.

In the United States, it has been nearly 200 years since the adoption of the First Amendment to the Constitution which strongly asserts freedom of the press in its simple declaration: "Congress shall make no laws . . . abridging the freedom of speech, or of the press . . ." Over the years, the First Amendment has given rise to innumerable court cases involving access to information, advertising, prior restraint, censorship, the fairness doctrine, libel laws and closed court hearings, among many other matters. The court decisions have provided direction in the evolution of the free press principle as it adapted to the era of the multi-media.

Canada's constitutional provision is not as strong as the American version, nor does it have a similar legal orientation. Nevertheless, it sets the stage for a more active role by the courts in conflicts involving encroachment on the free press guarantee. The constitution now places the free press guarantee beyond the ordi-

---

2. *Ibid.*, S.1. The power to override inherent in S.1. is designed to deal specifically with emergency situations, e.g. invocation of the War Measures Act.
3. R. Gordon Fairweather, "Press Freedom: More than a Platitude." Lecture in honour of the 20th Anniversary of York University, Gerstein Conference on Mass Communication and Canadian Nationhood, York Univ., April 10, 1981.
4. *Associated Press et al. v. United States* (1945).

nary reach of the federal Parliament or any of the provincial Legislatures, except by way of the *override* provision, whose impact remains unknown. (There may, in fact, be a built-in obsolescence in the *override* provision in relation to the freedom guarantees for the mass media, except in time of emergency.)[5]

Until 1982, the legal support structure for free press was thin despite the recognition by the courts that a free press is essential to the democratic practices in Canada's parliamentary system.

A quarter of a century earlier, Prime Minister John Diefenbaker wanted to entrench freedom of speech and freedom of the press in a Bill of Rights, but it was clear that he could not get the necessary provincial support for an amendment to the British North America Act. Instead, Mr. Diefenbaker had to be satisfied with having the Bill of Rights enacted as an ordinary statute of Parliament, which meant that Parliament could remove press protections or limit them by simply passing new legislation on the subject. Furthermore, the law did not apply to the provinces. (Three provinces—Alberta, Quebec and Saskatchewan—have their own bill of rights with freedom of the press provisions.)

The most important legal support for freedom of the press comes out of a Supreme Court ruling in the 1938 Alberta Press Act reference case. The Alberta legislation, called "An Act to Ensure the Publication of Accurate News and Information," provided for outright censorship and governmental intervention in the editorial content of newspapers. Social Credit Premier William Aberhart had argued in his attacks on the "so-called free press" that the press was not at all free, for the reporters and publishers tended to "heed the dictates of the money barons." This statement has a familiar ring today. As Professor G. Stuart Adam has observed, Premier Aberhart had been thoroughly harassed by the press and the Alberta Press Act was a retributive action.[6]

The Lieutenant-Governor of Alberta declined to give the legislation the necessary Royal Assent and reserved it, as well as two other pieces of key Social Credit legislation, for the "signification of the Governor-General's pleasure." The Ottawa government promptly sent the legislation to the Supreme Court for a ruling of its constitutionality. It was found to be unconstitutional (*ultra vires*).

The Chief Justice of the Supreme Court, Sir Lyman Duff, literally turned the BNA Act on its head in his interpretation of freedom of the press in Canada. He noted that the preamble of the BNA Act declares that Canada has a constitution "similar in principle" to that of the United Kingdom, meaning that Parliament works under the influence of public opinion and public discussion. The judge said further:

> There can be no controversy that such institutions [Parliament] derive their efficacy from the free public discussion of affairs, from criticism and answer and counter-criticism, from attack upon policy and administration and defence

---

5. For a counterview on the implications of S.33. see Linda Silver Dranoff, "Override: Menace to Basic Rights?" *Globe and Mail*, December 23, 1981, p. 7.
6. G. Stuart Adam, "The Sovereignty of the Publicity System: The Case of the Alberta Press Act," in Adam (ed.), *Journalism, Communication and the Law, op. cit.*, p. 153.

and counter-attack; from the freest and fullest analysis and examination from every point of view of political proposals . . .[7]

Mr. Justice Cannon, in support of Sir Lyman Duff's argument, declared: Democracy cannot be maintained without its foundation; free public opinion and free discussion throughout the nation are all matters affecting the state, within the limits set by the criminal code and the common law.[8]

The Supreme Court's ruling meant that the provincial legislature did not have the powers to control the content, the publication and distribution of newspapers.

The quick action by Ottawa on the Alberta Press Act is in stark contrast to the failure of the federal government to take similar action against the Quebec Padlock Law, enacted also in 1937 by Premier Maurice Duplessis' Union Nationale government. *The Padlock Law* outlawed the use of any property in Quebec for disseminating Communist propaganda: the building would be padlocked—hence the name of the legislation.[9] It was used as an instrument of censorship and repression for 20 years until it was finally ruled unconstitutional in 1957 after lengthy action through the courts by private parties.[10] Political party interests were behind Ottawa's decision not to intervene in the Padlock Law, although Justice Minister Ernest Lapointe thought it was unconstitutional.[11] It may be concluded that at both the federal and provincial levels, Canada has a spotty record on press freedom.

The new constitution will make it far more difficult for legislative encroachment on press freedom. The courts will play a major role in the further evolution of the free press guarantee through court cases.

GOVERNMENT POLICY

SECRET GOVERNMENT AND FREEDOM OF INFORMATION

Freedom of the press guarantees are incompatible in spirit—if not in law—with secretive or closed government. Our analysis (Chapter III) showed that it has been a painstakingly slow process (more than a dozen years) from the acceptance of the principle of ''open government'' to the adoption of Bill C-43, The Access to Information Act, in the summer of 1982. Numerous delays beset the legislation: the provinces were unhappy with some of the provisions and a number of government departments and agencies requested changes right up until the last moment. Some Cabinet Ministers were opposed to the bill.

---

7. Reference re Alberta Statutes [1938] S.C.R. 100 The ruling by the court did not mean necessarily that freedom of speech and discussion were entrenched in the BNA Act. See Mallory, *The Structure of Canadian Government, op. cit.*, p. 307.
8. *Ibid.* S.C.R. 148. See also *Constitutional Freedom in Peril: the Jehovah Witnesses' Case,* Winnipeg Free Press Pamphlet No. 48, January 1954.
9. The law did not define Communist propaganda. The Attorney-General of Quebec determined what constituted such propaganda.
10. *Switzman v. Elbling and A.G. for Quebec* [1957] S.C.R. 285.
11. Mallory, *Structure of Canadian Government, op. cit.*, p. 312.

A leading international authority, Professor Donald C. Rowat of Carleton University, regarded the legislation as too restrictive; it has some exemptions that "go against the whole spirit of a Freedom of Information Act by prohibiting certain types of records from being released," even where these documents might formerly have been released by custom.[12] All the same, the legislation moves in the direction of greater openness "and with some key amendments" could have resulted in a strong law.[13] Communications Minister Francis Fox, who steered The Access to Information Act through Parliament, indicated as late as March 26, 1982 that he favoured new legislation which would apply to both the federal and the provincial levels of government. "The country as a whole would be the winner," Mr. Fox said, "if you had a [federal] law that somehow could apply to provinces."[14]

There are indications that the trend toward "open government" in Canada has lost momentum. In the United States, where there is a strong Freedom of Information Act, President Ronald Reagan has tightened the rules on disclosing secret information, reversing a 25-year trend toward a less restrictive government information policy.[15]

At the provincial level of government, the move to greater disclosure of information is unimpressive. Three provinces—Nova Scotia, New Brunswick and Newfoundland—have freedom of information acts, but the legislation is not sufficiently strong to provide "open government." Manitoba and Quebec are planning to introduce freedom of information legislation. Ontario, which has spent close to two million dollars in the past five years studying freedom of information, still has to decide on the form of the legislation. As the New Democratic Party member of the Ontario Legislature, Donald MacDonald, put it, "The process [of delay] could go on forever."[16] For the time being, "closed government" remains the practice in Canada.

LEGAL RESTRAINTS

Our examination of legal restraints shows that there are significant limitations on the freedom of the press principle when it is in conflict with the higher interests of the government (especially in matters relating to national security and public policy), free parliament, the administration of justice and individual reputations. The Official Secrets Act, parliamentary privilege, the laws of libel, the laws relating to fair trial and the dignity of the court, and the "revealing of sources" practices are among the most significant legal restraints in the interaction of media and politics. Some of the restraints (for example, libel and fair trial requirements) seek to establish a sensible balance between freedom and responsi-

---

12. *Toronto Star*, November 22, 1981.
13. *Ibid.*
14. *Globe and Mail*, March 27, 1982, p. 12.
15. *New York Times*, April 3, 1982, p. 1.
16. *Donald C. MacDonald, "Freedom of Information Delayed to Death," Globe and Mail*, August 25, 1981, p. 7.

bility of the media. Others do not have a comfortable fit. The Official Secrets Act, in particular, creates serious obstacles to the free flow of political information in that it is a support structure for secrecy in society. Certainly, Section IV of the Secrets Act, which contains the leakage provision, is incompatible with the freedom of the press guarantees in the constitution and the newly enacted Access to Information law.

THE PROPOSED CANADIAN NEWSPAPER ACT

In 1982, it became government policy to regulate aspects of the newspaper industry under a comprehensive federal statute, namely the Canadian Newspaper Act.[17] Newspapers have, of course, been subject to regulations under the Income Tax Act, the Excise Tax Act, the Canada Post Corporation Act and the Combines Investigation Act, among others. In opting for a Newspaper Act, the government has formally decided to make the newspaper field a policy area in its own right. This has implications for the interaction of press and politics, since it breaks new ground in the government's approach to dealing with the printed press.

The Minister of State for Multiculturalism, Jim Fleming, who is also the minister responsible for newspaper policy, announced the government's plans in the long-awaited Cabinet response to the Kent Commission recommendations. He provided in broad outline some of the government proposals that will shape the Newspaper Act that Parliament will be asked to pass.

The federal policy on newspapers can be summarized as follows:

—A 20 per cent rule on ownership. No newspaper chain in future will be allowed to control more than 20 per cent of national newspaper circulation. This rule is not retroactive.

—The two largest chains, Southam and Thomson, each of which controls more than 20 per cent of national newspaper circulation, will not be allowed to expand. If either of these chains is sold in the future, it will be broken up.

—Non-media companies who want to buy newspapers will first have to demonstrate to the Restrictive Trade Practices Commission that the newspapers will be operated independently of the companies' other interests. (A non-media company is one whose non-media assets are of greater value than its media holdings.)

—Establishment of a Canadian Advisory Council on Newspapers. This 50-member council, consisting of 10 part-time members from each of five regions, will have some of the characteristics of a national press council: it will handle public complaints, especially where there are no press councils already performing this function. The Advisory Council will be made up of

17. Speech by Jim Fleming, Minister of State for Multiculturalism, at the University of Western Ontario, London, Ont., May 25, 1982. For further details of government policy see Jim Fleming, *Government Proposals on Freedom of the Press in Relation to the Canadian Daily Newspaper Industry* (Ottawa: Supply and Services, May 1982).

representatives of publishers, journalists and the public. It will be funded by an endowment fund established by the government and there will be other insulating mechanisms to keep the council independent of political interference.

The council will report bi-anually on the state of the newspaper industry on the basis of its own research and analysis.

—Cross-media ownership (that is, newspapers owning broadcast outlets) in the same community will be discouraged. The CRTC will be directed to enforce this principle when considering broadcast licence renewals and applications. In markets where there is considerable media competition and in special hardship cases, there will be exemptions to the cross-media ownership restraints.

—News bureau proposal. The government is willing to spend one million dollars a year over five years in a cost-sharing program to encourage newspapers to set up new out-of-province and foreign news bureaus. (There is a $50,000 annual limit for three years per newspaper.)

The proposed Newspaper Act will not incorporate the far-reaching recommendations of the Kent Commission, which included some newspaper divestments by chains, the selling of the *Globe and Mail* by the Thomson chain and financial incentives in the form of tax credits and surcharges aimed at raising ''journalistic standards.'' Nor will the Newspaper Act seek to safeguard freedom of the press, as recommended by the Kent Commission, by insulating editors-in-chief from owners who control more than one newspaper or have other significant business interests. The complex framework of accountability of newspapers to Parliament through a Cabinet-appointed Press Rights Panel will not be instituted.

In turning its back on the most controversial of the Kent Commission recommendations, the government seems to have been influenced by a number of factors. Firstly, there were indications of strong public opinion opposition to policies which could have been interpreted as government meddling in the newsroom operations of newspapers. Secondly, the Kent recommendations would have faced constitutional obstacles on at least two grounds: (1) the Charter guarantees for freedom of the press and (2) federal versus provincial jurisdiction in the newspaper field. Thirdly, there were tax policy problems in the proposed ''editorial spendings equalization formula'' (discussed in Chapter VII) and in the tax incentives aimed at making it financially attractive for persons to invest in their local daily.

The constitutional guarantee of freedom of the press would have been an empty exhortation if the Press Rights Panel, proposed by the Kent Commission, became a national supervisory body for newspaper performance.

Our analysis of the history of mass communications in Canada (Chapter V) shows that freedom of the press was never a gift from the authorities. It evolved as a result of persistent and often dangerous encroachments by editors, including Joseph Howe and William Lyon Mackenzie, against government controls. Suspicion and dynamic tension between politicians and journalists, as argued in

Chapter II, are important elements in the interaction of media and politics in democratic societies. Government benevolence toward the media is more likely to undermine the credibility of the press than the economic factors that, in the view of the Kent Commission, damage the legitimacy of newspapers. The Canadian experience makes us suspicious of government intentions in legislative action to ''free the press.''

THE ECONOMICS OF THE MASS MEDIA

ECONOMIC RESTRAINTS

The mass media in Canada are a huge business largely but not wholly financed by advertising. Gross advertising spendings in 1982 are projected at just under $5 billion. On a per capita basis, Canada ranks third (behind the United States and Holland) in advertising spendings: $200 per person, compared to $35 in 1962. In the decade of the 1970s, advertising revenues were 1.3 per cent of the Gross National Product. This pattern is continuing in the 1980s. Projections are that by 1985, gross advertising revenues will range between $6.5-$7 billion.

In 1982, $1.1 billion, or 24 per cent of advertising revenues, will flow into the daily newspaper industry. The industry will have further incomes of about $400 million from subscriptions and street sales. The fact that it is owned and controlled in large part by a half-dozen chains is but one troubling facet of the newspaper industry. Another serious problem is that, except in a handful of cities, competition is nonexistent. Thus, the newspapers have a monopoly which is almost certain to be highly profitable.

In the decade of the 1970s, such papers as *L'Action* of Quebec City, the Quebec *Chronicle-Telegraph, Montréal-Matin, Montreal Star, Ottawa Journal,* Toronto *Telegram* and the *Winnipeg Tribune* closed down in a continuing trend of declining competition. In some cities, however, a new breed of successful papers, the tabloids, emerged.

Concentration of ownership is a problem in many countries but nowhere has it reached Canadian levels. A series of take-overs and mergers in the late 1970s that extended into 1982, with the $54 million purchase of the half-interest in the *Toronto Sun* chain by the communications conglomerate Maclean Hunter, has heightened concern about the potential threat to freedom of expression.

Concentration of ownership becomes an even more complex problem as a result of cross-ownership in the media, where newspaper companies own broadcast companies and cable operations, sometimes in the same cities. As shown in Table XI.1, there is significant media cross-ownership in at least 12 cities. This is not the full depth of the problem because the media conglomerates are also involved in magazine publishing, book publishing, community newspapers and other ventures in the communications industry.

An often overlooked matter is concentration of ownership in the broadcast industry. In 1975, 56 per cent of television stations, 81 per cent of radio stations

TABLE XI.1 Cross-Media Ownership in Selected Canadian Cities
Daily Newspapers, Radio, Television and Cable TV (May 1982)

CITY	OWNER	NEWSPAPER	BROADCAST OUTLET	OBSERVATION
Saint John, N.B.	Irving Group	*Telegraph Journal* *Evening Times Globe*	CHSJ-TV CHSJ-AM	
Moncton	Irving Group	*Daily Times* *Transcript*	CHMT-TV CHMT-AM	
Granby, Que.	Desmarais	*La Voix de L'Est*	CHEF-AM	
Shawinigan-Trois Rivières	Desmarais	*Le Nouvelliste*	CKSM-AM	
Ottawa	*Southam	*Ottawa Citizen*	Ottawa Cablevision Ltd.	Selkirk owns 50% of Ottawa Cablevision.
Belleville	Thomson	*The Intelligencer*	Cablevue (Quinte)	Thomson owns 50% of Cablevue.
Toronto	Maclean Hunter	*Toronto Sun* *Sunday Sun*	Maclean-Hunter Cable TV Ltd. CKEY-AM	Maclean Hunter is parent company of Key Radio Ltd., owners of CKEY.
	Torstar	*Toronto Star* *Sunday Star*	(none)	Torstar is not in broadcast field. It controls 27 community newspapers in Toronto region.
	Thomson	*Globe and Mail*	Classic Communications Cable	Thomson owns 50% of Classic Communications.
Hamilton	*Southam	*Hamilton Spectator*	CHCH-TV	

London	Blackburn Holdings Ltd.	London Free Press	CFPL-TV CFPL-AM CFPL-FM
Regina	Armadale	Regina Leader-Post	CKCK-AM
Edmonton	Maclean Hunter	Edmonton Sun Sunday Sun	CJAX-FM
	*Southam	Edmonton Journal	CJCA-AM
Calgary	Maclean Hunter	Calgary Sun Sunday Sun	CFCN-TV CFCN-AM CJAY-FM
	*Southam	Calgary Herald	CFAC-TV CFAC-AM
Vancouver	*Southam	Vancouver Province Vancouver Sun	CKWX-AM CJAZ-FM CHAN-TV

*Southam is the largest shareholder in Selkirk, which operates the listed broadcast stations.

and 53 per cent of the cable systems were group-owned.[18] The cable industry exhibited the greatest concentration of ownership, followed by radio and TV. In television, the top 10 per cent of the owners accounted for 40 per cent of the industry revenues. At the time of the 1975 analysis—and concentration has increased since then—newspaper ownership was less concentrated than that of either radio or television.[19]

There can be no denying that Canada must take forceful steps not only to avoid further newspaper concentration but also to stimulate a more competitive media industry. It is an economic problem that requires, among other measures, effective Anti-Combines legislation (which has been long delayed by government deference to the business community), intervention by the CRTC, and strong action by the Restrictive Trade Practices Commission.

THE DOMINANT ROLE OF TELEVISION IN ELECTION CAMPAIGNS

While Canadians continue to be ardent newspaper readers, their enthusiasm for the electronic media, especially television is tremendous. The national public opinion survey carried out for the Royal Commission on Newspapers in 1981 yielded the following information:[20]

—Nearly 80 per cent of Canadians say that the electronic media keeps them up-to-date on information.

—About 85 per cent consider the electronic media the most fair and unbiased.

—Eighty-one per cent regard the electronic media as the most influential.

—Sixty-six per cent consider the electronic media as most essential to Canadians.

—Eighty-two per cent describe the electronic media as the most believable.

In each of the five categories listed above, television ranked considerably ahead of radio and newspapers.

It is only natural that politicians would turn to the electronic media in election campaigns. When Canadians went to the polls twice within a 10-month period, in May 1979 and February 1980, television was by far the most important medium in the campaign. It is characteristic of public affairs television programmes to present information in a confrontation context in order to hold the attention of the audience: "everything must be made dramatic."[21] Conse-

18. *Ownership of Private Broadcasting: An Economic Analysis of Structure, Performance and Behaviour.* Report of the Ownership Study Group to the Canadian Radio-television and Telecommunications Commission, (Ottawa: CRTC, 1978).
19. *Ibid.*, pp. 6-8.
20. Royal Commission on Newspapers, *Report, op. cit.*, pp. 33-38. For a more detailed analysis, see Leonard Kubas with the Communications Research Center, *Newspapers and their Readers*, Research Publication, Vol. I, the Royal Commission on Newspapers.
21. Jean-Louis Gagnon, "Communication, Identity, Unity," Gerstein Lecture at York University, *op. cit.*, p. 17.

quently, the elections were "treated like horse races."[22] The time constraints of television and the estimated audience interest span in a topic meant that the emphasis was on the 90-second news clip. Ralph Hancox, the President of Reader's Digest Foundation of Canada, says, "Issues were oversimplified and like individual candidates hardly received any attention. Newspapers, caught up in the party strategy, became adjuncts to the instantaneous television coverage."[23]

John Crosbie, the Conservative Minister of Finance whose budget had precipitated the February 1980 elections, said afterwards, "It is obvious that the importance and weight of the media with reference to news and politics has shifted to television and radio."[24]

The research of Professor Fred Fletcher of York University confirms the views of Hancox and Crosbie about the role of television in the elections. "More than ever before," says Fletcher, "these election campaigns were run for the news media." The emphasis was not on convincing live audiences on the hustings. Rather, the campaign energies, including some 500 speeches by national political figures, were aimed at "making images on a million feet of video tape and film" used in the campaign coverage.[25]

Since the early 1970s, a group of communications scholars and political scientists at the University of Windsor—Professors W.C. Soderlund, W.I. Romanow, E.D. Briggs and R.H. Wagenberg—has carried out a series of studies on media coverage of Canadian elections. In 1975, Wagenberg and Soderlund reported that their content analysis studies of seven chain-owned newspapers did not indicate any evidence of collusion in the parties they endorsed or in the choice of issues raised in editorials.[26]

In the most recent of their studies, the four Windsor scholars report on the media coverage of the 1979 elections.[27] They found that region, language and ownership did not affect significantly the campaign coverage in the press. In analysing radio and television content, they found some differences between French and English coverage, but their overall conclusion was that there existed a common electronic agenda. Furthermore, the coverage in the print and electronic press was fairly similar. Their overall conclusion was that "with respect to the 1979 election at least there was far more of a single, national agenda

22. Ralph Hancox, in Foreword to *Politics and the Mass Media*, (Montreal: Readers Digest Foundation of Canada and Erindale College, University of Toronto, 1981), p. 5.
23. *Ibid.*
24. John Crosbie, "Politics and the Media: Is the Public Well Served?" in *Politics and the Mass Media, op. cit.*, p. 7.
25. Fred Fletcher, "The Contest for Media Attention: The 1979 and 1980 Federal Election Campaigns," in *Politics and the Mass Media, op. cit.*, p. 125. See also William O. Gilsdorf, "The Liberal Party and the Media in the 1979 Canadian Federal Election: Some Preliminary Thoughts." Paper presented to Canadian Communication Association, Halifax, May 1981.
26. R.H. Wagenberg and W.C. Soderlund, "The Influence of Chain Ownership on Editorial Comment in Canada," *Journalism Quarterly*, 52, 1975, pp. 93-98.
27. W.C. Soderlund, W.I. Romanow, E.D. Briggs, R.H. Wagenberg, "Newspaper Coverage of the 1979 Canadian Federal Election: The Impact of Region, Language and Chain Ownership," Paper presented to Canadian Communication Association, Halifax, May 1981.

across all regions of the country and all mass media than we or anyone else would have expected."[28]

The Windsor scholars suggest two possible explanations for the remarkably homogeneous election coverage. One possibility is the influence of "pack journalism," which does not result from collusion, but flows from media practices in the Parliamentary Press Gallery. Another possibility is "that in an election campaign it is the parties and their leaders who are to a great extent responsible for setting the agenda which the media are largely compelled to adopt."[29]

There is considerable evidence that party strategists have learned how to "use the media." In opting for television and thus bypassing newspapers and journalists that may be unfriendly, Canadian political leaders try to reach out to the public directly. This gives party leaders an enhanced power in setting the political agenda.

Senator Keith Davey, who was a principal architect of the Liberal Party strategy in the 1980 elections that brought Mr. Trudeau back to power, has provided insights into a contemporary campaign.[30] The emphasis in the elections was on television and public opinion polling. The Liberal strategy included:

(i) Making Conservative leader Joe Clark the central issue.
(ii) "Low-bridging" Pierre Trudeau: keeping him at a distance from the media.
(iii) Using public opinion surveys to determine the platform. The polls showed the New Democratic Party doing extremely well in Ontario. The Liberals promptly adopted new issues (foreign ownership, guaranteed income supplement) and thus outflanked the NDP. As Senator Davey put it, "It worked."

The former Leader of the Progressive Conservative Party, Robert Stanfield, believes the media today "are forcing politicians to oversimplify the discussion," and if they can, to manipulate it.[31] "Frankly," says Mr. Stanfield, "I am mad as hell, and I'd like to see a few more journalists as mad as I am." For his part, Geoffrey Stevens of the Globe and Mail says that "considerable damage has been done to the political system." He continues:

A leader seems to be primarily accountable now to his strategists, his organizers, his back-room boys. Their bottom line is not good government or constructive opposition. Their bottom line is winning the election.[32]

TECHNOLOGICAL CHANGE

Since the start of electronic communications, Canada has been at the forefront in the application and/or development of new technology. Our analysis, however,

28. *Ibid.*, p. 17.
29. *Ibid.*
30. Keith Davey, "The Anatomy of a Campaign: The Federal Election and the Referendum, or Who Manages Whom?," in *Politics and the Media, op. cit.*, pp. 53-57.
31. Robert Stanfield, "Summing Up," in *Politics and the Media, op. cit.*, p. 124.
32. Geoffrey Stevens, "Prospects and Proposals," in *Politics and the Media, op. cit.*, p. 102.

has shown that with almost each embrace of new technology, not only did we fail to ensure that it would bolster Canadian interests in mass communication flow, we actually moved in the wrong direction and increased our dependence on the United States.

The telegraph provides a shocking example of the abuse of technology in Canada: the wires and poles went up alongside the railway tracks in the east-west bonding of the country, but the mass media messages they carried came largely from the United States, with only minimal Canadian content.

The concern for Canadian unity created by World War I was the catalyst in the establishment in 1917 of a national news agency (CP) with government subsidies. Sixty-five years later, the international news flow into Canada continues to be of largely American origin. Economic realities and a degree of indifference about the national implications are as much the main reasons for this situation today as they were a century ago. There has been a high price for what the media industries see as a free ride. The dominance of the global news agencies in world news flow is a fact of life for mass media in nearly all countries, but CP's efforts at international news collecting are little more than tokenism.

Radio provided perhaps the best opportunity for stimulating a national mass communication flow, as the dynamic efforts of the CNR clearly illustrated. It was a Canadian who invented modern radio (in the United States, because he could not find support at home) and Canada had the first radio station in the world. Also, we pioneered radio on the railways and long-distance radio. In the absence of a meaningful policy, radio stations had the freedom to plug into the American radio system and provide radio on the cheap. Canadian communications tastes were nurtured from outside sources and it was only natural we would crave American TV when it became a mass medium in 1948. When Canada introduced its own TV in 1952, it was not long until we built up a relationship dependent upon the American networks, not only for entertainment programming but also for international and U.S. news coverage. The incredible success of Cable-TV in Canada was due in most part because it could give us more and sharper U.S. television signals, even in communities far removed from the U.S. border.

We were the first country (in 1972) to employ space communications satellites and they have helped us to conquer the enormous distances and difficult terrain, long regarded as the most difficult of the major communications problems facing Canada. The incredible number of broadcast stations, both originating and repeater, bolstered by cable and communications satellites has also helped us deal with another of the great obstacles to mass communication flow: the uneven population dispersion. But they were, in part, superficial solutions. We conquered space by supplying entertainment programming from largely foreign sources. At the same time, Canadian-produced news and information did not cater to the distinctive regional interests.

Communications satellites, on the whole, have not contributed significantly to the Canadianization of TV. In fact, while Canada remains a major force in space communications, we have an insatiable thirst for the programming carried by American communications satellites.

Communications is of course vital to all societies; to Canada, it is a question of survival as a nation. Electronic communications was envisaged even in the nineteenth century as providing the panacea for the future development of a sense of culture and identity. We have a formidable electronic communications system that is second to none. It includes 65 telephones for every 100 people, 3,000 broadcasting operations, 38 million radios, 12 million television sets, three national and several regional TV networks, three transcontinental microwave systems, the world's first network of communications satellites, Cable-television available to 80 per cent of Canadians, and more fibre optic cable (where light is used to transmit electronic signals through hair-thin fibres made of glass) in place than any other country. Between 1982 and 1985, Canada is slated to launch three additional Anik satellites that will enormously increase our space communications channels. In 1983, we are adding Pay-TV—a national French and national English system as well as a series of regional operations—that will provide yet another dimension to our television programming structure.

Since 1978, Canada has helped revolutionize thinking about videotex systems, the interaction of computers and our television sets, with the introduction of Telidon. Described as a second-generation videotex system, Telidon provides high-quality graphics with other services (for example, teletext and person-to-person communications) provided by other videotex systems.

Telidon, developed by the Department of Communications in Ottawa, has been called the key to the wired city. It is appropriate that the most wired country in the world per capita would develop the best technical system for linking the household and store-houses of information (data banks). A fully operational system, to be operating within the next five years, would provide access to millions of pages of information stored in computers by governments, universities, publishing houses and newspapers. It is estimated that by 1984 the price of a Telidon decoder—the attachment that converts the TV set into a data-receiving instrument—will cost about $300. This price projection is based on mass production and will materialize only if Telidon is adopted as quickly as TV was 30 years ago. (Complete Telidon units with colour television monitors, teletex receiver and key capability will cost well over $1,000 even after sales pass the 50,000-a-year level.)

There are signs that some of the major problems facing the broadcast system may resurface with this new technology. There is an English-language bias in computer systems. There are indications that the system may become largely a supplier of data from outside Canada. There is a trend toward conglomerate ownership. Canada was the first country to begin examining the policy implications of the information society and is sensitive to the problems, but hard decisions have to be made.

In 1949, the Massey Royal Commission declared that Canada will flourish in the future in proportion to "our belief in ourselves." Canada was at the time preparing itself for the adoption of television and sought to take steps to ensure that television would be operated in line with the national interest. Since the introduction of television, however, we have become increasingly estranged from ourselves. The chairman of the Canadian Radio-television and Telecommunications Commission, John Meisel, referred to this estrangement when he declared in 1981 at the Gerstein Conference on Mass Communications and Canadian Nationhood, "The electronic media, and television in particular, have contributed significantly to the loss of regional and national identities; they have been among the principal agents of denationalization and of the Americanization of our airwaves."[33] Indications are that if the present broadcast policies and practices continue, the worst is yet to come. The new technologies—some already in use, others about to become operational—"provide threatening avenues for the complete annihilation of what remains of a distinct Canadian culture, of its regional and other unique components, and, in the final analysis of an independent Canadian state."[34]

Canadians need to know more about each other and about their politics and their society to make informed decisions regarding the country's future. The media, preoccupied with their own economic interests and popularity ratings, have not given sufficient emphasis to their political and social functions in society. Considering the advanced state of our communications technology, we deserve to be better informed about Canada. Good journalism is not in conflict with the national interest; rather, it promotes it.

Technology in itself, the Canadian experience shows, is not the answer to stimulating a meaningful exchange of ideas, views and information on a national basis. The information flow appears to have become increasingly fragmented as communication systems have become more numerous, complex and sophisticated. The Canadian communications challenge in the 1980s is to create a conduit for the dynamic harvesting of values that reflect the regions, the languages and the cultures of Canada.

---

33. Meisel, "Five Steps to Survival," Gerstein Lecture, *op. cit.*, p. 2.
34. *Ibid.*

INDEX